Watteau's Shepherds

Watteau's Shepherds: The Detective Novel In Britain 1914-1940

LeRoy Panek

Bowling Green University Popular Press
Bowling Green, Ohio 43403

Cover design by Linda Marsano

Chart design by Kas Schwan

For My Parents

Contents

Preface   1

Backgrounds and Approaches   5

E.C. Bentley   29

Agatha Christie   38

A. A. Milne   64

Dorothy Sayers   72

Anthony Berkeley Cox   111

Margery Allingham   126

John Dickson Carr   145

Ngaio Marsh   185

The End   198

Appendix I: Detective Plots   200

Appendix II: Chronology and Titles   219

Index   228

Preface

After forty years of criticism, the detective story is still an unexamined form; the handful of books and several hundred articles written about detective fiction have not gotten very far in coming to terms with it. This is not for want of zeal or lack of supple minds. Few writers are as ardent about tracking down bibliographical minutiae or as conscious of the philosophic implications of their subject as detective story critics. The problem is that serious writers have too few tools with which to explore the literary side of the detective story. Since the late twenties, most critics have been mesmerized by the idea of the puzzle and its relationship to the form. It is not difficult, then, to guess that in the following pages I will suggest a number of alternate ways of approaching the detective novel, ways which, for me at least, explain the principal features of the form more consistently and more elegantly than the unalloyed idea of the puzzle does. Detective novels are games, jokes, reactions to the adventure thriller, and reactions to the established form itself. This is the hobby horse that I ride, and I would like to persuade readers that puzzle analysis used by itself is an inadequate way of seeing the detective novel. But this is not all that I try to do: in the body of the book I take a look at detective novels from a literary point of view. That is, I pay some attention to literary history and look at the materials and patterns from which detective writers created their fictions.

Another of the fundamental problems confronting the criticism of detective fiction is its field of focus. To date it has largely been very broad or very narrow: from general historical surveys and philosophic reactions to articles on single writers or books. These approaches have their virtues, but at this stage of development of detective criticism they have some serious drawbacks. I have decided, therefore, to shape my study around a group of novelists working during a specific period in

1

Britain. Not all of these writers are British (one is an American and one a New Zealander), but they all worked in Britain during the "Golden Age" and they were all influential in making the detective novel what it was between the two Wars. As a consequence of this I have purposely omitted a great deal of important and interesting material from this study: there is little about novelists working in America in either tradition of the detective novel, little about the short story, little about novels written after 1940, and little about important but lesser British detective writers like Ronald Knox or the Coles. Even in Milton there is a limit to the fall. There is still, however, plenty left to cover—the writers I have selected produced one hundred and seven novels before the Second World War, and I have tried to mention and provide some insight into all of them.

Detective criticism has traditionally been different from regular, academic literary criticism. For one thing, characters tend to become more important than their creators or literary technique. Sherlock Holmes is a case in point, but this is equally true of Wimsey and other Golden Age detectives. For another thing, detective critics have traditionally avoided any mention of the endings of detective stories so as not to spoil surprises for readers. I have followed, to some extent, both of these conventions: I have paid some attention to the cult interest in detective heroes and I have not revealed the endings of any but the best known detective plots. In some ways these practices deny the critic some of the most useful tools of the trade, but from another perspective they make detective criticism into an exercise in ingenuity like the detective story itself.

Readers, though, should not be misled by these opening remarks. I enjoyed detective novels before I started this project and I enjoy them still. This book is not intended as a tight historical study or a one thesis tract. Not enough is yet known about writers of the Golden Age for the complete and final history to be written, and I have not the patience to write a single thesis book, which I inevitably find boring and repetitious. I have instead tried here to approach each chapter from a slightly different angle, keeping in mind Bacon's advice that "studies serve for delight." I would, in fact, like readers to find in the following an essay in Montaigne's original sense of that word—something which outlines tentative ideas and opinions on an engrossing subject.

3   Watteau's Shepherds

I would like here to acknowledge the help of the librarians at the Enoch Pratt Library in Baltimore, and the Western Maryland College Library, especially Carol Quinn, who have helped me track down fugitive books and obscure facts. My thanks too go to Del Palmer and Bob Sapora who have listened to me and suggested ways of attacking and handling popular fiction. Finally, my deepest appreciation goes to my wife, Susan, whose firmness draws my circle (and my orthography) just.

Chapter 1

Backgrounds and Approaches

Detective novels, however, were no more to be judged by realistic standards than one would judge Watteau's shepherds and shepherdesses in terms of contemporary sheep-farming.
Robert Graves and Alan Hodge
The Long Week-End

The Thriller

The adventure story, especially the blood and thunder, harum-scarum variety, goes at least back as far as Heliodorus' Hellenistic Greek prose romance, and probably much farther. To trace it through all of its permutations from Sidney to Mme. D'Aulnoy would take us too far afield from the beginnings of the novel of adventure as it stood in the teens—at the advent of the detective novels of the twenties. We do, however, need to go back to the Victorian novel of adventure, because it was these wild fictions which would eventually give part of the impetus to Dorothy Sayers, Agatha Christie, and many of the other Golden Age novelists. This idea to some extent violates conventional wisdom, which sees the modern detective novel developing directly from Edgar Allan Poe to Gaboriau to Conan Doyle to R. Austin Freeman and G.K. Chesterton, and so on. This line of development is very important and it has received plenty of attention from E.A. Murch, Howard Haycraft, *et. al.* But the development of a vigorous literature for adolescents and the working class in the mid-1800's, which was modified by Robert Louis Stevenson, Rider Haggard and Anthony Hope in the 1880's and 1890's, and again modified by Edgar Wallace, E. Phillips Oppenheim, Sax Rohmer, LeQueux, John Buchan and others in the first decades of the twentieth century, is almost as important to the development of the detective novel in the 1920's as was Conan Doyle's detective.

In *Great Expectations* when Pip goes to be formally apprenticed to Joe, an evil-minded crank shoves him a moral tract about conduct in prison. For a long time this was the only kind of reading material which adolescents and self-educated men like Adam Bede could find. Their first real chance for escape came in the 1830's and 1840's, when publishers and writers produced the penny dreadful. A group of publishers on Salisbury Square, abetted by others, began to titillate the lower sections of the reading public with cheap editions of wild, pseudo-gothic and Newgate calendar adventures or with periodicals which featured this kind of fiction. The book publishers produced titles like *Varney the Vampire, Wagner the Wehr-Wolfe, The Black Tower of Bransdorf* and *The Secret of the Grey Turret,* and in newspaper form there were vehicles like the *Penny Sunday Times and People's Police Gazette* which carried the same kind of fiction. What sort of fiction? First of all, fiction about bad people from Vampires and Wehr-Wolves to criminals like Dick Turpin or Spring-Heeled Jack Sheppard. And, surprisingly enough, considering the Victorian propensities for moralizing, fiction with remarkably little of the sunday school in it. In Reynold's *Wagner the Wehr-Wolf,* for instance, neither being a Wehr-Wolf, a murderess, a fornicator, nor a convert to Islam receives much opprobrium. The important thing in this and other fiction of this sort was a dash of sensuality, complete with bared bosoms, and a monstrous great deal of life-and-death action: capture, escape, fights, and threats. There is even a mystery or two upon which the story is suspended. Penny dreadfuls thus gave their readers an unqualified dose of adventure—significantly, adventure in which monstrous villainy often played a key role.

Faced with boys sneaking off to revel in the luxurious excitement of the penny dreadful, Victorian moralists were quick to respond with an antidote to the poison of immoral adventure. This took the form of the juvenile paper or the schoolboy novel which were intended to provide healthy and instructive outlets for children's imaginations. From the 1850's onward a whole bookstall of juvenile papers appeared, papers like the *Boys' Own Paper* which stressed useful knowledge and Christian character-building (not surprising, as it was published by the Religious Tract Society through a subsidiary). Quite the same thing happened in the schoolboy novels of Hughes *(Tom Brown's School Days, Tom Brown at Oxford,* etc.), Ballantyne *(The Lifeboat,* etc.) and others. These novels stressed the character-building of the upper-class English boy and developed a new moral hero for the adventure story—one whose fiber needed to be tested because of his eventual responsibilities as a white, male leader of the Empire. Howarth describes this new hero as the Newbolt man (after the moral qualities advocated in the poetry of Sir Henry Newbolt):

Imbued with a strong sense of institutional loyalty, upper middle-class by background, conformist in belief, dedicated to a concept, not simply "my country right or wrong," but of a nation enjoying a natural moral prerogative, accepting ungrudgingly the demands of service and duty, inclined to treat women either as companions or as unmentionable; add to this a natural power of command, some degree of worldly success, a distrust of latter-day politicians and a tendency towards philistinism in artistic taste, and we have the species *homo newboltiensis.*[1]

Take these internal qualities and combine them with various physical characteristics (a frame six feet tall, with broad shoulders, rugged features) and make him a rugger blue, and we have a hero who stretches like Banquo's heirs through English fiction.

It is this character who carries his Christian Imperial morality through so much Victorian and Edwardian fiction and who also carries his schoolboy associates with him. The group of schoolboy friends with its natural leader, the older boy guiding and protecting the younger boy, were transposed from school fiction to the world of the adventure novel by any number of writers, but most notably it was done by Rider Haggard and Conan Doyle.

During the late 1880's and the 1890's what had formerly been considered largely boys' literature began to be seen as popular literature. Perhaps the rise of adventure stories in these years was due to the maturation of the first generation to receive the benefits of the Education Act of 1870; at any rate, a number of the classic English adventure stories were written during this period: *Kidnapped, Treasure Island, King Solomon's Mines, She, The Prisoner of Zenda,* to say nothing of *Rodney Stone, The White Company* or *A Study in Scarlet.* These books simply took over the earlier Victorian adventure material—often with a glance at an energetic villain like Rupert of Heintzau or She—but with the focus on a moral English hero whose character is buffed to shining by his adventures. Almost inevitably these stories contain not only the grown-up schoolboy hero, but his school associates as well.

8   Watteau's Shepherds

In *King Solomon's Mines* there is the Allan Quartermain clique with tubby Captain Good and noble Sir Henry Curtis, and in Conan Doyle's adventure novels from *The White Company* through *The Lost World* one finds the teacher—Sir Nigel or Professor Challenger—surrounded by his best and brightest students. Even the Holmes-Watson relationship is that of the older boy and younger boy, which P.G. Wodehouse eventually apotheosized in the Psmith-Mike Jackson relationship. The difference with Conan Doyle is that he also introduced Joe Bell, Poe, Gaboriau, and Vidocq. And thereby hangs a tale.

Once Sherlock Holmes caught on, he caught on like a million pounds. If not for the potential sales and the cash, then for the fun of working with a detective story, a flock of short story writers turned to the detective story in the late Victorian and early Edwardian years, so we get the short fiction of R. Austin Freeman, Baroness Orczy, G.K. Chesterton, Ernest Bramah and a number of others. The only trouble was that Conan Doyle could never figure out how to successfully extend his detective story ideas into novels; he approaches writing a unified novel in *The Hound of the Baskervilles,* but the rest of the Sherlock Holmes novels are flops. The first solution to the problem of how to write a detective novel was forged by a group of writers in the first decades of the twentieth century—Edgar Wallace, E. Phillips Oppenheim, LeQueux, Sax Rohmer, John Buchan: the thriller writers. They combined certain traditions of the adventure story with those of the detective story and created a form which runs through Bulldog Drummond, the Saint, James Bond and all of their sons and heirs, and against which the novelists of the Golden Age reacted.

The thriller writers accepted *in toto* the ideals of character which had been developed in the boy's papers, schoolboy novels, and the works of Conan Doyle, Rider Haggard, and their fellow imperial romancers. All of the thriller heroes of the early 1900's are from the same mold: magnificent physical specimens, they are not hulking but strong-thewed as average Englishmen, they are seasoned by adversity and duty, are natural leaders, quick-thinking, fast-fisted, ready to right wrongs and to suffer privation and torture for the salvation of the world (or the salvation of the Empire, which amounts to the same thing). Virtually every one of these qualities is seen in characters like Rohmer's Sir Dennis Nayland-Smith, the agents in LeQueux, Oppenheim's Sir Everard Dominey, or Buchan's Richard Hannay. They are strong, resourceful he-men who exude a sort of tweedy macho. Never silly, never wrong, never depressed, these men do a great deal to create the Golden Age detective.

Virtually as important as the heroes are the villains. Heirs to the penny dreadful behemoths, the thriller villain was no penny-ante crook but rather a giant of evil, a master criminal whose evil ambitions shake the foundations of the very civilized world. Even before British writers invented Germans in the teens, monstrous, titanic evil stalked the pages of the thriller—there were Sexton Blake's nemeses Dr. Huxton Rymer and Prince WuLing, of course, Fu Manchu, Umkulunkulu the Zulu chief in Buchan's *Prester John* (1910), and the Oxford-educated Albanian brigand chief Remington Kara in Wallace's *The Clue of the Twisted Candle* (1916), to mention only a few. These people are so ineffably nasty that they a) are above the law, b) subvert society with their massive intellects and thick bank rolls, and c) want to dominate the world. They possess superior intellects, unlimited wealth, the aids of advanced technology to supply them with fiendish weapons, as well as innumerable hulking toadies who do their bidding without thinking. To complicate issues further—and to help to squeeze in some detection—these villains are usually disguised (usually obvious to the reader) and often have secret and inaccessible lairs. Against them the hero must struggle, and this struggle provides the thriller plot. Against them the novelists of the twenties also did battle, but with sodawater siphons and custard pies; but this is getting too far ahead of the argument.

This struggle provides the thriller plot. Thrillers rely on two metaphors coming from the struggle of the hero and the villain: the hunt and the chase. One of the principal shifts that happens in most thrillers is that these metaphors change, and hunt becomes chase, and hunter becomes the object of the chase. For example, in Buchan's *The Thirty Nine Steps* (1915), Hannay is hunted by Blackstone and his minions for three-quarters of the novel, and 'hen he hunts them in the last quarter. Essentially, as John Cawelti suggests,[2] the thriller runs on a plot in which the hero overcomes obstacles to w _n a victory which has moral significance. In the vast majority of thrillers—even before 1914—it is the duty of the hero to save his country from destruction. There are various kinds of obstacles which he needs to surmount:

> 1. Obstacles presented by the villain—the villain's inaccessibility, attempts on the hero's life, capture, etc.
> 2. Obstacles presented by time and space—there is usually a given date when the villain's plan will be effected and the hero must get from, say, Barundi to Limehouse to thwart it.
> 3. Obstacles presented by physical nature—the hero usually finds himself in a situation in which hunger or cold threaten him and his physical strength ebbs.
> 4. Obstacles from psychology—the hero, being after all average, may have a momentary tick of doubt or fear.

In addition to these obstacles there must be danger or the threat of danger. Of course there is the danger of the imminent destruction of the world in the background, but there are also dangers to the hero's life and to the lives of innocent friends and bystanders. The central problem for the thriller writers is to pack in as many obstacles and dangers as possible, and to do this they adopt episodic plots and *ad hoc* art describing new attributes of character and inventing background which each new action demands. Consequently most thriller writers depend on the idea of the hunt or the chase from one locale to another in order to unify what otherwise would be too baldly episodic.

It is possible for the thriller to exist without the detective story: Victorian adventure stories operated with only a modicum of detective interest. After Conan Doyle, however, thriller writers latched onto detective story elements, and their novels became the detective novels of the early 1900's, copying characters and plot devices from Holmes and the detective tradition, and mixing in the obstacles and dangers of the thriller. For example, take Rohmer's first novel, *The Insidious Fu Manchu* (1913). Here Holmes and Watson become Nayland-Smith and Petrie, and in the course of the novel they solve four separate locked-room murders with such panache that they make Carr's detectives look slow-moving and dim-witted. Add to the locked-room murders Dacoits, a beautiful slave girl, botany gone berserk, torture and escape, disguises, and you have the makings of a real thriller. Or take Wallace's *The Clue of the Twisted Candle* (1916): here there is a locked-room murder with clues for the reader, but there is also a prison break, dungeons in Albania and Grosvenor Square, political blackmail, an Albanian bandit, and heartless minions. These writers saw the detective elements developed by Poe and Conan Doyle as providing episodes or affording organization to their larger enterprise of selling sensation to the lower spectrum of the reading public. And sell it they did. Oppenheim and Wallace earned and spent fortunes, and we can assume that their publishers did too. So, in the commercial lending libraries, it was Rohmer, Wallace, LeQueux and Oppenheim who were advertised, and it was these writers who the vast majority of the public saw as detective novelists at the beginning of the Golden Age of the detective story and continued to see as detective novelists through the 1930's.

The Golden Age: Reactions

The standard view is that the detective novel of the Golden Age was invented by E.C. Bentley in *Trent's Last Case* in 1914, and then was taken up in earnest after the war, by Christie, Sayers, *et. al.* This is largely true, but it does not tell us very much about the detective novel or the germs from which it grew. In part, the new detective novel was a reaction against the thriller. If the thriller reflected the English view of the world as their oyster during the Edwardian years, then surely the Golden Age detective novel reflects the peculiar atmosphere of England between the two World Wars—an atmosphere which Graves depicts in his book, *The Long Week-End.* World War I left England in a strangely paradoxical position. The War undermined many institutions on which the English and their popular fiction ran: honor, heroism, individual effort, trust in authority, and the absolutely fixed class system. No one, however, wanted to realize this. It was not until 1928, for instance, that the bitter accounts of individual soldiers' experiences in the War began to appear in print. Instead of the War, people turned more and more to entertainment: Hollywood movies, jazz, dancing, cricket, football, musical comedy. Entertainment, though, had to walk a narrow line of upholding values without being Victorian, of being sophisticated without being snobbish, and of being exciting without being heroic. The new detective novel fit the bill.

Before the War, popular fiction, the thriller, had come

largely from lower-class writers who had had only casual educations and, but for the vogue for their books, would have continued doing hack journalism, selling shoes or clerking in banks. The popular thriller writers were also all men. This changed. After 1920 new groups of writers began writing the detective novel. First, there were the women (Christie, Sayers and later Margery Allingham, Josephine Tey and Ngaio Marsh). Next, there were the academics (Ronald Knox, the Coles, and later C.P. Snow and Michael Innes). And finally, there was a group of bright young men (Anthony Cox, Nicholas Blake, Philip MacDonald, John Dickson Carr, etc.). There was also a group of hangers-on (those writers whom Julian Symons calls "humdrums") like Freeman Wills Crofts and John Rhode, but it was the women, the academics, and the bright young men who gave talks about the detective story on the newly-founded B.B.C., who wrote articles on detection, who reviewed mystery novels, who—in short—remade the detective novel.

When considered by sensitive, intelligent or even educated people, the thriller is bad art, bad morality, bad education, bad everything: its hero is a lout, its villain a Guy Fawkes' dummy, and its plot a rhapsody of nonsense hidden under the pretense of presenting important social-or-character-molding points. After World War I, people in England wanted to forget about international horrors and characters acting as if Victorian, imperial standards were still valid. Since the new generation of detective writers came from or wished to appeal to this group, it is not surprising to find that one of the first targets of the new detective novel was the thriller. A basic premise of the new fiction was "this is a detective novel and not a thriller. It is not like Wallace, Oppenheim, Buchan, or LeQueux."

The initial reaction against the thriller was against the thriller hero, the Newbolt Man. All one has to do is to compare the old heroes with the new ones: Nayland-Smith with Wimsey, or Richard Hannay with Poirot. When the Golden Age writers built their characters, they included a wide variety of traits which separate them from the heroes of the thriller. Bentley began the whole movement by making Trent fallible, and the other writers followed this lead. New heroes were purposely made physically different from the stereotype, from the miniscule Poirot to the obese Gideon Fell and Nero Wolfe. Characters like Wimsey are substantively cultured and aristocratic versus the superficial veneer of these things in the old heroes. Some Golden Age characters, like Roger Sherringham, are frankly noxious. Opposed to the prickly heat felt around women by the thriller heroes, the new men are agreeable and at ease with them, often having real wives like Mrs. Bredon, Mrs. Gethryn, Mrs. Strangeways, Mrs. Campion, Mrs. Alleyn, and Mrs. Wimsey. Sometimes the new characters are intellectuals like Appleby or Strangeways, and most of them are partly comic—based more on Wodehouse than Wallace. And they all possess some sensitivity to the human predicament of both the criminal and the victim. They are different, defiantly different, indeed. In all of these cases, moreover, it is significant that the new generation of writers created these characters, since the women went after the rampant masculinity of the old hero and others followed. They all singled out that which was patently fake and obtuse and made their people comic, sensitive, intelligent, and at times tender—things which the thriller hero and his bulldog successors could never achieve. One can see this shift codified in the various burlesque passages in the novels of the twenties and thirties, and in the tongue-in-cheek rules appearing in the late twenties, which specified that the detective writer must never use 1) Chinamen or 2) Master Crooks. This took away the thriller antagonist without whom the thriller hero could not exist.

After the hero came the plot. No one who had been to university and had had Freytag drummed into his head could possibly plot a novel full of tenuously connected episodes made upon the spur of the moment. Why not? Because it would be laughably improbable. Thus, in addition to the attack on the thriller hero, one often finds burlesques of thriller plots in Golden Age detective novels. One of the best of these comes in Sayers' *Have His Carcase* (1932), when Harriet talks to Leila Garland:

> "I mean, they might have been a gang, you know, like in that story, *The Trail of the Purple Python.* Have you read it? The Purple Python was a Turkish millionaire, and he had a secret house full of steel-lined rooms and luxurious divans and obelisks—"
> "Obelisks?"
> "Well, you know. Ladies who weren't quite respectable. And he had agents in every country in Europe, who bought up

compromising letters and he wrote to his victims in cipher and
signed his missives with a squiggle of purple ink. Only the
English detective's young lady found out his secret by disguising
herself as an obelisk and the detective who was really Lord
Humphrey Chillingfold arrived with the police just in time to
rescue her from the loathsome embrace of the Purple Python."[3]

Instead of writing unbelievable collections of bizarrarie like
this, the writers of the twenties and thirties focused on one or
two crimes, and they made them much more domestic; the body
in the library may be a cliche today, but in the twenties it was a
relief from multiple bodies flopping out of secret passages,
shadowy doorways, abandoned houses, and hidden dungeons.
This is not to say that these writers entirely gave up the idea of
adventure and excitement in the detective story—far from it.
But the adventure came in smaller doses, and these writers
evolved a pattern for the detective story which was more
flexible than that which the thriller writers used (see Appendix
I).

The Joke

Take a woman who strode about Somerville College
chomping on a cigar, a man who explained Berkeley's
philosophy of perception in a comic poem, another after whom
a comic verse form was named, combine them with an editor
and several contributors to *Punch*, and one must expect high
spirits and high jinks. And that is exactly what one finds in the
Golden Age detective novel.

Standard histories of the detective story usually ignore one
thing about the founder of detective fiction, Edgar Allan Poe,
which Poe scholars are now beginning to realize more and
more;[4] Poe was not only interested in problems of logic and
perception but he was also a hoaxer, a diddler, and a joker.
Every one of his detective tales is a cheat which dupes the
readers into thinking that they are receiving fair treatment
when they are being flim-flammed. Just examine the narrative
placement of the ribbon and the orangutan hair in "Murders in
the Rue Morgue," and you get an example of the trickery. The
detective writers of the twenties and thirties took off from the
jokes in Poe as well as the intellectual problems.

Consider these items: there was an Irishman, a kangaroo,
and a Rolls Royce locked in a deserted ballroom in Croydon.
Two things can be made out of these disparate elements, a joke

and a detective story. The key to both is that the ending reconciles the differences which are apparent in the items in the series, and reconciles them by narrating a story which ends in a surprise and which, in spite of its shock, makes sense upon consideration. This is basic joke theory explained by, among others, Jerry Suls in *The Psychology of Humor*.[5] Not only do jokes (and detective stories) reconcile seemingly impossible elements, but they also provide signals that the listener/reader is experiencing something which a) is not real and b) is comic. They begin with the expression "now I am going to tell you a joke."

Apply these things to the fiction of the Golden Age. Most of the novels revolve around zany incongruities—a naked corpse in an unsuspecting architect's bath, a toe-print on the rung of a banister, a man wearing four watches—which the story reconciles. Further, the novelists felt that one of their chief functions was to upset expectations. They dealt with readers experienced with detective stories who expected something fresh from their reading. Thus we find writers consistently bamboozling readers by making stories in which the narrator is the murderer, novels where there are six credible explanations for a crime, and novels in which the least-likely character is guilty. All of these, and all of the art of the detective writer, were pointed toward hoaxing the readers and disconfirming their expectations. Just as in the joke the most important part is the listener's reaction to the punch line ("Because the book was already colored in; ah yes, that means that the populace is illiterate and the destruction of the library is not really a tragedy"), the most important part of the detective novel is the unravelling ("Ah yes, the refrigerant in the air conditioner turned to phosgene gas and that's how she died in the locked room"). And most importantly, integral to every joke is the presence of comic cues, the announcement of the comic intent of the whole (I will deal with the announcement of the unreal world below), and I think that they can be found in many detective novels of the Golden Age. Take, for instance, Josephine Tey's first novel, *The Man in the Queue* (1929). This book turns on a bilious pun on the name Ray Marcable; perhaps not a pun for all tastes, this certainly does something to the overall tone of the novel when it is given at the end. In an era in which most of the detectives are partly comic, and when writers not only began writing for diversion but also frequently tell their readers that the detective story is not real, it seems safe to say that detective characters, like Roger Sherringham, and whole novels began as and functioned as jokes.

Seeing the detective novels of the twenties—and some later ones too—as jokes provides a ready and easy, patent method of analyzing them which makes more sense than seeing them simply as intellectual puzzles in fiction. It explains the ambience of silliness in so many of them, and it sufficiently explains what goes on in terms of plot. Take, for example, Christie's first novel, *The Mysterious Affair at Styles*. Here we have a comic foreigner, Poirot, with all that that entails: language gaffs, wry observations about English culture, physical differences. His companion is the frankly comic Hastings, who bungles and bumbles about. In the end of the novel we discover that the one person who has earlier been demonstrated to be innocent is, in fact, guilty. Given this fact, we think back to the earlier parts of the text and find that, yes, the solution jibes with earlier facts which are there but placed in such a way that we (from the writer's point of view) should not notice them. Wait. What if we do notice these facts or guess the culprit without them? Then the detective story fails and we lose interest, just as we do when we know the punch line to a joke ("I know. It's a long way to tip a Rary").

Play

The joke is, after all, only part of that larger human activity called play, which is intimately connected with all detective stories. Among others, Ed McBain makes this clear in his police procedural novel *Jigsaw* (1970):

> It was the belief of every detective on the 87th Squad that the real motive behind half the crimes being committed in the city was *enjoyment* pure and simple—the *fun* of playing Cops and Robbers.[6]

The Golden Age detective novel not only portrayed human activity which can be described and analyzed as play, its very form grew out of play, and playing was one of its functions. At the start of the period, A.A. Milne reacted against what he saw as the weakness of Edwardian detective fiction by asking,

> What satisfaction is it to you or me when the famous Professor

examines the small particle of dust which the murderer has left
behind him, and infers that he lives between a brewery and a flour
mill? What thrill do we get when the bloodspot on the missing
man's hankerchief proves that he was bitten by a camel?
Speaking for myself, none.[7]

Here even Raymond Chandler might agree with Milne—if not
for the same reasons. For Milne and his fellows, writing
detective novels was to be fun for both the writer and the
reader: they were to be games. And in doing this they simply
did what their culture moved them to.

The period between the two wars in England was a time for
playing games. This era gave us Mah-jongg, the cross-word
puzzle, the scavenger hunt, contract bridge, bingo, Monopoly,
the pogo stick, miniature golf, and many other games. Play
fever swept much of Europe and the U.S.: according to
Sussman, there were six hundred books published on play in
the U.S. during these years (and probably a like number in
Britain).[8] In 1921, Sir Herbert Nield inveighed that "we have
gone recreation mad," and in 1924, Rev. H.L.C.V. de Candole
preached a sermon on "Why are the Churches Empty? Craze
for Exciting Pleasures." In Britain, public tennis courts were
built, Greyhound racing was introduced (proving how stupid
dogs are), and Association Football spread into country
districts. Oxford undergraduates formed a Hide-and-Seek
Society in 1921. On the continent, Morgenstern and Von
Neumann formulated Game Theory, which has become a part
of modern mathematics and social sciences, and in 1938,
Huizinga assembled his classic work on play, *Homo Ludens*.
Play was certainly in the air.

And play certainly exists in the detective books of the
Golden Age. The game of murder (about which I have
something to say later) appears in *The Crime at Black Dudley*
(1929), *Enter a Murderer* (1935), and *The Ten Teacups* (1937).
Hide-and-seek is played in *The Beast Must Die* (1938), Pin-the-
tail-on-the-donkey in *To Wake the Dead* (1937). Blake's *Malice
in Wonderland* (1940) takes place at one of those typically
British holiday spas, and almost every novel of the period has a
game of chess, tennis, or golf in it. *Murder Must Advertise*
(1933) ends with Wimsey of Balliol swatting out a century or
two for Pym's cricket team. Virtually every detective is some
sort of game player. Reggie Fortune is described as "the eternal
child" in *The Great Game* (1939), H.M. trained for three

seasons with the Athletics and is a great, natural hitter. Dr. Fell dresses up as Professor von Hornswoggle in *The Eight of Swords* (1934) and as a cop in *The Mad Hatter Mystery* (1933). Robert Sherringham is accused of "making fun of everything," and Albert Campion carries a squirt gun. Knox's Bredon plays patience, and Poirot builds card houses. Even prigs like Philo Vance play cards.

This, I venture, tells us something. It tells us that games and play dominate the exteriors of Golden Age novels, but it gives shape and form to their interiors too. Play explains a good deal of what happens in these books, for in many ways they *are* games. But since I am going to pursue this, a caution is needed. The concept of play is a useful tool for analysis of various human activities, but like other tools (Marxism, Freudianism, Structuralism, etc.) it can be taken too far. Some play theoreticians can see the rudiments of play in all human activities—war, law, and probably even work. I am not going to go that far and will try to be measured and relevant in what follows.

Above I mentioned Huizinga and his *Homo Ludens*: almost every contemporary discussion of play begins with his definition and criteria, which were formulated in the thirties. Huizinga states that play has certain marked characteristics. They are that 1) play is voluntary, 2) it exists outside of the normal routine of life, 3) it is repetitive, 4) it operates according to rules, 5) it moves in fixed boundaries of time and space—play time and the playground, 6) it fosters associations among people, 7) these associations are exclusive, distinguishing between playmates and others, 8) it rests on competition, 9) it allows exhibitionism on the part of the successful player, 10) it gives vent to tension and release [without effect in terms of things made or work done], and 11) it is fun. Taken individually these points have little force and can describe many things which are manifestly not play—a visit to the dentist, for instance, involves tension and release—but taken together they have a great deal of argumentative force.

I have no wish to belabor all of these points and their presence in detective fiction, since some of them are fairly obvious. No one, I suppose, would deny that detective novels contain tension and release, or focus on competition between the criminal and the detective and among the detectives. Few can listen to Poirot's boasts or sit through the lecture in the unravelling without noting a tincture of exhibitionism. It is further clear, considering the preponderance of amateur detectives during the period, that the heroes of these books get involved with crime voluntarily. I do, however, want to point out and stress the presence of some of Huizinga's criteria in the Golden Age story, because they add to the collective force of the play elements and because they explain some of the unique features of these detective novels.

Before 1920 and after 1940, almost all detective stories pretend that they are real, as do American, hard-boiled stories. They insist that they portray for the reader events and experiences which actually happened. Thus Poe, Conan Doyle, Freeman, and others use the fictional memoir of the detective's assistant, which tells the reader that "I was there with the great man." On the other hand, American writers like Daily, Dashiell Hammett, and Raymond Chandler, through Mickey Spillane and Ross Macdonald, use the voice of the detective himself to take the reader along with the actions and reactions of the hero. Golden Age writers, however, although they sometimes use the first person—as Christie occasionally uses Hastings—usually write their fictions using a variety of third person narrative techniques. This, to some extent, prevents full identification with the characters and removes the readers from direct involvement in the action. There is this distancing in Golden Age novels, and there are constant reminders to readers that *they are reading a detective story:* this is not life, they say. It is a detective story. To get this point, note the following narrative interruptions in a cross-section of Golden Age novels.[9]

> I oughtn't explain 'til the last chapter, but I always think that's so unfair.
> > A.A. Milne, *The Red House Mystery* (1922)

> ...you're not beginning to look on yourself as a story-book detective, and all the rest of the world as the Scotland Yard specimen to match, are you?
> > A.Berkeley, *The Wychford Poisoning Case* (1926)

> To show you how minutely I've searched—I even thought of that favorite stand-by of our friends the fiction writers: curare, the South American toxin which makes the grade in four out of five

detective novels.

E.Queen, *The Roman Hat Mystery* (1930)

You don't know what you're talking about. And besides, *get back to the subject*. This is the last chapter, and we want to get it over with.

J.D. Carr, *The Eight of Swords* (1934)

This is a mere sampling, for this sort of reference frequently crops up in Golden Age fiction. These and other references by detective stories to detective novel practices can hardly be seen as metaphors. They are reminders that we are reading a fiction. Further, the books of the Golden Age constantly allude to other detective works: Philip MacDonald refers to Gaboriau in *The Rasp* (1924), Christie to Sayers in *Appointment with Death* (1938), Sayers to Bentley in *Whose Body?* (1923), Van Dine to Freeman in *The Kennel Murder Case* (1931), and everyone to Conan Doyle and Poe. This confirms that these writers wrote for the experienced reader, but it points out that Golden Age writers did not try to absorb their readers in the actuality of a fictional world. The reverse is true: writers remind us of the artificiality of the form—that it is not normal life or even normal fiction. It is Huizinga's point about play existing in a realm separate from normal routine. The Golden Age story is a game in this respect.

Another constituent part of playing is the limitations in time and space: playtime and the playground, or Prince Hal's "if all the year were playing holidays,/ To sport would be as tedious as to work." The formal detective story from Poe onward has existed in clearly defined spaces—the locked room, Dupin's chambers, Minister D—'s flat. To tone down thriller plots, Golden Age writers returned to this and severely limited the geographical scope of their plots, focusing on one crime and covering a reasonably limited period of time. In short, they followed the Aristotelian unities of the drama. But it did not stop there. One of the peculiar features of Golden Age fiction is the appearance of architectural drawings, room plans, and village maps. This can be seen as an artistic failure of nerves on the part of writers who did not trust their own descriptions, a scrupulous exactitude on the part of fastidious writers, or (and this conjunction is meant to be "or") an attempt to include a game board upon which the writer (and perhaps the reader) can place and manipulate the figures in the novels.

And finally, every game must have rules. Game rules are logically consistent but arbitrary strictures which players establish and agree upon, in order to make the game function and to disqualify those who do not play according to the spirit of the group. Try to imagine a game of chess in which each player can make the pieces move in any direction he or she chooses, and the point becomes clear. Leafing through Haycraft's anthology, one finds sets of detective writing rules by Knox and Van Dine, and in her introduction to the *Omnibus of Crime* (1928), Sayers adds her own. In the twenties and thirties there was the Red Badge test of eight points, formulated by Dodd and Mead, as well as the "How To" sections in Haycraft's *Murder for Pleasure* (1941) and Carolyn Wells' *The Technique of the Mystery Story,* in 1929. These sets of rules generally do two things—they exclude thrillers from any claim to respectability, and they set down the standard of fair play in the relationship between the reader and the writer. Significantly also, the American literary umpires are largely in earnest in their promulgation of rules, while the British writers, those with whom this study is concerned, saw them as a lark. Margery Allingham saw Chesterton laugh while she swore the oath of the Detection Club. The rules were part of the game (as was the Detection Club itself).

All of these things taken together make a strong case for a lively play element in the Golden Age detective novel. The atmosphere of play, combined with the joke, and the rejection (burlesque and serious) of the thriller give us much of what is unique in Golden Age fiction. The other part is supplied by the domestication and regularization of plot and character inherited from the detective and thriller tradition. This combination gives us the form which was initially used by novelists in the twenties, and which continued to color detective novels for years to come. There were, however, other influences which modified the Golden Age novel as it moved toward the 1930's.

The Puzzle Story

The problem with the term puzzle story is that no one has really, scrupulously defined exactly what it means when applied to Golden Age novels (not short stories for, because of their length, they present different problems). It has been applied to the detective's role, the reader's role, and it can be used to describe a small class of novels written during the late twenties which, in turn, influence later views of detective fiction and writers' views of their own genre. To start this section, then, it would seem profitable to turn to a definition of what puzzles are and then try to place the operations of puzzling in detective fiction before 1920.

The word "puzzle" as a noun for a class of games did not come into English until the nineteenth century—presumably because earlier people did not have the leisure to play with puzzles, or paid so little attention to children's pursuits that puzzles were included in the words "toy" or "game." The two favorite kinds of puzzles referred to in detective fiction of the twentieth century, the jigsaw puzzle and the crossword puzzle, did not appear until the 1900's: the jigsaw itself was not introduced into England until the late 1800's—the Oxford English Dictionary does not contain the term jigsaw puzzle— and the crossword puzzle did not appear until 1924 when it was invented in New York.

Puzzles, as games, are either physical, verbal, or mathematical constructs which the player must assemble in order to form the shape implied by the puzzle (a picture in a jigsaw puzzle, regular words in crosswords, or a mathematical solution in the case of mathematical puzzles). As games they have certain specific criteria: they ask the player for the solution, all of the pieces must be available, and there must be only one possible solution. In the puzzle, the finished construct is of greatest importance, and players do not review the mental operations which either they or the puzzle manufacturer engaged in. Finally, puzzles are created in order to be solved. If one fails to complete a jigsaw puzzle then no satisfaction is gained. Puzzles are very different from jokes and other games.

Going back to Poe, the detective story has puzzle potential—Poe even notes that the analyst likes to solve enigmas—for they contain facts which, if arranged correctly, will supply answers to the questions of who, why, and how. Fate, combined with the actions of the criminal, offers a problem to be solved, and the hero (the detective) does just this. Poe does not invite the reader to solve the puzzle but displays the hero's intellectual acumen in its solution. Conan Doyle does the same thing. He constructs narratives intended to evoke admiration of Holmes' intellect and not for the readers to solve. In *A Study in Scarlet,* for instance, the reader does not know of Holmes' telegram to the police in Ohio until after Jefferson Hope is caught, and without it cannot duplicate Holmes' deductions with the detective. Conan Doyle's successors did not use the detective tale as a puzzle for readers either. R. Austin Freeman's predilection for the inverted tale eliminates puzzle-playing by the reader and focuses attention on Thorndyke's methods. In all of these cases there is a puzzle which is solved, but it is solved solely by the fictional detective and all that is asked of the reader is admiration of the detective's perspicacity.

Things stood this way at the beginning of the 1920's when the Golden Age novel began to develop. Writers had not begun to pretend to take readers into the puzzle-solving in the novel. Christie, borrowing the Watson character from Conan Doyle, continued to twit the observer in the novel for not seeing the keys to the solution, and all of the novelists began to make the puzzle in the book more consistent and logical—Sayers, for instance, includes the air-locked motorcycle in *Unnatural Death* to provide the springboard for Wimsey's imaginative leap—but they never intended to involve the reader in solving the problem. First, they do not tell the readers that they are supposed to try to solve the puzzle, and without the challenge one cannot expect the game. Second, *they never expect that the reader will be able to anticipate the solution to the puzzle.* People began writing detective stories because they felt that they had invented a new device or expository technique which would completely befuddle, perplex, and thwart any attempt to forecast the solution: the most talked of novels of the Golden Age, novels like *The Murder of Roger Ackroyd* and *Unnatural Death,* do exactly that. Compare this to the jigsaw or crossword puzzle which fail for the players if they cannot achieve the solution; on the contrary, few people wish to read a detective novel which they can demonstrably forecast before the denouement. At any rate, the most important things in the novels of the early twenties were the reader's admiration of the detective's skill and his delight in the style, characterization, and surprise ending of the novel: all things which the traditional novel accomplished and which the thriller did not.

During the late 1920's, however, some detective writers began to consciously construct their books as puzzles for the readers. These books are clearly different from the standard detective novel of earlier in the decade. For one thing, they

contain specific puzzle signs: perhaps the most apparent of
these is the cast of characters and "challenge to the reader"
included in the Ellery Queen novels. These puzzle signs usually
involve a break in the normal narration and the intrusion of
another voice in parentheses or footnotes telling the reader to
consider certain objects or to come to certain conclusions. They
are also manifested in the missing object in Sayers' *Five Red
Herrings* (her only real puzzle story), and in various publishing
gimmicks like sealed pages, which are spoofed by Michael
Innes in *Hamlet, Revenge* in the piece of wire included in *Death
Laughs at Locksmiths*. Perhaps the earliest and most tedious
example of puzzle devices is in S.S. Van Dine's *The Greene
Murder Case* (1927), where there is a list of ninety-seven points
for the reader to rearrange with the solution ("3, 4, 44, 92...")
provided in a footnote to chapter twenty-six.

Concentrated attention to puzzles and the involvement of
the reader was perhaps a natural extension of the game spirit
of the genre. It grew particularly after the concerted attention
to rules in the late twenties—rules in every case which specified
that 1) all of the evidence must be available and 2) the writer
must play fair with the reader. The puzzle element which
stressed the reader's intellectual exercise was also a defense to
justify the detective novel: a defense similar to the crossword
player's position that these games "improve the mind."
Further, the stress on the reader's intellectual engagement had
something to do with the development of the hard-boiled
detective story in the U.S.. Van Dine and the Queens, who were
most dedicated to puzzle apparatus, were, after all, Americans
writing for the American middle-class, and in both America
and England writers of Golden Age fiction object to what
Ellery calls "the so-called realistic school of fiction" in *The
Chinese Orange Mystery,* and which Sayers labels as "light
reading for the masses" in *Unnatural Death.* Hammett,
Chandler, Whitfield, Daily, and others write for the lower-
class, whereas our detective stories are intellectual—they
develop the mind.

The rage for "pure puzzle stories" probably has its origins
in various party games which grew up along with charades in
the early twenties. The most popular of these, the game of
Murder, appears in detective novels by 1928 but no doubt was
invented somewhat earlier. In Murder, one guest is secretly
assigned the role of the murderer, and then he or she

unobtrusively nominates another guest to be the corpse. When the "body" is discovered, the remainder of the party assembles and asks questions in order to identify the "murderer" in their midst. This party game prompted a number of very popular puzzle books which frankly evolved from it. These books provided crime puzzles for the readers, encouraged them to figure out the solutions and gave the right answers in another section of the book—usually printed upside down to make "cheating" and access to the answers more difficult. The most successful of these was *The Baffle Book* (1928), by Lassiter Wren and Randle McKay; new editions appeared in 1929, 1930, and 1933. This volume contains narratives which include maps, charts, timetables, and fingerprints for the reader to ponder, and it not only asks the reader to solve the crime puzzle at the close of each story but also asks questions about chains of evidence. An even more popular example of this genre is H.A. Ripley's *How Good a Detective are You?*, which went through five printings from 1934 to 1937. These books came from America—S.S. Van Dine, in fact, wrote the introduction to the 1933 edition of *The Baffle Book*—but the fad spread to England too. Dennis Wheatley's "crime files" *(File on Bolitho Blane,* 1936; *File on Robert Prentice,* 1937; *Malinsay Massacre,* 1938; *Herewith the Clues,* 1939) are the ultimate extensions of the puzzle book. These were not novels but rather looseleaf binders containing "the complete dossier of a crime, with every clue preserved in its original, physical form, exactly as received at police headquarters."

These pure puzzle entertainments embodied the intellectual, problem-solving part of the detective story, and it is to them that people interested only in the puzzle turned. The detective story flirted only briefly with the idea of being an exclusively intellectual, problem-solving, crossword medium.

Devotion to the detective novel which featured the puzzle game between the writer and reader to the exclusion of all else did not last long. In 1931 H. Douglas Thompson, in *Masters of Mystery,* began inveighing against "puzzle fever," and novelists deserted the puzzle story or severely subordinated it. Ultimately the form failed, because no first-rate detective novelist was committed to it. Vestiges continue in Queen's challenges, Marsh's mid-book surveys of evidence, and Carr's warning footnotes, but each of these writers felt that in spite of the puzzle apparatus, the majority of readers did not read their stories for the sake of the puzzle games in them.

Puzzle Reactions

By the early thirties, the short life of the writer-reader puzzle novel was sick if not dying: most of the major crime writers gave it up for other kinds of detective forms. Partly this was due to the tedium of the pure puzzle story, but it was also due to the notion that, as J.B. Priestly suggested,[10] the detective novel could step out of popular fiction and become regular literature. Sayers makes this point in *The Omnibus of Crime* (1928), and A.B. Cox sums it up in terms of the puzzle story in the preface to *The Second Shot* (1930):

> I am personally convinced that the days of the old crime-puzzle pure and simple, relying entirely upon plot and without any added attractiveness of character, style, or even humour, are in the hands of the auditor; and that the detective story is in the process of developing into the novel with a detective interest, holding its readers less by mathematical [i.e. puzzle] than by psychological ties.

Writers were deserting the puzzle story in droves.

The first destination was the country of psychology. After the war the impact of psychology, especially Freudian psychology, hit England. One can see this on one hand in the novels of D.H. Lawrence and on the other hand in Sayers' unshakeable hatred for everything that Lawrence and psychoanalysis stood for. In spite of Sayers' antipathy, some very watered-down psychology enters the detective novels in the thirties. Christie, for instance, begins using megalo and other assorted manias as the motivation in her plots, and she adds "the psychology" to Poirot's arsenal of stock remarks. Most writers and most readers were, however, out of sympathy with probing libidos or analyzing mother fixations— Lawrence's early novels were, after all, banned in England. Detective writers turned instead to psychological thrillers built around detective story motifs which exploited and examined not sex but fear. Cox led the way in this. Under the pseudonym Francis Iles, he wrote *Malice Aforethought* (1931) and *Before the Fact* (1932) which ignore detective puzzles and watch instead the reactions of the murderer and his victim. Novels like these and Philip MacDonald's *Murder Gone Mad* (1931) intend to catch the reader up in the oppressive danger of crime rather than in intellectual analysis. They remind one very much of Alfred Hitchcock, whose 1926 film of Marie Belloc Lowndes' *The Lodger* (1913), along with that novel itself, may have influenced some writers to move to the psychological thriller.

If the English (and American) reading public would not tolerate the direct Freudianism of Lawrence and his followers, they would and did admire the repressed sexuality of the romance. E.M. Hull's *The Sheik* (1922), along with the works of Elinor Glyn and Ethel M. Dell, sold like hot cakes during the twenties. Detective writers from Collins on had introduced the motif of love into their detective stories, but in the twenties, probably in reaction to the popular romance, they drew back, and one finds Van Dine decreeing that "there must be no love interest" in the detective story. The sea of passion was, however, too strong, and in the thirties it swept into the detective novel. Sayers led the way with her Harriet Vane-Wimsey books, and others followed: Allingham with *Dancers in Mourning* (1937), *Fashion in Shrouds* (1938), and *Traitor's Purse* (1940); Marsh with her books from *Vintage Murder* (1937) to *Death in a White Tie* (1938); Ellery Queen with *The Door Between* (1937); Christie with *Death on the Nile* (1937). Much of this may have been due to the interest in "romance" stirred by the abdication of Edward in 1936, but whatever the cause, one finds love dominating or co-equal with the detective interest in these books. Most of the writers also adopt some of the patterns familiar to the romance: the pains of love, the accidental misunderstanding, the tragic past and rescue from it, and the issue of giving one's self to another. All of these flash on the screen, making the detective story of the thirties into a different kind of fiction.

But most of the writers were aware that the romance could never be important literature, and while they wrote romance elements into their novels, they also nudged them toward a more acceptable literary tradition—the novel of manners. This can be seen especially in Sayers' portrait of the advertising industry in *Murder Must Advertise,* and in her last two works, *Gaudy Night* (1935), and *Busman's Honeymoon* (1937). Allingham and Marsh later did the same thing in exploring the milieu of the theater, the art world, publishing, and fashion design. These writers in the thirties turn from the detective story in its pure state and spend much more effort on drawing background and character than on articulating their detective plots.

Finally, some of the detective writers who took up the craft in the thirties took up the bubbling high spirits with which the Golden Age began. Carr shot off a pair of comic detectives, whose gambols in the fields of the puzzle story not only bring it to its highest achievement but also turn it back to the tongue-in-cheek hijinks of the early twenties. Likewise Michael Innes, with the exception of his tribute to Collins in *Lament for a Maker* (1938), capered about creating excruciating puzzles and laughing at them at the same time, as did the American Anthony Boucher in *The Seven of Calvary* (1937).

At the end of the long week-end between the two World Wars, the detective novel had developed into a flexible medium which could entertain people in many different ways. It brought pity and fear as well as sighs and belly laughs to a class of people who were either discomfited or bored by other kinds of literature. The Golden Age detective novel attracted a generation of witty, ingenious, and sometimes sensitive writers who reveled in the form until it bored them or they became mesmerized by it, or until the world of the Golden Age story came to an end. The end was announced by the thunder of German panzers striking into Poland.

Chapter 2

E. C. Bentley

"Remembering that well-thought-out little work of Mr. Bentley's I examined Levy's mouth for false teeth."
> Dorothy Sayers, *Whose Body?* (1923)

Gott had risen and was prowling around the room. Coming to the bookcase, he found himself confronted, as had Appleby the night before, with *Trent's Last Case*. He picked up this bible of his craft and, opening it at random, seemed absorbed for a space of minutes.
> **Michael Innes,** *Death at the President's Lodging* (1936)

These are not bad reviews to get. They show pretty clearly the place of *Trent's Last Case* in the development of the detective novel between the wars.

Of course Bentley had no idea that his detective story would make such a splash. After St. Paul's School and Merton College, Oxford, Bentley settled into journalism, having already gained some reputation among his friends as a wit and a poet through the invention of the nonsense verse form, the Clerihew (Bentley's middle name). A boyhood friend of Chesterton, he was one of those Edwardians who "splashed about in intellectual life in a thoroughly carefree way."[1] *Trent's Last Case* was a result of all of this. Bentley dedicated his detective novel to Chesterton, suggesting that they had discussed the story's concept in France in 1910, and he also dedicated it to "the spirit of youth." The spirit and idea of *Trent's Last Case,* however, transcend the spirit of youth. True, the book is youthful in its high spirits and love of melodrama, but it is also self-conscious and, in a way, serious at the same time. *Trent's Last Case* suited so many readers and writers between the wars because it is a blend of the serious and the comic: Bentley ridicules and appreciates, parodies and imitates. And his principal material is the traditions of the detective story from Poe to Collins to Conan Doyle.

29

Before coming to *Trent's Last Case,* we need to be aware of what had happened to the detective story when Bentley came upon it. After Conan Doyle's Juggernaut got under way in the 1890's, a number of writers began to create characters and plots exploiting the separate parts of what Eliot calls Holmes' manifold "abilities, accomplishments and peculiarities." The characters of Sexton Blake, Nayland-Smith and others capitalized on the adventure potential in the Holmes stories; Drs. Thorndyke and Craig Kennedy followed up on the scientific potential latent in Holmes; Max Carrados and The Old Man in the Corner developed as eccentric detectives following the pattern set by Conan Doyle. As Raffles might have said, they were *post Holmes ergo propter Holmes.* All of these characters were created in businesslike imitation or serious reaction to the Great Detective in hopes of capturing or sharing some of Conan Doyle's success with the public. Simultaneously, a number of writers, including Mark Twain, realized the unreality, absurdity, and pure comic potential of the "Great Detective." Thus in the early 1900's we get a whole list of comic detectives with names like Herlock Sholmes, Hemlock Shears, Picklock Holes, Shylock Homes, Shamrock Jolnes, Sherlaw Kombs, etc. These detectives appear in stories which were outright comic reductions of Conan Doyle's detective. One only has to look into Mark Twain's "Double-barreled Detective Story" (1902) to get the jist of the full-bodied burlesque of the infallible, unflappable, universally accomplished detective.

What Bentley did when he composed *Trent's Last Case* was to combine both of these reactions to Holmes, the serious and the comic, in a single book which blends parody with imitation and thus satisfies the demands of the intelligent reader who, to relieve his boredom, would like to read detective stories but is put off by their pomposity or embarrassed by their naivete. To this end he shapes the dialogue, the characters, and the plot of *Trent's Last Case.*

In the opening sections of the novel, Bentley presents his detective hero as a man of demonstrated competence but also as a comic character (in the early portions of the novel, in fact, most of the characters and events have a light tone). As the text introduces him to the reader, Philip Trent has all of the qualifications of the renaissance man and, in the context of the detective story, the Great Detective. He became involved in criminology "very much [as]...Poe" did by acting as the armchair detective, analyzing newspaper accounts of a crime and finding the solution which the others had missed. As a consequence of this, a newspaper baron made him a special correspondent for crime and he has a remarkable history of success. Not that he does it for the money, mind you, for Trent is a young man of independent means who directs his major energies toward his chosen profession, painting. So far, so good; Trent could have been any of the contemporaries of Sherlock Holmes. Bentley does provide a quick laugh for middle class readers by pointing out that Trent not only paints but also sells his pictures. The real shock, however, comes upon Trent's first entrance. He enters with cap and bells, prattling a language full of burlesque literary allusion and self-conscious parody. Take this example of Trent's speech to Mr. Cupples:

> I should prefer to put it that I have come down in the character of
> the avenger of blood, to hunt down the guilty, and vindicate the
> honour of society. That is my line of business. Families waited on
> at their private residences.[1a]

Most of this passage could have come straight out of the thriller with the speaker righteously stating his moral position. The inclusion of the advertisement in the last line, however, overthrows this and gives the reader the signal that the whole passage is facetious.

Trent's persiflage is simply part of his character early in the novel. He is an intelligent young man to whom everything comes easily, who skips through problems and plays at those things at which others must work. This is apparent in his first conversation with his publisher, Sir James Molloy:

> "Trent," said Sir James impressively," it is important. I want you
> to do some work for us."
> "Some play, you mean."[2]

Precisely the same issue arises when Trent meets the Scotland Yard drudge. Here he says

> "Well now, inspector, I suppose we play the game as before."[3]

His language is simply part of Trent's overall attitude toward himself and toward life.

The whole business of making your hero blithely talk nonsense plays an important part in the detective novel after the First World War, what with Wimsey and Campion as well as the wise-cracking hero of the thriller (especially Simon Templar) and the American hard-boiled story. Part of the impetus of this, of course, comes from writers' attempts to capture current slang in order to build contemporary characters. Then, also, there is the impression of ease and nonchalance when a character under stress can be witty and facetious. Bentley knew this last point because he must have read it in one of friend Chesterton's earliest works, *The Defendant* (1901) in which G.K.C. describes the detective story as a romance and the hero as the "knight errant" who stands

> ...somewhat fatuously fearless amid the knives and fists of a thieves' kitchen.[4]

Fatuous, but purposely fatuous, is a good way in which to describe Trent early in the novel, and Bentley purposely builds up both his fatuous frivolity and his over-confidence in order to reverse them in the end. One can, in fact, graph the major reversal in the plot by tracking the changes in Trent's speech. The novel closes with his sophisticated poses removed and his nonchalance bridled. At the end he is the Great Detective no more and this is his last case.

Bentley cuts Trent down to human size through two major turns in the plot. The first, and the most famous, shock to Trent's character as the Great Detective comes from the demonstration that his finely wrought analysis of the crime was built on false assumptions and is, therefore, demonstrably wrong. One can hardly go on as the perfect thinking machine after one has produced a faulty product. But before Trent discovers that he is wrong, he falls in love and as a result of the apparent impossibility of his passion he travels to the continent. In a chapter entitled "Evil Days" Trent suffers from his hopeless love, but he also enters the real world of violence and bloodshed:

> He was the only correspondent who saw General Dragilew killed in the street of Volmar by a girl of eighteen. He saw burnings, lynchings, fusillades, hangings; each day his soul sickened afresh at the imbecilities born of misrule.[5]

Playing detective and mouthing witty blather in the idyllic puppet theater makes no sense when compared with man's inhumanity to man. Human misery is something which cannot be punned away or even shut out of the consciousness once it has taken root. The next generation of detective story writers would slowly learn this for themselves, but Bentley knew it in the teens. That is, he knew about the implications of real violence for the detective story. He did not, however, impress this on the form itself, for whatever may happen to Trent's consciousness in the middle of the novel, it does not cloud the end of the story, and the plot remains, in many ways an excellent demonstration of what the Golen Age detective novel should be.

Before *Trent's Last Case* the detective story was written principally as the short story, and this has certain consequences for the writer's purpose. In the detective short story the writer simply does not have the time or space to do more than establish the facts of the problem, render the confusion which it causes in most characters, and expound the solution through the detective hero. In short stories from Poe through Freeman the chief reaction expected in the reader is either confusion or wonder, or both. The novel, on the other hand, provides an opportunity to toy with the reader's reactions. Collins, for instance, sets in motion several lines of false conjecture for the reader to follow (did Rosanna Spearman or Rachael or the Indians steal the Moonstone?) only to undercut them all with the revelations about Franklin Blake's complicity and the guilt of an unsuspected individual. Reversal of expectations lies at the center of *The Moonstone*— and at the heart of *Trent's Last Case* as well. In Bentley's memoir, *Those Days* (1940), he writes a rambling and somewhat self-congratulatory chapter on the composition of *Trent's Last Case.* Here he reveals that during the composition of the novel he decided that it would be amusing if Trent's meticulous deductions turned out to be completely wrong. The novel, of course, does exactly this and it reverses our expectations about the detective story in which the hero never fails. On one hand, *Trent's Last Case* defeats readers' expectations about the hero, but on the other hand it confirms them about the detective story through the workings of the plot. The plot confirms our preconceived notion that the detective story will unravel the true facts about the commission of the crime that started the whole business off. Bentley has it both ways.

Trent's Last Case runs on the major reversals in Trent's character, but these are only part of a whole complex of reversals which pervade the plot of the novel. Bentley turns many things upside down during the course of the story and listing all of them would spoil the anticipation; a list of a few of the reversals will show their number and variety:

> 1. In the opening remarks about Sigsbee Manderson, it seems as if he will become a wild speculator on Wall Street and an uncontrolled gambler, but instead he turns into a disciplined financier.
> 2. The public believes that Manderson is a stabilizing force in an insecure market, but it is not Manderson but Jeffrey who is holding up the market.
> 3. Jeffrey should be safe and successful from his heroic saving of everyone else's bacon, but he fails.
> 4. Manderson's death should create a crash of epic proportions, but it does not. There is no crash.
> 5. We expect some moral comment on Manderson's death (*sic transit,* and all that), but Bentley only shows Sir James Molloy gloating over the fact that he can turn it to his own financial advantage.
> 6. Manderson being, after all, an American tycoon, should be a big spender, a loudmouth, and live on a lavish scale, but he is an ascetic whose only extravagance is shoes, and this comes more from the detective plot than from the character.
> 7. Mabel Manderson should be in love with Marlowe; this is not the case.
> 8. Marlowe should be the murderer, but he is not.
> 9. Manderson should have committed suicide, but instead he got murdered.
> 10. The murderer ought to be vindictive or unrepentant, and should be carted off to jail at the close, but at the end of the novel he is satisfied, happy and free.

And there are more reversals than these. Bentley springs surprises at the beginning, middle and end of the novel; it is the principle upon which the book works.

Seeing all of this one can hardly say that Bentley intended to "play fair." Neither this nor about ninety percent of the novels written from 1920 to 1940 intends to take the readers into the writer's confidence and let them solve the crime. If there is anything in the traditional identification of the reader with the hero, then Bentley intends to befuddle, confuse, dupe and surprise. One simply cannot figure out the solution to the crime in *Trent's Last Case* before it is given at the end. Naturally, the whole thing makes some sense after Bentley unwraps the conclusion, but as the narrative unfolds, there are quirks and gaps which make pre-solution based on inductive or deductive logic impossible. For one thing, the story rests on a culprit who does not have a trace of a guilty conscience and who, after the murder, does not think about it at all. Here is a look into the murderer's mind on the morning after the crime:

> He was thinking about breakfast. In this case the colloquialism must be taken literally: he really was thinking about breakfast.[6]

Therefore, although Bentley gives us a glimpse into the murderer's consciousness, it does not help us in gaining a solution of the crime—a device which Christie would later make famous in the twenties. Further, Bentley omits a great deal of important material from the first part of the plot and saves it for the summary. A small instance of this comes when Trent fires off a telegram about Marlowe and its contents are withheld. Another, and more important fact that Bentley omits is that Manderson's body has been moved. The moved body is a technique, like disguise, which would be liberally used by writers in the twenties and thirties, and which is ideal for the detective writer's purposes since it means that the murder could have been committed somewhere, anywhere, else, by someone, anyone, other than the chief suspect. It also means that the writer can either mock the use of physical evidence or use the technique of the moved body to shoehorn in even more physical evidence. At any rate, Bentley does not intend to "play fair;" he intends to confuse his readers and surprise them with the grand turnabout. The plot, the characters, and much of the effect of *Trent's Last Case* depend on the reversal.

When Bentley began *Trent's Last Case,* the detective story was just that, the detective short story. The most famous detective writers, Poe, Conan Doyle, Freeman, Bramah, Orczy, *et. al*, wrote short stories, and when some of them like Conan Doyle turned to the novel their story telling gifts failed them. Even the French *roman policier* was hardly what one would like to call a unified novel. There had been, however, one well constructed detective novel—Wilkie Collins' *The Moonstone.* When Century accepted Bentley's novel for publication they made him change the hero's name to Trent, and they changed the book's title to *The Woman in Black*. This title is not only more romantic but it may have also been the publisher's play on the title of Collins' first novel, *The Woman in White*—if it was not it should have been, for there is a lot of Collins in *Trent's Last Case*. From one perspective, Bentley's book is simply a remake of *The Moonstone*. Consider the story of *The Moonstone*. The hero, Franklin Blake, who is, among other things, a painter, gives up his investigations into the loss of the diamond because of a romantic snub. He lounges about the continent without enthusiasm, returns to England, confronts the woman he loves, and takes up the investigation again. He gathers more facts but cannot solve the theft without the intervention of Ezra Jennings. Now consider the story of *Trent's Last Case*. The hero, Trent, who is, among other things, a painter, gives up his investigation into Manderson's death because of his romantic attachment to Mabel Manderson. He travels around the continent, returns to England, confronts the woman he loves, and takes up the investigation again. He gathers more facts (chiefly from Marlowe), but is unable to solve the mystery without the intervention of Mr. Cupples who unravels the whole mystery. Pretty similar. There are some other details too: the Indians in Collins become the hypothetical union thugs lurking about to exact revenge upon Manderson for his shoddy practices in America, and the melancholy Mabel standing on the cliffs reminds one of Rosanna Spearman contemplating the quicksand. From the historical view point, all of this makes sense. Bentley carries the tradition of Collins to a new generation of writers in the twenties and the thirties, and he streamlines the tradition too: he cuts down on the sentiment (which later writers would completely kill off only to rejuvenate), brushes up the character of the hero, and crystallizes the playful manipulation of the reader's expectations.

It is in this last respect, the playful manipulation of the reader's expectations, that Bentley fathers the writers of the Golden Age. Upon opening *Trent's Last Case* one immediately experiences a tone which is aloof, wry, and playful. The opening chapters on Manderson flicker back and forth between objective reportage and gagged satiric laughter, and, although we descend into sentiment in the middle of the novel, the twinkle comes back at the end. Through all of this the book works in the unique roller coaster third person point of view which would become the standard in the twenties, now dipping into characters' minds, now presenting dialogue, now showing facts, now excluding them or covering them up. If one has the patience and knows where to look, *Trent's Last Case* is, indeed, the bible of the detective writer's craft.

Chapter 3

Agatha Christie

Agatha Mary Clarissa Miller Christie Mallowan, C.B.E., has a sufficient number of names. To these journalists have added the titles of "Mistress of Mystery," and "Queen of Crime." After Bentley she is the first of the new detective writers and she is, no doubt, the most successful, having turned out best-selling detective fiction for over fifty years. Early in the twenties she proved conclusively that the detective story could be turned into the short novel—all of Christie's novels are short—and it has flourished in this form ever since. Forgetting for the moment writers like Wallace, Oppenheim, and Creasy, Christie was by ordinary standards a prolific writer: from 1920 to 1940 she wrote twenty-six detective novels, several collections of detective short stories, two romantic novels under the name Mary Westmacott, and a memoir. During this period she also, no doubt, wrote the story of Poirot's death, *Curtain*, which remained unpublished until after her death. *Sleeping Murder*, the second posthumous novel, was probably written shortly after World War II.[1] She is clearly the most popular of all of the detective writers of the era—shown by the fact that four of her books (*The Murder of Roger Ackroyd, And Then There Were None, Peril at End House*, and *Easy to Kill*) have sold over a million copies in the U.S. while none of her fellow writers has reached this level of sales. Christie's popularity, however, sometimes puzzles critics. It certainly puzzled me for a long time. Why do people read her books? The novels lack any sort of stylistic distinction, as she would have admitted, her characters are vapid or superficial, hardly any scene setting or atmosphere comes into her novels, and the consideration of moral or social issues is banal. Readers for fifty years have forgotten or overlooked this and identified Christie with Hercule Poirot's idiosyncratic character, and the pace of the action in her plots. Her reputation and popularity rests on these things, and Christie knew it; she used Poirot in thirty-five novels between 1920 and 1975, and prided herself on the fresh surprises provided by the least likely character routine. Looking back at her production during the first twenty years, I hope, gives some perspective on Christie and the nature of her books, perspective which has been lost.

During the twenties Christie wrote nine detective novels. Four of these are what can be considered "straight" detective stories: *The Mysterious Affair at Styles* (1920), *Murder on the Links* (1923), *The Murder of Roger Ackroyd* (1926), and *The Mystery of the Blue Train* (1928). These novels focus on detection of the perpetrator of a murder and follow Poirot's efforts toward this end. During the same period, however, Christie wrote five other novels which mix detection with adventure, humor, and a touch of romance: *The Secret Adversary* (1922), *The Man in the Brown Suit* (1924), *The Secret of Chimneys* (1925), *The Big Four* (1927), and *The Seven Dials Mystery* (1929). To put it simply, Christie wrote more "fringe" detective stories during the twenties than she wrote straight ones. That she wrote five novels which can be considered thrillers disturbs orthodox commentators who wish to see Christie as a consistently orthodox writer of "classical" detective stories; they usually shrug these early books off as entertainments which are separable and separate from the detective stories—as Christie's Mary Westmacott romances are. Thus the standard biography of Christie holds that until 1930 and *Murder at the Vicarage* she fooled around a good bit and that, thank goodness, she finally settled down to standard detective works. Barzun, for example, notes that *Murder at the Vicarage* "marks a turning point in Agatha's output: henceforth Poirot and detection predominate, gradually replacing the earlier adventure stories and thrillers."[2] I have no wish to tackle Barzun on this point—it is probably true that 1930 is the watershed date after which Christie under her own name wrote detective books only. I do, however, wish to say a word for the much maligned thriller, for one can learn a great deal about Christie from her early thrillers. She did not see them as separate from the Poirot books, as she saw the romances which she published under a pseudonym. What happens in the five thrillers becomes a basis for what happens in the Poirot books. In looking at them we come a step closer to understanding the genesis of the detective story as written by

Christie for over fifty years—the genesis of plots, characters, narrative techniques, and stirrings of purpose. She intended to do—and did—the same things in her detective stories that she had done in her thrillers, only in a slightly different genre which grew more restrictive in the 1930's.

Christie's first thriller, *The Secret Adversary*, crosses the adventure thriller with various strains of the same breed. Like Oppenheim's *The Amazing Partnership* (1914), the main characters are two young people who form a partnership to have fun and do detective work—the amazing part for Oppenheim was that one of the partners was a woman, but this was not so strange for Christie. They place an ad in the newspaper, as Bulldog Drummond does in *Bulldog Drummond* (1920), announcing "Two young adventurers for hire. Willing to do anything, go anywhere. Pay must be good...no reasonable offer refused." They stumble into a plot to foment a general strike, motivated by an evil group which has in its possession an incriminating document which they will expose on a given date. Mr. Brown, the mysterious leader who no one knows since he is a master of disguise, leads a conspiracy filled with Germans and Russians. During the course of the book, the girl, Tuppence, poses as a maid to obtain evidence about Mr. Brown, and both she and the boy, Tommy, fall into the enemy's toils but manage to escape. The sinister Mr. Brown turns out to be one of the people who had been helping Tuppence and Tommy with their detection. Setting a trap of their own, the good people catch Mr. Brown, avert disaster, and move inexorably toward the altar. Loud Cheers. The novel has little subtlety or cleverness in it; it is just the story of two nice youngsters chasing about, saving their country from the Reds. But it is a bit more than this, for the novel contains Christie's first least likely suspect who is concealed because he works with the detectives. It would become one of Christie's standard devices. Also, Christie clearly understands the book's purpose: fun and excitement. Thus Tuppence and Tommy form their partnership "for the fun of the thing" and Christie dedicated the novel to:

> All those who lead monotonous lives in hope that they may experience at second hand the delights and dangers of adventure.

The next book, *The Man in the Brown Suit*, exudes a bit

less naivete than the first thriller—for one thing the domestic political connection of *The Secret Adversary* has disappeared—and a bit more romance has been added. In this novel, Anne Beddingfeld, a retreaded Tuppence, witnesses a murder, follows a cryptic clue to South Africa where she tries to track down the Master Crook and revolution fomenter whose identity is hidden from all. Evil minions capture her, but she escapes by cutting her bonds with a broken glass, and with the help of an enigmatically romantic man (who will become her husband) and Colonel Race, (who is something in the Secret Service) she runs the enemy to ground. As in the first thriller, the story begins with the heroine's search for excitement and adventure to relieve the boredom of normal life. More importantly, Christie introduces for the first time another of what will become her standard techniques. *The Man in the Brown Suit* contains a mixture of third person narrative, Anne's narration of her adventures, and extracts from the diary of Sir Eustace Pedler, M.P., a nice enough old codger who is delivering some papers from the Government to South Africa. Only Pedler is the Master Crook, and Christie fools the reader by giving innocent snatches from his diary worked in with the other kinds of narration. Here is the germ of *The Murder of Roger Ackroyd,* Christie's best known deception, written in a thriller fully two years before the publication of the straight detective story.

In 1925 Christie's thrillers took a new turn; not only did they become less naive, they became chiefly comic, burlesque versions of popular literature. The essentials of the thriller still remain: the murder, the stolen document, the terminal date, the disguised master criminal. But now they appear as jokes. *The Secret of Chimneys* contains two murders, political intrigue, a disguised international jewel thief, a document which, if published, will overturn governments, and a secret society. Christie, however, sets these in a comic atmosphere. Lord Caterham putters around his estate grumbling about being put upon and being invaded by politicos from Whitehall, and Lomax from the Foreign Office persecutes every available ear with windy political speeches. Moreover, the main plot burlesques Anthony Hope's novels about Ruritania. (In *Passenger to Frankfurt* [1970], Lady Matilda, no doubt speaking for Christie, says that reading *The Prisoner of Zenda* was "about the only taste of romance we got" growing up in

Edwardian days).[3] As Hope's novels, beginning with *The Prisoner of Zenda,* deal with the dynastic problems of a mythical European kingdom, *The Secret of Chimneys* chronicles the adventures of Anthony (note the name) Cade, heir to the Herzlovakian throne, who is surrounded by various Herzlovakian politicians, including one nobleman with the patently ludicrous name, Count Lolopretjzyl. To this Christie adds a dash of *The Moonstone* with some business about the stolen Koh-i-noor diamond, which Superintendent Battle, a remade Sergeant Cuff, eventually finds buried in the rose garden. Chesterton, too, comes in, for the French detective who arrives to catch the elusive jewel thief is much like Flambeau in "The Blue Cross." The tone of the whole book can easily be gauged from the fact that when Cade arrives in London he registers (unconscious of future irony) not at the Ritz, but at the luxurious Blitz Hotel. The novel bubbles with playing and burlesque.

Precisely the same thing holds for the next thriller, *The Big Four.* In Poirot's only thriller appearance he foils four, count them, Master Criminals who attempt to dominate the world through new inventions, radio waves and atomic power. A super-intellectual Chinaman who has his secret lair in Limehouse leads the four crooks. During the course of the book Poirot and Hastings discover the identities of the villains and eventually destroy them in their mountain hideout. Here the burlesque is so thorough that it is difficult to pick out one writer who is consistently lampooned. To start, the adventure begins with a secret service agent stumbling into Poirot's flat and dying, leaving an enigmatic clue—comparable to what happens to Hannay at the beginning of *The Thirty Nine Steps.* Conan Doyle comes in too. One simply cannot see Poirot's invention of a smarter brother, Achille, as anything but a laugh about Mycroft. How could it be serious imitation? And Fu Manchu plays a large role too. In the persons of the Big Four, Christie simply split Fu Manchu up into his constituent parts. One villain is a vastly intellectual Chinaman, another is a master of disguise, and a third is a scientist who perverts science from its pure course. During one part of the adventure the villain lures Hastings to a labyrinth in Limehouse, Fu Manchu's haunt, and threatens him with a watery grave; this repeats Nayland-Smith's and Petrie's encounter with the Master Villain in *The Insidious Fu Manchu.* Christie also has all writers knowledgeable about China threatened, just as Fu Manchu threatens Parson Dan in Rohmer's book.

The spirit of burlesque and hi-jinks carries over into the last thriller of the twenties, *The Seven Dials Mystery*. This book takes up characters from *The Secret of Chimneys* and involves them in an even more improbable situation: suppose that Sapper's Bulldog Drummond story *The Black Gang* (1922), in which Drummond and his adventure-loving chums go about beating sense into communists and other criminals, had been written by P.G. Wodehouse. This was the premise of Christie's novel. A group of young adventurers form a secret society—the Black Gang to Sapper, the Seven Dials here—to fight crime. But Christie's heroes are hardly hulking brutes. They are patently Wodehousean characters with names like Pongo, Codders, Bundle, and Socks: these sound a bit like Stinker Pinker, Stiffy Byng, Bongo Little or Oofy Prosser from the master. Christie's characters also act like people in Wodehouse. To avoid Codders' noxious embrace, for instance, Bundle simply jumps out of the window and runs. Lord Caterham and his mansion, Chimneys, have become very much like the Earl of Emsworth and Blandings Castle in the Wodehouse saga. Christie even tries to write Wodehouse:

> I congratulate you on the handling of Pongo. O'Rourke was probably a sitter—but Pongo is made of other stuff. There's only one word for that lad—it was in the *Sunday Nosebag* crossword last week. Word of ten letters meaning everywhere at once. Ubiquitous. That describes Pongo down to the ground.[4]

This is not good Wodehouse, which only he could write, but here wish and act go together. The linguistic imitation is only one part of the complex of items which combines to give the flavor of a Wodehousean burlesque. There is even one character with a valet who has exquisite taste and is ruthlessly efficient!

Now that we have skipped through all of Christie's early thrillers it seems clear that they present the reader with a number of *caveats*. Since the thrillers were the laboratory in which Christie tried out some of the standard turns of her regular detective books, they ought not be dismissed as her frivolous practices of the twenties. With this in mind the reader needs to ask about the writer's purpose in all of her detective novels, and whether the aim of providing diversion and excitement extends from the thrillers into the other books. Also, Christie wrote a number of thrillers which blatantly parody the popular fiction of the era. Do parody and burlesque play a part in the detective novels too? The rhetoric is transparent: obviously the form and techniques of her early thrillers shaped the kind of detective stories which Christie turned to in the thirties.

How does one establish that Christie's novels of the thirties, which seem to be respectable, well-made detective stories, were in reality domesticated thrillers? First of all, it can be done by looking for statements of the detective story's purpose and the effect which it is supposed to have on its readers. Like other detective writers of the period, Christie included a number of fictional detective story writers and people who read detective stories in the novels which she wrote in the thirties. The first of these fictional writers, Mr. Daniel Clancy (author of *The Clue of the Scarlet Pedal),* pops into the plot of *Death in the Air*—a work written five years after Christie officially dropped the thriller. Mr. Clancy writes books about a detective named Wilbraham Rice:

> The public have taken very strongly to Wilbraham Rice. He bites his nails and eats a lot of bananas. I don't know why I made him bite his nails, to start with; it's really rather disgusting, but there it is.... The bananas aren't so bad; you get a bit of fun out of them—criminals slipping on the skin.[5]

After talking about his slap-stick hero, Mr. Clancy goes on to discuss the attraction of certain subjects in detective fiction:

> You can't write anything too sensational...Especially when you're dealing with the arrow poison of the South American Indians. I know it was snake juice really, but the principle is the same. After all, you don't want a detective story to be like real life? Look at the things in the papers—dull as ditch water.[6]

At least Mr. Clancy describes detective stories as needing both comedy and excitement to compensate the readers for their trouble.

The other detective writer created by Christie in the thirties appears in *Cards on the Table* (1936). Here we meet Mrs. Ariadne Oliver, who has written thirty-two detective novels, including *The Lotus Murder, The Clue of the Candle*

Wax (which even Poirot has read), *The Death in the Drain Pipe,* and *The Body in the Library* (a title which Christie herself would use for one of her real novels in 1942). All of these fictions within fiction feature a Finnish detective named Sven Hjerson. Christie makes Mrs. Oliver's opinions about the nature of the detective story largely echo what Mr. Clancy had said the year before:

> What really matters is plenty of bodies! If the thing's getting a little dull, some more blood cheers it up. Somebody is going to tell something—and they're killed first! That always goes down well. It comes in all my books—camouflaged different ways of course. And people *like* untraceable poisons, and idiotic police inspectors and girls tied up in cellars with sewer gas or water pouring in...and a hero who can dispose of anything from three to seven villains single-handed. I've written thirty two books by now—and of course they're all exactly the same, as M. Poirot seems to have noticed—but nobody else has—and I only regret one thing—making my detective a Finn. I really don't know anything about Finns.[7]

Or, one might add, Belgians. Whether or not this is an accurately autobiographical portrait, it gives perspective on the detective writer's purpose. Mrs. Oliver does not stress ratiocination, though she does not scorn it, but insists that detective stories need sensation and excitement. They differ from thrillers because the thrill and sensation are hidden by conventions like alibi and motive hunting.

Writers of popular fiction put into their works what their readers want, or what they perceive that their readers should or do want. Christie depicts several characters in her works of the period who are detective story addicts. All of them read detective stories for diversion and excitement. Thus, Mrs. Croft, a disabled and retired lady in *Peril at End House* (1931), says,

> I've read all the detective stories that ever were, I should think. Nothing else seems to pass the time so quick.[8]

Detective stories provide her with diversion, not intellectual exercise, since Mrs. Croft hardly would seek that. The other reason for turning to the thriller, excitement, is mentioned in *The Boomerang Clue* (1933), where Christie couples it to the detective story. In this book, when Bobby Jones is hospitalized he finds the available books not to his taste.

> To a mind nourished on *The Third Bloodstain, The Case of the Murdered Archduke* and *The Strange Adventure of the Florentine Dagger,* Mrs. Mulock Craik's *Halifax* somehow lacked pep.[9]

These all seem to be detective titles, titles to which the reader looks for excitement. Realistically, few of Christie's readers, in the novels or out, read with pad and pencil making notes or compiling lists and they do not compare complicated alibis or dog ear pages with significant points on them—look through a second hand Christie novel and you will find none of these things. Reading is not an exercise in logic or at least Christie does not approach it as such. Thus neither Mr. Clancy nor Mrs. Oliver writes for this kind of reader. Their stories exist for diversion and excitement, and so do Christie's. But these things can take any number of forms.

One constant in Christie's regular detective novels from 1920 to 1940 grows from her aim to excite and divert. She wishes to involve the reader in the movement of the action. One way in which she does this is through her heroes. In thrillers, heroes go into detection for fun and adventure, whereas in straight detective stories the hero is typically aloof from the action. Christie's novels from *The Mysterious Affair at Styles* onward bring in subsidiary detectives who serve several purposes. Of course they serve a number of classical roles in her detective books: they are sounding boards for Poirot, they are collectors of information, and they attract the reader's attention so that the chief detective's work can legitimately be done off-stage. Almost always in Christie, however, they experience the thrill and excitement of the plot. They obviously function as surrogates for the reader. In spite of his stolidness, Hastings sometimes serves this purpose, but there are lots of other subordinate detectives who highlight the excitement latent in the novels: Katherine Grey in *Mystery of the Blue Train;* Dr. Constantine in *Murder on the Calais Coach* (1933); Bobby Jones and Lady Frances in *The Boomerang Clue* (1933); a whole group in *The ABC Murders* (1935); Jane Grey in *Death in the Air* (1935); Egg Gore in *Murder in Three Acts* (1935); Mrs. Oliver in *Cards on the Table* (1936); and Bridget in *Easy to Kill* (1938). Each of them feels the thrill and threat of the thriller in the detective story. Poirot gives the equation of the reader's

attachment to the detective story in two conversations with
Katherine Grey in *The Mystery of the Blue Train:*

> "I see madame, that you have a *roman policier.*
> You are fond of such things?"
> "They amuse me," Katherine said.
> The little man nodded with the air of complete understanding.
> "They have a good sale always, so I am told. Now why is that, eh
> Mademoiselle? I ask it of you as a student of human nature—why
> should that be?"
> Katherine felt more and more amused.
> "Perhaps they give one the illusion of living an exciting life," she
> suggested.[10]

Later, after the action begins, Poirot tells Katherine

> "Excellent," said Poirot, and gave her a friendly nod. "This shall
> be a *roman policier a nous.*"[11]

Katherine as well as the reader supposedly plunge into the
vicarious excitement of the detective story. Even if Christie's
books of the thirties stopped being literal thrillers, her
characters expect them to serve the same purposes. The fact is
that you can take Christie out of the thriller but you cannot
take the thriller out of Christie. It creeps in even when it is
rejected and reviled.

By 1930 Christie was in a strange position. She was a
prominent detective story writer who had received a good deal
of publicity and notoriety, but she had written a lot of books
which "purists" did not consider detective novels and snubbed
as thrillers. This put Christie into a peculiar position,
especially since in the 1920's the new detective writers made a
concerted effort to separate the detective story from its low-
brow kin. Sayers traced the detective story back to the Greeks,
and W.H. Wright in America emphasized its intellectual,
problem-solving side. The thriller was passe. So in 1930
Christie turned exclusively to the regular detective story and,
with the exception of *The Boomerang Clue,* dropped the
thriller. In fact, signs of outward conversion appear in her
novels of the early thirties. Confession, contrition, and public
penance mark most conversions, and these signs appear in the
novels written after 1930. More than in *Murder at the Vicarage*
the new attitude comes into *Peril at End House* (1931). This
book marks a new approach for Christie: *Murder at the*

Vicarage was largely an experiment with a new character, Miss Marple, while *Peril at End House* gives a slightly different slant to the nature of Christie's detective story. It shows the external signs of conversion. In conversion one must first publicly confess his error and embrace the dogma of the new faith—this happens in *Peril at End House* first with the rejection of the thriller:

> I have let myself go to the most absurd suppositions. I, Hercule Poirot, have descended to the most ignominious flights of fancy. I have adopted the mentality of the cheap thriller...He was a traveller. Supposing, I say to myself, that he has stolen a jewel— the eye of a God. Jealous priests are on his track. Yes, I, Hercule Poirot, have descended to depths such as these.[12]

This public abasement—before Hastings even—has a touch of laughter about it in the oblique reference to *The Moonstone,* but still it shows rejection of the thriller mentality. A bit later in the same novel, Poirot sets out for Hastings the narrow limits of murder in the detective story: he says that maniacs are out, the murder must be cold-blooded and committed deliberately, and that it must be based on one of four motives: gain, hatred, envy, or fear. This is Christie's statement of the Rules of the Game so popular among critical detective writers of the late twenties. She echoes this same conversion in *The Boomerang Clue,* ironically itself a thriller, when the characters eschew gangs:

> "It's probably a gang. I like gangs."
> "That's a low taste," said Frankie absently.[13]

In the same novel, Christie goes so far toward the critical espousal of the regular detective story that for the first time she uses the comparison of the detective story to the crossword puzzle:
> It's [solving murders] like making crossword puzzles.[14]
Thirteen at Dinner (1933) also takes up the new cause and shows the effects of conversion in the proselytizing of heretics. Here Poirot accuses Hastings of being

> Like someone who reads the detective story and who starts guessing each of the characters in turn without rhyme or reason. Once, I agree, I had to do that myself.[15]

This seems to be a clear conversion to the ratiocinative story.
With these novels, Christie left behind the outward form of

the thriller, and she wrote no more adventure yarns like *The Secret Adversary* until after the war. She seems to take up the cause of the ratiocinative story, in which the writer sets out clues for the observant reader to notice and deduce from. No more flights of fancy, stolen Indian jewels, Master Crooks, or gangs. Her new novels are like stories which can be tabulated—the kind which Colonel Carbury asks for in *Appointment with Death* (1938):

> "I suppose you couldn't do the things the detective does in books? Write a list of significant facts—things that don't seem to mean anything but are really frightfully important?"
> "Ah!" said Poirot kindly. "You like that kind of detective story? But certainly. I will do it for you with pleasure."[16]

Through Poirot Christie suggests that now that the fashion is for the kind of story with lists of clues, she can write that sort of story too—or one which seems to be that kind of story.

Seems to be that kind of detective story, because Christie never stopped writing thrillers. Recalling Mrs. Oliver's term, Christie's novels of the thirties, after she had ostensibly converted to the straight detective story, are camouflaged thrillers. Thriller characters and techniques seep into all of her novels despite protests to the contrary. Take characters. Colonel Race, who is Something in the Secret Service (if we knew exactly what his position was it would not be secret), and helps to save Africa from revolution in *The Man in the Brown Suit*, walks on in *Cards on the Table* as a sort of prop and he actively protects the Empire from sedition in *Death on the Nile* (1937). He moves easily from the thrillers into Christie's straight novels of the thirties. If it is not Race who is mixed up in international intrigue, it is Poirot, for in both *Murder on the Calais Coach* and *Murder in Mesopotamia* (1936), Poirot is abroad because he has been mixed up in spy stuff. From the beginning, Christie loved to bring in loads of extraneous criminals. In *The Mysterious Affair at Styles* there is an extraneous German spy, and in the thirties, supernumerary criminals pop into *Murder at the Vicarage*, a dope dealer turns up in *Peril at End House*, three extraneous murderers appear in *Cards on the Table*, nine murderers appear in *And Then There Were None*, and jewel thieves crop up in *Death on the Nile*. None of these books zeroes in on an one-on-one duel between detective and criminal; Christie peoples her novels with thriller types.

As important as these thriller characters are, Christie never really gave up other thriller conventions. One commonplace of the thriller is the use of disguise: Master Criminals are masters of disguise. Christie, of course, used disguise in her early thrillers—it appears in *The Secret Adversary, The Man in the Brown Suit, The Secret of Chimneys, The Big Four* and *The Seven Dials Mystery*. It comes into many of the regular detective books, too. People operate in disguise in *The Mysterious Affair at Styles, The Mystery of the Blue Train, Murder at the Vicarage* (where a burglar is disguised as an archeologist—no doubt a gift to Christie's new archeologist husband), *Thirteen at Dinner, The Boomerang Clue, Death in the Air, Murder in Three Acts,* and *Murder in Mesopotamia.*

Even though one of her characters has denounced the predilection for gangs as a "low taste," a modified form of the gang shows up in many of Christie's works which are not supposed to be thrillers. As a rule, most writers of the period used accomplices sparingly since using them was too much like the old thriller technique of plotting by pulling rabbits out of hats: the use of an accomplice means that anyone can be the criminal. Christie, however, often depends on pairs of people in her legitimate detective works. Accomplices do their dirty work in *The Mysterious Affair at Styles, The Mystery of the Blue Train, Thirteen At Dinner, Murder at the Vicarage, Murder on the Calais Coach* (in which there is a gang, of sorts), *The Boomerang Clue, Death in the Air,* and *Death on the Nile.* Of course it helps the plotting to have gangs—or accomplices. They function as ready and easy ways to unravel plots, and more complicated plots can be produced with an accomplice than with a single murderer. Gangs in thrillers provide excitement, partly because they make the hero an underdog, but partly because they can be at more than one place at once, and because the hero cannot zero in on the leader because of the dispersal of evidence and motive which a gang provides. The same holds true for accomplices in Christie's books.

The thriller depends very heavily upon suspense, but it also depends on surprise. The collision with the unexpected occurs in almost every thriller—the ordinary traveller is an enemy agent, the First Sea Lord is not the First Sea Lord but an international plotter in disguise, the kindly gentleman helping the hero is really the Master Crook, the hero traps foreign villains but a trap door bangs open and he is dropped into the Thames. They were, after all, called shockers. Christie's consistent purpose in her thrillers as well as her detective novels was to shock the readers with the denouement. "The least likely suspect" formula with which Christie has been tagged is really "the most surprising solution" formula. She continuously worked out solutions which would surprise, and, because they infuriated many people who hollered about "playing fair," shock. When one of the detectives commits the murder, when the narrator is the murderer, when the "victim" is the one, when everyone in the plot has bashed, stabbed, or shot the corpse, the reader must be surprised and in most cases shocked—in a more emphatic way than one is shocked in the thriller. In thrillers we expect it, for the whole fictional world is hostile to the hero struggling toward his goal. Detective stories supposedly have more normal values, where crimes occur because of explainable, domesticated motives. When the detective story's narrator whom we have trusted turns out to be a blackguard, or a subsidiary detective turns out to be a murderer, and all of our best guesses are wrong, we are shocked (but not too deeply, for this is, after all, fiction) and surprised, because we never expected it to happen. Thus the surprise ending for Christie functions not as the solution to a puzzle which we might have, or could have, solved, but as a diversion—and diversion was the overriding purpose of Christie's straight detective tales as well as her thrillers.

Plenty of readers have overlooked the lifeless prose, the meagre atmosphere, and the cardboard characters because Christie entertains them by surprising them at the end with something which they did not expect. Christie's work in the thirties centered on variations of plot formulae which she adjusted so that she could continue to pull off what seemed to be new surprises. Her plot patterns, however, are really fairly simple, and she invented them early and merely worked out variations over and over throughout the period. Her favorite plot is that in which a detective is the guilty party. The idea goes back to *The Secret Adversary,* and it is the reason that so many of her books have subsidiary detectives in them who either help Poirot or go off detecting with another character. Simply, they intend to mislead the chief detective and the readers by gaining their confidence and feeding them malarkey. Thus, detective figures are the culprits not only in *The Secret Adversary* and *The Man in the Brown Suit*, but also in *Peril at End House, The Boomerang Clue, Murder in Three Acts, The ABC Murders, Murder in the Air, A Holiday for Murder, And Then There Were None*, and *Easy to Kill*. In each case someone who apparently helps to investigate the crime is actually the criminal. A variant of this criminal-as-detective plot appears in the novels in which the narrator commits the crime—it is a variant since we expect the narrator of the story to be interested in solving the crime and to be on the right side. Christie introduced this gambit in *The Man in the Brown Suit*, which followed *The Secret Adversary*, the first criminal-as-detective plot. We can almost see her looking for a variant. She carried this device to its fullest fruition in *The Murder of Roger Ackroyd*, where, instead of having the criminal narrate only parts, he narrates the whole novel. Finally, she reversed the process in *The ABC Murders*, in which the narrative of Cust seems to be that of the criminal, but turns out to be Christie's ruse to cover the straight criminal-as-detective plot. I have already provided lists of the works in which Christie employs her other stock plot devices: murder in disguise and murder with an accomplice. These are really about all of the patterns which she used in the twenties and thirties. Throughout the period she works with these basic formulae, using them in variations: sometimes combining two basic devices, sometimes, as in *Murder on the Calais Coach* and *And Then There Were None*, extending the idea to its furthest limit. The total effect of the plotting, however, is to provide sanitary thrillers in the guise of regular detective stories in order to divert her audience.

One final point about surprise, upon which all of Christie's books depend for their effect. Ought we to have tried to figure it out? Can or should one read her books the same way that we would read the early Ellery Queen novels? I think not. First of all, in the comments which Christie puts into the mouths of her detective novelists, Mr. Clancy and Mrs. Oliver, she discredits this approach. During the formative years of the twenties Christie seems, in fact, to shrug off the puzzle story which presents the readers with clues which they are to find and attempt to interpret. Few of Christie's novels, if any, when examined with any sort of objectivity, can be considered as puzzles which the readers are supposed to solve. They do not yield the solution to the enigmatic circumstances until the final chapters when Christie chooses to present it herself. Otherwise they would lose all of their force.

Consider the case of *And Then There Were None*. In this novel ten people die while they are trapped on an isolated island to which they have been lured by person or persons unknown. At the end of the book readers hear the musings of police officials who cannot solve the murders. The police continue at sea until a note in a bottle washes ashore and outlines the truth about the events on the island (which exemplifies the readers' position—or the position which Christie would like her readers to be in). If this is a puzzle story, where are the clues which should lead the readers to a logical interpretation of the facts and events which have been presented? There is no material evidence, there are no meaningful alibis, and the crimes have no internal similarities (poisoning, sandbagging, pistol shot, hanging, drowning, and stabbing all appear). The physician who pronounced the deaths could have been in cahoots with any one of the victims. All of the characters are in the same circumstance: each is accused of having committed a murder in the past by a mysterious recording. The psychological evidence is useless; the narration penetrates the consciousness of some people (including the murderer) but this does nothing to reveal the truth. Any of the victims could have feigned death and done the murders. Most of the characters have vocations which might lead them to this sort of mass judgment and execution, but this is moot, since each of us judges countless people daily, and this hardly makes us murderers. Upon what clues ought we to base our solution if we try to figure it out before the book provides it? There is, given retrospect, one clue—Christie describes one death (the fake one) in figurative language while she depicts the others in physical detail. Ought we to see that? I would like to say of course not, but I will waffle and say I think not. We don't see the miniscule, isolated clue for any number of reasons, but chiefly because the novel is three quarters thriller. If this were a *bona fide* puzzle detective novel, there would be ten deaths to be thought through and solved; instead, here, there are ten episodes in a thriller plot which pushes the readers on to the end even if they would otherwise incline to look for and analyze the events and facts in the story. With only one hundred and seventy-one pages in the book, divided into extremely short chapters, we know that we can finish the book tonight if we go on, and that she'll give us the answer at the end without making us think, and the chapters fly by so quickly, why bother? Not many people really do try to puzzle out the answer. It is the psychology. It is the thriller psychology and not that of the puzzle story: all of the facts are not in our possession.

And Then There Were None shows one way in which the techniques of the thriller overcome any claims of the ratiocinative story. Christie uses other thriller techniques in other books to bring about the conclusion, and none of them plays fair. Poirot holds out a bit of information about someone's past, or the telegram containing the pertinent information does not arrive until the last chapter, or the existence of an accomplice (like a husband or wife) whose presence has never been hinted stays unannounced, or the story has multiple endings with multiple solutions (as in *Cards on the Table*). We are not allowed to know the realities of the situation, and if an odd reader happens to uncover the criminal in the book before the last chapter, it can hardly be due to the operations of logic.

The books are not fair—but this is hardly important. The bodies of Christie's novels do not provide clues to follow because their chief function is to titillate the reader by holding off the ending. In this connection, Hastings takes Poirot to a detective play in *Poirot Loses a Client*. After the play Poirot complains that the problem was so simple that it should have been solved in the first act. What he does not appreciate is that if it were solved in the first act, there would be no play, no story, no novel. Aesthetically, the key to the detective story, and the only area in which a writer has freedom, is the middle. The form demands that there be a crime (or the appearance of one) at the beginning and a solution at the end. The writer's freedom lies in developing the middle. What can a writer do with the middle in relationship to the problem initiated by the beginning? There are three alternatives. The writer can sprinkle clues amidst irrelevant material and focus on winnowing, the writer can make the action exciting so that the reader is pulled to the end without much bother, or the writer can combine logical winnowing with action. Christie's books always choose to emphasize action; there has got to be excitement. As Mrs. Oliver says,

If the thing's getting a little dull, some more blood cheers it up:
give them another body to keep the excitement going.

Christie literally does just this in a number of her works. For
instance, in *Poirot Loses a Client* we find that Miss Arundel
has died by page thirty-six. Poirot then starts to nose around
for a hundred-odd pages and then he says

> "Do we not know, you and I, Hastings, how often a murderer, his
> confidence disturbed, turns and kills a second—or even a third
> time!"
> "You are afraid of that happening?"
> He nodded.

Poirot reminds the readers some thirty pages later that

> "I am afraid of a second tragedy."
> "You mean—?
> "I am afraid, Hastings, I am afraid.
> Let us leave it at that."

and again twenty pages later he says,

> "This business complicates itself. . . we must step very carefully. If
> not—the murderer will strike again."

Forty pages later, sure enough, we get another body. Christie's
books, in fact, usually contain multiple murders: ten people die
in *And Then There Were None,* seven in *Easy to Kill,* four in
The ABC Murders, three in *Thirteen at Dinner,* two each in *The
Boomerang Clue, Murder in the Air, Murder in Three Acts,
Cards on the Table, Poirot Loses a Client,* and *Murder in
Mesopotamia,* and several attempts leading to a murder in
Peril at End House and *Death on the Nile.* She follows her own
advice and plugs in a body to keep the excitement going.

The very titles of the books tell something about their
purpose. None of Christie's novels in either its British or
American edition contains the puzzle words "case," or "clue"
or "problem." Instead they have titles which suggest mystery
or the macabre: thus the terms "death," "mystery," and
"murder" label most of the books. Titles like *Easy to Kill,
Appointment with Death,* or *Peril at End House* suggest
sensational contents like those in the thriller. Even before her
Middle East books (which began with *Murder in Mesopotamia*

in 1936), Christie leaned toward the exotic in her titles as in
Murder on the Calais Coach and *Death in the Air.* These surely
are not titles of puzzle books. Her publishers picked up the hint
from the titles and the contents and advertised the sensational
side of Christie's books. Thus the end papers of the Dodd and
Mead Red Badge edition of *Poirot Loses a Client* announce that
Miss Arundel's letter . . . "embarked Hercule Poirot on his most
thrilling case." If Christie's books had not been what the titles
suggested, she could never have turned them into stage plays
or motion pictures, for neither of these mediums is particularly
suited to presenting intellectual puzzles. That is why *The
Mousetrap* is still playing and there are no dramatic
productions of, say, R. Austin Freeman who is usually
described as the "father" of the inverted tale.

Beside using thriller techniques to fill out the middle of her
novels, Christie uses characterization to the same end.
Naturally, Hercule Poirot is Christie's chief character. Poirot
fills out the middles of seventeen books written between 1920
and 1940. The remaining novels introduce a group of assorted
detectives from Miss Marple's only appearance of the period in
Murder at the Vicarage, to the assorted young people in *The
Man in the Brown Suit, The Secret Adversary, The Secret of
Chimneys, The Seven Dials Mystery, Murder at Hazlemoor,
The Boomerang Clue,* and *Easy to Kill,* to *And Then There
Were None* in which there is no detective. Hercule Poirot made
his first entrance in *The Mysterious Affair at Styles* in 1920.
Here he belongs to a group of Belgian refugees who have been
evacuated from their homeland because of the German
invasion of August, 1914. Christie introduces him as

> . . . an extraordinary looking little man. He was hardly more than
> five feet, four inches, but carried himself with great dignity. His
> head was exactly the shape of an egg, and he always perched it a
> little on one side. His moustache was very stiff and military. The
> neatness of his attire was almost incredible. I believe a speck of
> dust would have caused him more pain than a bullet wound. Yet
> this quaint, dandified little man who, I was sorry to see, now
> limped badly, had been in his time one of the most celebrated
> members of the Belgian police.[17]

Compared with Hastings' later descriptions of Poirot, this
introduction is fairly subdued. Only some gentle ridicule of his
fastidiousness contrasts the general impression of dignity and

pathos accorded by most Englishmen to Belgian refugees during the First World War. Hastings even brushes over Poirot's moustache without any special attention. This, however, would change.

Poirot was, like most detectives created after Sherlock Holmes, in large measure a reaction to Conan Doyle's creation. In the thirties, Nurse Leatheran, the narrator of *Murder in Mesopotamia,* makes clear what had been evident for a long time:

> I don't know what I'd imagined—something rather like Sherlock Holmes—long and lean with a keen, clever face...When you saw him [Poirot] you just wanted to laugh.[18]

Poirot serves as a comic reduction of the Great Detective. From her original description, Christie developed various specifically comic traits for Poirot. She plumps up his fastidiousness into a mania. His moustaches grow into comic vanity, and he pampers them through all of the succeeding books as carefully as he pampers his health. He continually wraps himself up in mufflers whenever there is a hint of change in the weather. Poirot becomes incredibly vain about both his appearance and his abilities in the later books. In all he is, as one of the characters in *Murder on the Calais Coach* says, "a ridiculous looking little man. The sort of little man one could never take seriously."[19] Although he can at times speak flawless English, at other times Christie makes his language the butt of jokes: witness this passage from *Cards on the Table:*

> "True," murmured Poirot, "one must play the cricket. As one of your poets so finely says, 'I could not love thee, so much, loved I not cricket more.' "[20]

This typically English literary jibe at a foreigner who massacres the idiom is the exception in Poirot's speech; Christie usually introduces his gaffes in smaller cliches and English proverbs. Such is the fate of the foreigner in popular fiction. Of course Poirot is not really Belgian—he is supposed to be but he is not. He may insist that he is a Belgian to people who mistake him for a Fenchman, but he is wrong. Poirot is really French. Mrs. Oliver, we recall, regretted that she had made her detective a Finn as she knew nothing about Finns; Christie, I think, also regretted making Poirot Belgian since she knew

little of Belgians, and because Belgians do not, after all, have a
national identity which is well-enough established to provide
attitudes which can be successfully burlesqued. Poirot's
Watson also points to this gallic origin; the English did lose a
major battle to the French at Hastings. At any rate what we
find is that Poirot is a stage Frenchman with quaint attitudes
toward life, women, food, *le bon Dieu,* rationality, and
everything else.

Still connected to the reduction of Sherlock Holmes,
Christie developed in the early novels Poirot's aversion to the
activist detective who crawls about on his hands and knees
with magnifying glass in hand looking for minute clues.
Holmes' tobacco ash knowledge and his tendency to rush off to
the railroad station on the least provocation become two
symbols of Poirot's distaste for the activist detective.
Typically, Hastings wants Poirot to get off of his duff and to
participate in this sort of action, while Poirot counters with
lectures about order and method and using the little grey cells.
In the early work, *Murder on the Links,* the attack on the
activist detective comes out in the contrast between Poirot and
Inspector Giraud, "the human foxhound," who crawls about
on all fours looking for tiny pieces of evidence. There is,
however, a good deal of sham and a twist of humor in Poirot's
professed distaste for active detection which depends on
physical evidence and on rushing about the countryside. First,
Poirot's contempt for tobacco ash and footprints is not real.
Virtually all of the books hinge on Poirot's discovery and
interpretation of small bits of evidence: a nail driven into the
skirting, the length of a top coat, the details of a portrait, etc.
Somewhat belatedly Christie revealed her joke about the
second point—Poirot as the sedentary thinking machine. In
Poirot Loses a Client, Poirot and Hastings have the following
colloquy about Poirot's detective practices:

> "that is because you have the mistaken idea implanted in your
> head that a detective is necessarily a man who puts on a false
> beard and hides behind a pillar! The false beard, it is *vieux jeu,* and
> shadowing is only done by the lowest branch of my profession.
> The Hercule Poirot, my friend, need only to sit back in a chair and
> think."
> "Which explains why we are walking along this exceedingly hot
> street on an exceedingly hot morning."
> "That is very neatly replied, Hastings. For once, I admit, you have

made the score off me."[21]

In fact Poirot does listen at key holes (in *Cards on the Table*), assume false identities (in *Poirot Loses a Client)*, and typically chases around the countryside. He is the antithesis of the static and cerebral detective. Oh yes, he talks about the little grey cells continuously, but the grey cells lectures boil down to statements urging that the detective should think, and there is hardly anything new or exclusive in that.

Poirot embodies the two fundamental, relatively serious issues which Christie treats in almost all of her novels: the difference between generations, and the role of psychology. In virtually every book, including the thrillers, Christie introduces characters who highlight the differences between generations. In this respect she is slightly influenced by the Edwardian drive to reject Victorian manners and morals. Typically in Christie's novels there is a survivor of the Victorian era who has established wealth and position and has definite opinions about morals, behavior, dress, furniture, cosmetics, and cocktails. Opposing this fossil, young people crop up with the different attitudes: they prefer hot cars, angular furniture, cocktails, slinky clothes, and uninhibited behavior. Unlike most Edwardians, however, Christie presents the contest between the generations as a draw, for sometimes the young folks win with their spunk and pluck and the old fogies who are stiff, grasping and self-righteous lose; sometimes the old people with their concepts of tradition and morality win over the rootless and frivolous youngsters. This less than controversial stand shows up in Poirot, who mediates the differences between generations. Poirot is from the beginning an old gaffer—in the first novel he has retired from the Belgian police. But he acts as a kind of gallic elder who stands aloof from the combat even though he participates on both sides: on the side of the Victorians with his fixed ideas about crime and justice and other eternal verities, and on the side of the jazz age with his romanticism and some of his tastes. In *The ABC Murders* Poirot's avant-garde furnishing shocks the traditionally minded Hastings.

In the thirties there was a concerted effort on the part of some detective writers, led by Anthony Berkeley, to move the detective novel away from the game and toward a more serious probing of human motives, toward the psychological novel.

Not one to be exempt from popular tendencies, Christie caused Poirot to devote himself to psychology in the thirties. Ostensibly this is because she felt the need to explain why people acted as they did—to remove the detective novel from the realm of the thriller in which people act the way they do because they are simply good or bad. Thus Poirot finds it necessary to diagnose specific mental illnesses for the culprits in the later books so that these will seem more like fashionable detective novels. He is by no means a subtle diagnostician. The mental illnesses which Christie uses are familiar and easy to recognize: kleptomania appears in *Cards on the Table* and *Poirot Loses a Client,* lust for dominance in *Murder in Three Acts,* possessiveness in *Murder in Mesopotamia,* and inherited criminal natures in a number of novels. None of these aberrations really needs to appear in the books, since motives like greed and revenge usually suffice to explain the characters' actions. They are there to raise the tone of the books and to give Poirot's character an added fillip. This shows in books like *Death on the Nile,* where Papa Poirot runs a sort of floating psychologist's clinic curing a thief, an alcoholic, and a manic-depressive. "The psychology" also becomes a ready and easy way of drawing subsidiary characters by showing them as deviant types—and it helps, of course, to fill out the middle of the book.

The other character whom Christie treats with regularity during the period is Poirot's friend, Hastings. Captain Arthur Hastings narrates seven of the seventeen Poirot books between 1920 and 1940 (eight if one counts *Curtain): The Mysterious Affair at Styles, Murder on the Links, The Big Four, Peril at End House, Thirteen at Dinner, The ABC Murders,* and *Poirot Loses a Client.* In the first book he has returned home from the war an invalid, in the second he is the secretary for an M.P., and in all of the subsequent novels he is visiting Poirot from his ranch in Argentina where he lives with his wife, "Cinderella," whom he met in *Murder on the Links.* Hastings, as I mentioned before, is the place where the English lost an important battle to the Normans, just as Christie's Hastings continually loses to his gallic friend. He is, at times, stupid, stuffy, vain, and childish. Christie introduced him partly to be the obtuse narrator, but largely to be a comic character. He is a burlesque of a thick, good-natured country squire. As every comedian needs a straight man or an audience, Poirot needs Hastings to point out his linguistic gaffes, to chide him about his inactivity, and to react with outraged morality when he listens at key holes or ogles skirts. The fact that Hastings appears in *The Big Four* after an hiatus of several years underlines Poirot's need for him. Christie had apparently planned to dispose of Hastings after *Murder on the Links* by marrying him off to his Cinderella at the end of the novel, but she felt that she needed him for the hijinks in *The Big Four,* so she brought him back. And she brought him back again in the thirties whenever she thought that the books needed comic filler or she got tired of playing with point of view and wanted to return to her old, safe formula.

In addition to Poirot, who appears in most of her books, Christie's favorite character type is the bright young woman. Spunky girls claim the readers' attention in almost every book from first to last. Usually Christie repeats the character of Tuppence from *The Secret Adversary*—a young woman full of energy and imagination looking for adventure and loving every second of her involvement with crime and detection. This type can be found in Lady Frances in *The Boomerang Clue,* Egg Gore in *Murder in Three Acts,* and in Bridget in *Easy to Kill,* to name only a few. The female adventurer sometimes coalesces with Christie's other stock female character, the confused woman in love. During the thirties Christie branched out from writing the detective story to write two romantic novels (*Giant's Bread,* 1930, and *Unfinished Portrait,* 1934) under the name Mary Westmacott. One could almost have predicted this since, from the strained relations between John and Mary Cavendish in *The Mysterious Affair at Styles,* Christie had paid some attention to the kinds of characters and situations which one finds in popular romances. This interest increased in the thirties, when Christie included in her detective novels characters like the lover turned murderer in *Murder in Mesopotamia* and *Death on the Nile,* and the cynical woman who is engaged to the rich old man in *Easy to Kill.*

Christie's novels generally have an amusing character or two and may deal with the generational conflict, but one element of fiction which receives scanty treatment is atmosphere. Many of Christie's books treat places which give opportunity for description, but it never comes. Most of the books have a great house, but there is never any architectural description beyond the bare minimum necessary to establish that it is a great house. Description simply was not Christie's *metier*. In her autobiographical book on the Middle East, *Come, Tell Me How You Live* (1946), Christie admits this fact early on when she warns that

> it will give you no interesting sidelights on archeology, there will be no beautiful descriptions of scenery, no treating of economic problems, no racial reflections, no history.[22]

This may as well have been a description of her detective novels. Even in the novels set in the exotic Middle East (*Death on the Nile, Murder in Mesopotamia,* and *Appointment with Death)* Christie does no scene setting beyond a cursory glance at a tomb or two. She does not, further, observe the relatively strict unity of place found in many regular detective stories: the books follow Poirot and the other detectives around England and over to the continent. Again it is the thriller coming in. Just as adding bodies quickens the pace, so does chasing about—as the jumps from Devon to the Riviera to Yorkshire to London to Yorkshire to Devon enliven the plot of *Murder in Three Acts.*

As a prose stylist Christie is hardly distinguished. From the beginning she wrote in a neutral, simple fashion using short sentences and brief paragraphs which do not tax the reader. Occasionally, however, she uses her lack of a prose style to spring traps on the readers: this is the case with the intrusion of figurative description in *And Then There Were None,* as well as the irritatingly simple-minded style adopted for *Easy to Kill.* If Christie has any particular claim to literary originality, though, it is because of her use of point of view. The important lesson which she learned early and well was that detective stories work chiefly because of the way in which they are told. Using Hastings as the narrator in *The Mysterious Affair at Styles* shows that from the beginning she liked Conan Doyle's method of hiding the obvious from the reader by using an obtuse narrator. She also realized, in the early twenties, that this technique was old hat and she started to poke about for alternate styles of narration which would obscure the facts which needed to be withheld until the conclusion. In *The Man in the Brown Suit* she mixed straight narration with extracts from two diaries, covering the facts by switching the point of view. This mixture of points of view, although it is not always so obvious, appears in most of the non-Hastings novels—and in *The ABC Murders* which Hastings narrates—written subsequently. The point of view of a typical Christie novel of the period usually shifts among 1) straight third person narration describing people and events from the outside, 2) third person narration over the shoulder of a particular character following him or her around, 3) selectively omniscient narration which probes some of the characters' minds, and 4) dramatic presentation of dialogue with little more than speech tags supplied. By switching from one point of view to another, Christie manipulates her readers in several ways. First, she gives the readers the false confidence that they can sympathize with and trust the judgments of the character whom the narrative follows. Almost equally important is the impression which the readers receive from the omniscient passages: they falsely believe that they receive insight into all of the characters' thoughts, while this never happens. By tossing together these different points of view, Christie can keep her important facts back and fool her readers almost every time.

Chapter 4

A. A. Milne

A. A. Milne wrote only one detective novel, *The Red House Mystery* (1922). Between 1922 and 1965 it went through twenty two printings, it was enjoyed by many readers, and it became for Raymond Chandler the essence of everything that was wrong with the detective novel between the two World Wars. Setting aside for the moment Chandler's objections to the book, *The Red House Mystery* and Milne's introduction to it written in 1924 stand at the beginning of the Golden Age of the Detective Story and go a good way toward setting the patterns which succeeding writers would follow.

After the Second World War there arose a running commentary in American magazines attempting to define and justify the detective novel. On one hand critics like Raymond Chandler and Edmund Wilson denigrated the form with essays like "The Simple Art of Murder," and "Who Cares Who Killed Roger Ackroyd?" while Jacques Barzun and W.H. Auden defended it. Auden, in "The Guilty Vicarage" (*Harpers:* May, 1945), sets out to establish the myth and ritual in the detective story, and he shows how even an intelligent and sympathetic critic can completely miss the boat about detective novels like *The Red House Mystery*. In his discussion of the setting of the detective story, Auden says that

> In the detective story, as in its mirror image, the Quest for the Grail, maps (the ritual of space) and timetables (the ritual of time) are desirable. Nature should reflect its human inhabitants, i.e., it should be the Great Good Place; for the more Eden-like it is, the greater the contradiction of the murder...the corpse must shock not only because it is a corpse but also because, even for a corpse, it is shockingly out of place, as when a dog makes a mess on a drawing room carpet.[1]

Looking at Milne's novel we find some of Auden's points borne out. Take the first paragraph of the book:

> In the drowsy heat of the summer afternoon the Red House was taking its siesta. There was a lazy murmur of bees in the flower-borders, a gentle cooing of pigeons in the tops of the elms. From distant lawns came the whir of a mowing-machine, that most restful of country sounds...[2]

If Adam and Eve came loping out of the bushes they would feel right at home. The trouble with Auden's mythologizing, however, is that there is no trouble. Sure, one man is murdered and another commits suicide, but these things make no impact upon the world of the novel or on the readers. The fact of murder has no moral implications and it upsets neither the bucolic idyll of the landscape nor the lives of the characters. In fact, the murder provides stimulation for the characters in the book—stimulation more exciting and more fun than the round of house parties to which Bill Beverley returns at the close of the novel. The action of *The Red House Mystery* is that of two boys romping about without a modicum of awareness of the social, moral, or theological issues which others might see implicit in the same events.

Milne's novel tells the story of the murder of Mark Ablett, a rather disagreeable, middle aged man, and of the unraveling of the crime by Antony Gillingham and his friend, Bill Beverley. Aside from the fact that during nine-tenths of the novel they pursue an obvious fact (that Caley is the murderer), their characters form the substance of the story. Antony and Bill—the narrator uses their christian names throughout the text while using other characters' surnames—are clearly schoolboy heroes and their adventures are those of a schoolboy story. In them we find the older/smarter boy's relationship with the younger/less bright admirer: Bill tags along after Antony, revelling in any scrap of approval which is tossed his way. This pattern extends to when Antony has something really important to do—he sends Bill off on a pointless errand. During much of the book their action involves sneaking off so that they can pursue some private adventure. In one instance, in typical schoolboy fashion, they make up dummies for their beds and creep out of the house as if to elude the proctor's supervising eye. Throughout the book they stalk Caley trying to discover exactly how he is connected with the crime and he, like the warty, disagreeable school boy, tries to break into their clique. Their attitudes toward Caley vary as the plot moves along—at one point Bill decides that sending Caley to the gallows is justified because he has eavesdropped on one of his conversations with Antony. At the end, however, both heroes learn to have sympathy for Caley when they learn that he was motivated by chivalry, much in the same way that the schoolboy heroes learn to pity the disagreeable boy who has been a pain because he has a consumptive sister and a father who died heroically in the Boer War.

The schoolboy atmosphere dominates the entire novel and clearly shows Antony and Bill gamboling with childlike abandon. Glance through the following passages to see how clear Milne is about what Antony and Bill do in the novel:[3]

> For he was taking himself seriously as a detective (while getting all the fun out of it which was possible)...
>
> "I say, what fun! I love secret passages. Good lord, this afternoon I was playing golf like an ordinary merchant."
>
> "So we've got to carry on secretly for a bit. It's the only way." He smiled and added "And it's much more fun."
>
> Bill nodded and walked off in the direction of the pond. This was glorious fun; this was life.
>
> People were always doing that sort of thing in books, and he had been filled with a hopeless envy of them; well, now he was actually going to do it himself. What fun!
>
> And then, when he had got back unobserved to the house and reported to Antony, they were going to explore the secret passage! Again, what fun!
>
> Well anyhow, they were going to watch him. What fun!
>
> "To-night," he said. "I say, to-night's going to be rather fun."
>
> "Well, dash it, it's our show. I don't see why we shouldn't get our little bit of fun out of it."

It should be taken for granted, I think, that fun is important to *The Red House Mystery*. And it is not simply a quirk of the characters either, for both they and the narrator shout out that the quintessence of being a detective is having fun.

Milne is perfectly clear about it; Antony and Bill are

playing detective. He may know the moral consequences and ramifications of violent death and crime, and he may realize the real danger and drudgery involved in police work, but they never appear in the novel. Whenever Antony and Bill start off on trains of thought which might lead them to consideration of serious issues, their trains are stopped or switched to another line. Odd? Morally irresponsible? Perhaps both, but, after all, war lies behind the game of chess and few would attack chess players for ignoring the issues raised by war. It is a parallel case. Milne tells us that Antony and Bill are playing a game: note the way in which he deals with the issue of tragedy in the following passage.

> Dash it, of course he had forgotten Mark. How could he think of him as an escaped murderer, a fugitive from justice, when everything was going on just as it did yesterday, and the sun was still shining just as it did when they all drove off to their golf, only twenty-four hours ago? How could you help feeling that this was not a real tragedy, but merely a jolly kind of detective game that he and Antony were playing?[4]

There is no irony here and Milne expects no self-righteous smirk or snort. He is talking to his readers, including his father (to whom the book was dedicated), and expecting them to agree. Antony's exclamation when he lights on the critical piece of evidence confirms this. He shouts "It's a game. What a game!"[5] If Milne wants to have it this way we need to grant him his premise.

And what are they playing? Well, of course, they spend a good deal of time playing schoolboy games—sneaking out of the dorm, maintaining the clique—as well as other children's games—hunting for secret passages, taking a forbidden dip in the pond—but principally they play at being characters out of a book; the book is *The Adventures of Sherlock Holmes*. Milne's treatment of Holmes in *The Red House Mystery* is not parody or burlesque or even criticism although there is a touch of each of these in the novel: Bill, for instance, burlesques Holmes' deductions when he says

> I perceive from the strawberry mark on your shirt front that you had strawberries for dessert.[6]

Antony and Bill play at being Holmes and Watson, adopting

the superficial mannerisms of Conan Doyle's characters and acting out the substantial detective story devices used in the Holmes stories. When they are reconnoitering the pond, for instance, Antony tries to lead Bill to the concept of taking bearings from the fence without stating the point, at which Bill bridles and Antony responds with

> "I love being Sherlocky," he said. "It's very unfair of you not to play up to me."[7]

They glide in and out of the characters of Holmes and Watson as they pursue their games, getting a double dose of excitement because they not only act the parts of the detective and his stooge but they also become them.

The Red House Mystery works to make Antony and Bill have fun and succeeds if it gives the readers some fun too. As an intellectual problem it is not much, and Milne knew it. This is why the basic mystery of the book is kept under wraps until the last chapter, the mystery of the identity of the body, that is. If Milne wished to make the whole book scrupulously logical, if he wished to make it a "who done it," he would have considered that Mrs. Calladine, Mrs. Norbury, or Miss Norbury could have committed the murder, acting with Caley as the accomplice. But in this novel that sort of suspicion would be absurd. The only parts of the ratiocinative tradition which get any attention are a few snippets from Poe: Antony's trick of closing his eyes to summon up his photographic memory comes from Dupin, as does the question of finding the best hiding place. If Milne has done anything in the line of the problem solving detective story it is to pull a fast one on the experienced reader. For his mystery to work Milne assumes that his readers will have read other detective stories and will be conditioned to ask the question, who committed the crime, instead of asking what Antony later admits should have been the first question, who was the victim?

Antony and especially Bill get fun and excitement from playing detective—especially the part which allows them to play the roles of their story book favorites. Another part of their role playing is manifested in their use of a special kind of diction. They talk twaddle while the other people in the novel use standard diction. Both characters have extended passages of unique diction not only when they are playing Holmes and

Watson, but at other times, too. At the beginning of the novel, before Gillingham appears, Bill twits the Major with this stream of facetiousness:

> It's going to be dashed hot, but that's where Betty and I score. On the fifth green, your old wound, the one you got in that frontier skirmish in '43, will begin to trouble you; on the eighth, your liver, undermined by years of curry, will drop to pieces...[8]

There is even one chapter entitled "Mr. Gillingham Talks Nonsense" which includes snippets like

> Some talk of Alexander and some of Hercules, but nobody talks about—what's the Latin for trap-door? *Mensa*—a table; you might get it from that.[9]

The line from "The British Grenadiers" and the Latin business, combining classical learning with popular culture, is typical of the way in which a whole generation of detectives was to speak. Milne, of course, got this from Bentley, but he sets the facetious diction in a more appropriate background. He sets it in a world of playing and clearly shows it as a manifestation of the zest with which these young men approach life, and as a part of the games which they make out of life's problems and enigmas.

In all, *The Red House Mystery* yields its meaning easily, but after its publication the book assumed proportions far beyond its original mold. Two years after the book appeared, Milne wrote an introduction for it which gives a number of insights into the development of the detective story in the twenties. Forecasting the critical prescriptions of Van Dine, Knox, Christie, *et. al.,* Milne laid down some rules for the detective novel. The points which he makes boil down to these:

> 1. The detective story should be written in good, colloquial English prose.
> 2. It should contain no love interest.
> 3. The detective should be an amateur.
> 4. Scientific detection is too boring to be countenanced.
> 5. The detective should not have any knowledge which the readers do not possess.
> 6. There should be a Watson character.

Now these criteria seem to be fairly innocuous, but in fact they raise more problems than they solve—or rather point five

raises more problems than it solves. The rest are either obvious
(like the point about good prose) or were clearly dictated by
Milne's reactions to what he felt were abuses in popular fiction.
Thus he frowns on the love interest because he did not want the
detective novel confused with the romance, and he, like
Anthony Berkeley Cox after him, reacts against the scientific
detective stories of R. Austin Freeman. Point five, though,
hints that the detective story should be a reader-writer game, a
puzzle set by the writer for his or her readers to solve. This,
however, was certainly not Milne's aim in 1922 when he wrote
The Red House Mystery, and it is probably not what he was
driving at when he wrote the introduction in 1924. In neither
place does he insist that the pleasures of the detective story
spring from the analytical operations of problem solving. In
fact he inclines toward saying the reverse: that the art of the
detective story and the readers' pleasure come from being
well-deceived. Thus, in the Introduction Milne says that

> The reader must be made to feel that, *if* he had used the light of cool
> inductive reason and the logic of stern, remorseless facts...then
> he too *would have* fixed the guilt.[10]
>
> (my italics)

The subjunctives are imperative, for Milne knows that only a
tiny handful of readers wants to disassemble the toy while they
play with it for the first time; the rest prefer to play with it,
content with the assumption that it is well built. Readers take
up the detective story to find an animated plot and interesting
characters. Milne wrote stories like this for his son in the Pooh
books, and he did the same thing for his father, and other
"really nice people," in *The Red House Mystery.* There is
hardly anything stern or remorseless in the novel.

Another instance of *The Red House Mystery* being blown
up out of proportion came when Raymond Chandler used it as a
punching bag in his essay "The Simple Art of Murder." This
post-World War II piece shows, in many ways, how the milieu
which begat the Golden Age detective novel in England was
largely absent in America, and how the Second World War
destroyed some readers' sympathy for this kind of novel. Not
that Chandler is entirely negative (as Edmund Wilson is
toward virtually every Golden Age writer). He admits Milne's
craftsmanship in his ability to write

> ...Light, amusing [prose] in the *Punch* style...with a deceptive

smoothness which is not as easy as it looks.[11]

What Chandler objects to about *The Red House Mystery* is that
the problem is not scrupulously worked out, and that, even if it
were, the book would be useless because it is not real. This last
item, that "Fiction in any form has always intended to be
realistic,"[12] is the premise of his criticism. And a shaky premise
it is. Consider *Midsummer Night's Dream, Tristram Shandy,*
or *Through the Looking Glass.* None of these works is realistic
in Chandler's mundane view. There is a difference between
realism and verisimilitude. In terms of Milne's novel, it simply
makes no difference that a cigar chewing cop or a shabbily
dressed physician would have solved the Red House mystery in
about five minutes. Milne is not writing about the actual world,
just as Chandler's hero, Hammett, does not write about the real
world in, say, *The Red Harvest.* It is just that Hammett's
fiction contains violence while Milne's does not.

If *The Red House Mystery* should not be judged according
to the conventions of the American "hard boiled" story, neither
should it be judged by Auden's mythologizing scheme for the
detective story. *The Red House Mystery* does not recount the
Grail myth or give an account of the despoiling of Eden. It is
not that grand; its purposes are more modest. Rather, Milne
needs to be seen in the perspective supplied by Robert Graves in
The Long Week End. There Graves suggests that the Golden
Age detective story was like rococco art, art like that of
Watteau. These paintings are full of comfortable, pretty, mildly
exciting amusements which do not inspire sublime emotions or
probe the basic mysteries of life. This is what most people in
England wanted in their art after the Great War, and it is what
Milne gave them. He gave them a good read.

Chapter 5

Dorothy Sayers

Whose Body? (1923)

Starting a novel with "damn" had a good deal more punch in 1923 than it does today. This was only one of the shocks which Sayers put into her first novel. Another was putting the corpse, not in the conventional locked room or panelled library, but in ginky Mr. Thipps' bathtub—and the body is naked. If Sayers had had her way, moreover, the situation of the body would have been more shocking still: in her original version of the novel, Wimsey deduces that the body in the bath is not Sir Reuben Levy's because it is not circumcised. Her publisher demurred at this and forced a change in the physical evidence.[1] Even without the evidence of the foreskin, though, *Whose Body?* shocks because it takes the detective story as it had been written and stands it on its head; the book manages to mock the conventions of the form and to become a new kind of detective story.

This is due, in part, to Lord Peter D.B. Wimsey. Reviewers and critics have written a good deal of drivel about Wimsey—writers inclined to Marxism see him as the embodiment of Sayers' silly fantasies about wealth and aristocracy, and feminist critics see him as Sayers' design for the ideal man. Both of these views may have a tincture of truth in them, especially in the later books, but in *Whose Body?* Sayers began Wimsey as a parody and criticism of traditional detective heroes. In this sense, *Whose Body?* has the same motive as *Trent's Last Case* (to which Sayers alludes in this novel): to spoof detective literature. She purposely creates a hero who is in many respects the opposite of the standard detective hero. Compared with the strong, silent, quietly intelligent, stern-faced Englishmen who detect in the teens, Wimsey is a pipsqueak. He is short, 5'9" versus the standard 6', effete, pampered, and not much of a physical specimen compared,

say, to Harriet Vane's detective hero, Robert Templeton.
Sayers specifically deflates Wimsey's appearance rather than
inflating him into a ruthlessly handsome aristocrat. The first
physical description of Wimsey in *Whose Body?* significantly
notes that

> His long, amiable face looked as if it had generated spontaneously
> from his top hat, as white maggots breed from gorgonzola.[2]

Maggots in cheese is not a very attractive simile for a detective
hero. Neither is there much that is admirable in Wimsey's
relationship with his man, Bunter. The scene in which Wimsey
pleads with Bunter over his trousers only to be overruled by his
man undercuts the whole masterful impression which earlier
writers had tried to give their detective heroes.

So does Wimsey's speech. In this novel Wimsey's speech is
an amalgam of undetective diction. Sayers builds it out of
casual, lazy, upperclass speech habits—dropping g's, slurring
words into contractions, and the ready use of catch words like
"old Bird." To this she adds a tendency to burst into silly
rhymes and songs like

> We both have a body in a bath,
> We both have a body in a bath—
> For spite of all temptations,
> To go in for cheap sensations
> We insist upon a body in a bath.[3]

Also she uses patches of telegraphic, journalistic, advertising
phraseology, as in

> I trust you told her I had succumbed to lethargic encephalitis
> suddenly, no flowers by request.[4]

To this she adds frequent and casual literary allusion: here
Wimsey quotes Dickens, Gilbert and Sullivan, Shakespeare,
and Joel Chandler Harris. Finally, Sayers gives Wimsey Sam
Weller's habit of dropping absurd anecdotes into his speech.
Take this one from *Unnatural Death:*

> Shut up Sherlock...the doctor's story is not going to be obvious.
> Far from it as the private said when he aimed at the bull's—eye
> and hit the gunnery instructor.[5]

All of this combines to give the impression of a facetious, flighty, scatter-brained hero who runs his mouth at the slightest encouragement. The Great Detective would hardly warble about bodies in baths.

The burbling detective certainly goes back to Trent, but the grace notes in Wimsey's speech come from Wodehouse. It is obvious that Sayers put a good deal of Wodehouse's Bertie Wooster into Wimsey; he will later be compared to Bertie. And Bunter has a touch of Jeeves in his presence and attitudes. Probably more important for the creation of Wimsey, however, was Wodehouse's character R. Psmith. Beginning in 1908 with *Mike and Psmith,* Wodehouse developed this character through three other novels: *Psmith in the City* (1910), *Psmith Journalist* (1915), and *Leave it to Psmith* (1923). In his introduction to the omnibus volume, *The World of Psmith* (1974), Wodehouse describes the genesis of Psmith:

> A cousin of mine, who had been at Winchester, happened to tell me one night of Rupert D'Oyly Carte, the son of the Savoy opera's D'Oyly Carte, a schoolmate of his. Rupert D'Oyly Carte was long, slender, always beautifully dressed and very dignified. His speech was what is known as orotund, and he wore a monocle. He habitually addressed his fellow Wykehamists as "Comrade," and if one of the masters chanced to inquire as to his health, he would reply, "Sir, I grow thinnah and thinnah."[6]

Psmith's constant companion in all of the books is Mike Jackson, an enthusiastic young cricketer, who avidly follows Psmith; although Psmith can act, argue, and box, he leaves these things to Mike. It is here, in Psmith, that Sayers found the original for Wimsey's deportment, appearance and speech, and it is in Mike Jackson that she found the original for Parker.

Psmith and Dr. Thorndyke make strange companions, but they do actually combine in Sayers' creation of her hero. From the start Sayers put highly technical problems at the center of her mysteries; in *The Omnibus of Crime* (1929) she would later explicitly say that the *how* of a crime offered more possibilities than the *who*. Thus she made Wimsey in some external ways resemble Freeman's scientific detective. Wimsey carries with him tools for close observation and exact measurement: his monocle is a powerful lens, there is a torch in his match box, and his stick is marked off in inches. Just as Thorndykean is Bunter, whose role echoes that of Polton in Freeman. More than he is Jeeves, Bunter is the detective's scientific assistant who takes charge of the photography, and who actually spends much of his time in the dark room. This would later change, but in the beginning Bunter is very much like Polton.

Paradoxically, Wimsey is both the *reductio ad absurdum* of the fake aristocratic detective, and he is also more of an aristocrat than any of Oppenheim's jeweled elite against whom Sayers was reacting. Sayers understood the craft of fiction well enough to build characters and atmosphere through verifiable specifics. Thus Wimsey's milieu is full of specific luxuries which can be checked in Sotheby's catalogue: there are actual first editions, Sevres vases, Scarlatti sonatas, specific wines of identified vintage, furniture by famous makers, etc. Her readers, Sayers felt, would be educated enough at least to know the names.

The key to Wimsey's character, however, does not lie in Psmith or Thorndyke, or in the upholstery of his habits and tastes. It lies in his conscience. From first to last, writing about crime presented for Sayers certain moral considerations which emerge in the form of questions which her novels confront—do detective stories encourage crime? What business does one human being have hunting another human being down? Does one have the right or duty to send a man or woman to the gallows? What is sin? Sayers makes questions like these central to Wimsey's character in *Whose Body?* They come specifically into the novel in the confession scene between Wimsey and Parker. Here Wimsey sets aside his frivolity and confronts Parker with questions on the morality of detection. Parker answers Wimsey's doubts with a statement about responsibility and duty to truth and society. More importantly, though, Parker holds on his lap a commentary on Paul's Epistle to the Galatians. This suggests not only the social justification for detection but also that Divine will and Divine justice enter subtly into the human acts of the detective. Here is an essential departure in detective literature—it is part of Sayers' aim to broaden and deepen the moral and ethical background of the form. She does this in *Whose Body?* and in each subsequent novel in which Wimsey has doubts which are so essential to his created nature.

This moral concern also informs the plot of *Whose Body?* The novel on one level shows the struggle between the criminal and the forces of civil justice; on another level it shows the struggle between God and the pernicious forces of anti-God. Sayers puts her detectives solidly in the camp of God through the books which they read—Parker reads theology and Wimsey reads Dante throughout the novel. Evil resides in Sir Julian Freke (an unsubtle play on "freak") who has taken as his life's work the attempt to prove the physiological nature of conscience, hence morality, hence God—proving, if you will, that Marley's ghost is a bit of undigested gruel. Thus, unlike previous detective stories which approach good and evil on either too general or too specific levels and never grapple with real moral problems, Sayers made the basis of her first detective novel the Christian criticism of St. Julian Huxley—one of the deadly sins of twentieth century culture which she would later attack in her theological works.

Precisely because *Whose Body?* goes beyond the normal detective book, it is not a who did it problem. Sayers later admitted that she did not make most of her books turn on the identity of the criminal:

> I have been annoyed (stupidly enough) by a lot of reviewers who observed that in *Strong Poison* I had lost my grip because the identity of the murderer was obvious from the start (as it is also in *Unnatural Death* and *The Documents in the Case*...[7]

Most of Sayers' novels, in fact, introduce the murderer early and leave little doubt that he or she is guilty. She did this partly because it enabled her to work on causes and effects of evil in human beings, and partly because she was convinced that the mechanism of murder was a more interesting detective problem than the problem of identity:

> Personally, I feel that it is only when the identity of the murderer *is* obvious that the reader can really concentrate on the question (much the most interesting), *How* did he do it?[8]

Therefore, with a couple of exceptions, Sayers' mysteries must have begun with her acquisition of technical knowledge, frequently medical, which would form the intricate mystery to be solved.

Just as *Whose Body?* is not a traditional who did it book, it is not like older detective works which depend on rationality and logic. Sayers gives Wimsey, in fact, a parody presentation which undermines the mathematical logic of detective stories.

When considering poor, old Mr. Crimplesham, Wimsey begins
with

> Following the methods inculcated at the University of which I
> have the honour to be a member, we will now examine severally
> the various suggestions afforded by Possibility No. 2. This
> Possibility may be sub-divided into two or more hypotheses. On
> Hypothesis 1 (strongly advocated by my distinguished colleague
> Professor Snupshed), the criminal, whom we may designate as X,
> is not identical with Crimplesham, but using the name
> Crimplesham as a shield, or aegis.[9]

This sort of ratiocination leads nowhere. In *Whose Body?* when
truth comes to Wimsey it does not come as the result of tortuous
logic. It comes from

> ...not one thing, nor another thing, nor a logical succession of
> things, but everything—the whole thing, perfect, complete, in all
> its dimensions as it were and instantaneously; as if he stood
> outside the world and saw it suspended in infinitely dimensional
> space.[10]

It comes described in the language of a vision, the language
familiar to religious mystics and not that of Mill's Canons.

What Sayers has done in her first novel, then, is to combine
what she considered to be best in the traditions of the detective
story—R. Austin Freeman's science, G.K. Chesterton's
humane and spiritual concern, the how it happened story—
with a thorough debunking of the cliches of Wallace and
Oppenheim, the thriller writers of the last generation. To this
she added a morality play of good and evil adapted to twentieth
century problems. Later she discovered that the conflict of
good and evil went beyond this kind of presentation, and tried
again and again to adapt her fiction to it.

Clouds of Witness (1926)

In *Whose Body?* Wimsey answers his brother's complaints
about the crassness of playing detective by saying "you may
come to want me yourself, you never know." Prophetic words,
for what this means, of course, is that Sayers had planned her
second Wimsey story before the first one was finished—or had
at least selected the subject. Nevertheless, it took three years
for *Clouds of Witness* to appear. In telling the story of the trial
of the Duke of Denver for murder, Sayers further exploited two
elements which she had touched in the first novel: this book

gives an expanded view of the lives of the Quality, and it emphasizes the love lives of rich, aristocratic people. Viewed from the lowest perspective, Sayers is merely putting the gossip columns into fiction. From a higher point of view, this novel develops what the first novel gives and it introduces another important area of moral concern.

If in her first book Sayers gives her readers a picture of high life through the things which surround Wimsey, here she conveys the same world through portraits of people and places. In addition to Lord Peter, Sayers brings in the whole Wimsey family. There is the stolid Duke of Denver, his iceberg wife, Helen, the spoiled and confused Lady Mary, and the sprightly Dowager Duchess. She also brings in Murbles, the family solicitor, and Sir Impey Biggs, the advocate who defends Gerald in his trial for murder. The portraits, critical though they may be in showing the lack of direction and stupid mistakes of the aristocracy, are based on the idea that these people—with the exception of Helen—are basically sound in their values and honesty. Thus Gerald protects an injured woman, Lady Mary admits her mistakes in loyalty and puts her trust in proper objects, and Peter's mother shows the same adroitness and common sense that she showed in *Whose Body?*

In addition to the aristocrats themselves, Sayers expands on her emphasis on places in order to make one of her thematic points. She shows the kinds of places which the Quality frequent: Riddlesdale Lodge, Murbles' rooms in Staple Inn, Wimsey's hotel in Paris, The House of Lords, as well as Wimsey's flat in Piccadilly. Each place brims with historic association, fancy furniture, expensive art, good food, famous drink, and important books. But these places have more importance than giving the readers a tour of great houses. Contrasted to the aristocratic places are the sordid locales of Grimthorpe's farm, and the Soviet Club, where Wimsey suffers through a wretched meal in the interests of justice. The two sorts of locale reflect, on one hand, real human concern coupled with social amenities, and on the other hand, lack of human concern plus various stages of artificiality and brutality. Very simply, no one cares for others at the Soviet Club or at Grimthorpe's whereas each other place shows people concerned with others.

Romance in High Places provides Sayers with the other society page interest in *Clouds of Witness*. She fills the book with pairing and re-pairing of people: Gerald and Helen, Gerald and Mrs. Grimthorpe, Mr. and Mrs. Grimthorpe, Lady Mary and Cathcart, Lady Mary and Goyles, Lady Mary and Parker, Cathcart and Simone Vonderaa. The only people in the novel who are exempt from romance are Murbles and the Dowager Duchess who, presumably, are too old. Even Wimsey has been in love—here we learn that his slight case of melancholia is caused by the loss of the Great Love of his life, Barbara, who did not wait for him but married the other fellow. No one is exempt. Impey Biggs' eloquence takes second place to the fact that he is the most desirable, available man in the Kingdom.

All of this concern with love appeals to the same sympathies, fantasies, and identifications which the popular love story cultivates, but Sayers uses it for other purposes as well. She realized that the key to plotting a detective story is holding off the revelation of truth:

> ...your recipe for detective fiction [is] the art of framing lies. From beginning to end of your book, it is your whole aim and object to lead the reader up the garden, to induce him to believe a lie.[11]

Characters, however, must lie or refuse to talk for credible motives—Sayers was a traditionalist in this and most other literary matters. Having the suspects in love provides one possible basis for irrational, misleading behavior. Thus Collins, to whom Sayers returns again and again, based the whole fabric of *The Moonstone* on Rachael Verinder's refusal to tell what she knows. In fact, Rachael's behavior in *The Moonstone* probably gave Sayers the idea for both Gerald's and Lady Mary's characters in *Clouds of Witness*.

This book also shows Sayers' typical unwillingness to deal with issues on a solely superficial level. Granted, much of the love interest here is used to make the book work as a detective story or to decorate the world of the aristocracy. Sayers, however, looks into more substantial issues in the relationships between men and women in her treatment of the Grimthorpes. In these sections of the novel she portrays a marriage filled with fear and brutality, a marriage which is based solely upon male possessiveness. It is an obvious case in which divorce would be desirable or even necessary. But Sayers does not present the Grimthorpes as an argument for divorce. She treats the repulsiveness of Grimthorpe's brutality as a symptom of possessiveness which actually caused the rot in the relationship and the whole string of evil effects; it destroys both parties. It is also not something which can be expunged by a limited civil decree: the problem goes beyond the novel. Possessiveness was, therefore, to become Sayers' major concern when writing of human relationships throughout her books, culminating in the sections about it in the Vane-Wimsey novels.

In spite of or because of all the interest in values and the frosting of aristocratic manners, Sayers must have been unsure about how this book would be received as a detective story by her readers, so she spiced it up by mixing in more episodes of exciting adventure than one finds in any of her other novels. On the average, someone's life is threatened about once in every novel—usually near the end in order to hold off the conclusion and to generate suspense and excitement. In *Clouds of Witness* Sayers introduces four exciting incidents: the confrontation with Grimthorpe and his dogs, the bog at Grinder's Hole, the shooting outside of the Soviet Club, and finally the transatlantic airplane flight. Although these are not the elements which make the book a detective story, they do keep it from swinging too far toward the romance. They also show that Sayers was a bit leery about the ability of the romance material and the detective plot to stand by themselves, and to sell.

Literary reference in *Whose Body?* simply provides color for Wimsey's diction; the plot grew from Sayers' knowledge or guesses about medical school practice. Here, in addition to providing fuel for Wimsey's persiflage, literature lies under the conception of the plot. Of course it is all built on *Manon Lescaut*. The whole Cathcart-Simone Vonderaa business stems from Prevost's work, thus providing the major impetus to the mystery. *Manon* is also the chief clue which Sayers seeds throughout the novel to tantalize the readers: wherever Cathcart has been he has strewn his path with copies of the book. In this, Sayers approaches much closer the late twenties' guessing game detective story than she did in her first book.

Clouds of Witness also makes explicit Sayers' literary assessments and allegiances at the time, as well as her expectations about her audience. She expects some cultural sophistication, or at least education, from her readers. She reckons that most of them will be able to read the long letter in

French from Cathcart to Simone, and that they will know what *Manon* is all about. At the same time, moreover, she expects them to be traditional in their tastes and to agree with her ridicule of recent, radical trends in British writing. In this book the ridicule comes during Wimsey's visit to the Soviet Club where he overhears the following conversation between Miss Heath-Warburton, a sex-novelist, and her bearded companion:

> "—ever known a sincere emotion to express itself in a subordinate clause?"
> "Joyce has freed us from the superstition of syntax," agreed the curly man.
> "Scenes which make emotional history," said Miss Heath-Warburton, "should ideally be expressed in a series of animal squeals."
> "The D.H. Lawrence formula," said the other.[12]

Just as she would later attack modern poetry in the short story "Uncle Meleager's Will" as the "Whirligig" school, Sayers here appeals to the majority of British (and American) readers who were confused and irritated by Lawrence's frankness and Joyce's narrative technique. She later changed her mind about Joyce, but not about Lawrence. He, along with Freud, Marx, and Huxley remained for her the symptoms of what was wrong with modern life. The point is, however, that Sayers insists that detective novels do traditional things in traditional ways. She continually looked back to Dickens—and to Collins.

Unnatural Death (1927)

Clouds of Witness, to some extent, lies outside of the main development of the detective interest in Sayers' novels. In it, the cause of death is neither interesting or innovative: morgues full of people die of gunshot in detective stories. She made up for this in *Unnatural Death,* for here she returned to emphasizing *how* the crime occurred as she had done in *Whose Body?* In fact, either Sayers took advice from an agreeable physician like Robert Eustace, or she researched the method herself; gone are the days of *Whose Body?* when she was satisfied with using the old thriller standby, the poison unknown to science. Ironically, her murder method has become almost as popular and controversial as the unknown poison. It is alluded to both by Christie, in *Appointment with Death* (1937), and by Ellery Queen in *The Siamese Twin Mystery*

(1933). Sayers moved back to the unexpected means in this novel largely because, as in *Whose Body?,* there were several social and moral themes which she could only handle by having the evil localized in one person from the start. The detective interest, therefore, shifts back to the question of how the murder was accomplished, and the clues of the air-locked motorcycle, Mary Whittaker's hospital training, and the plethora of hypodermic needles appear so that when readers learn the actual cause of death they can see that it is consistent with the background which they have read.

In spite of the obviousness of the culprit, Sayers does include some embroidery to the questions of who committed the crime and why. The readers have Rev. Halleluja Dawson to ponder over and suspect, as well as the problem of Mrs. Forrest to solve, but, as we have seen above, Sayers never really intended these things to fool readers. The business about motive is almost analogous. For the detective plot, Mary Whittaker's motive lies in the change from the Old to the New Property Act, but this is embroidery. In the complete context of the novel the real motive is more than just the means of propulsion for the entertaining detective plot. Sorting out the crime and motives drives Wimsey and the readers into the ethical centers of the novel, ethical centers which could and do exist separately from the external motives for the murder.

One ethical center of the novel is Wimsey's concern with the propriety of being a detective—particularly in this case where an old, dying woman has been put out of her misery so that her fortune can be inherited by the person to whom she wished it to go and who has every legal and moral right to it. Earlier Wimsey had consulted Parker about a similar problem in *Whose Body?* where Parker gave his answer with a volume of Biblical commentary in his lap. Here Wimsey voices his doubts to a priest, Mr. Tredgold (another fairly obvious name), vicar of Leahampton. Tredgold broadens the answer which Parker gave by applying the issue of crime to the issue of sin, and by focusing upon the degenerating effect of both on the individual. This, in turn, becomes the characterizing principle for Mary Whittaker who throughout the novel grows more and more inhuman, going from one crime to another until her suicide at the end. Wimsey reacts to this as a detective by bringing the crime home and exonerating the innocent, but he also reacts as a Christian in his sorrow for sin and his acknowledgement of his identity with all humanity. This is particularly apparent in Wimsey's agonized reactions at the close of the book.

The other ethical center of *Unnatural Death* also reorganizes and restates a concern which Sayers had treated before. Part of the human interest in this book revolves around the issue of homosexuality. In the novel, Sayers draws two sets of women who give up the world of men and decide to make their lives together. One pair comes from the last generation, Clara Whittaker and Agatha Dawson, and one from the present generation, Mary Whittaker and Vera Findlater. A member of each pair acts a dominant, decisive, worldly, active role, while the other fills a passive, indecisive, and sheltered part. The older women, however, are markedly successful in business as well as life—they are respected by everyone in their community in spite of their unorthodox lives. The younger women are not successful; they are warped. The crux of the Findlater-Whittaker relationship lies not so much in Sayers' objection to lesbianism—the older women come in for no criticism—as with the problem of possessiveness. Thus, in addition to arguing for heterosexuality, Miss Climpson ties the failure of the girls' relationship to selfishness: "Love is always good, when it's the right kind...but I don't think it ought to be too possessive."[13]

Together with these themes, Sayers also touches on important social issues facing post-war Britain—the super-abundance of women, and the unmarried woman's situation in society. All of this resides in Miss Climpson. Alexandra Katherine Climpson began as a comic character, Sayers' redrawing of Miss Clack from *The Moonstone.* She took Collins' evangelical zealot and seized on the way that she speaks—her wandering irrelevancies, her concern for her own propriety, and the *implied emphases* on *noteworthy* words—and gave it to Miss Climpson whose letters delight both the readers and the people in the novel. Miss Climpson, however, is no evangelical humbug; just the reverse, she is a devout and sensitive woman. Granted, she is encumbered with all sorts of dowdy, Victorian conceptions of what women should and should not be, but she realizes this and tries to transcend her background. Her importance for the themes of the novel lies, in part, in her role as single woman for whom society has no use and consequently shunts from rooming house to rooming house. In the novel Sayers gives a fantasy solution for making this kind of woman useful and important, a scheme which will eventually become Wimsey's "cattery" in which he employs unattached women to right society's wrongs. But Sayers could not and did not mean this as a satisfying solution to this part of the women's problem. The problem was one which was so serious and complex that it must go beyond the comfortable, neat solutions of a detective novel.

In this book, in fact, Sayers begins to point out what she would later formulate as the chief defect of the detective story:

> *The detective problem is completely soluble:* no loose ends or enigmas are left anywhere. The solution provides for everything and every question that is asked is answered.... Now, our tendency to look for this kind of complete solution without lacunae or compensatory drawbacks badly distorts our view of a number of activities of real life.[14]

Life, she says, cannot be bundled and wrapped up as a detective problem can be. In these terms, *Unnatural Death* is an anti-detective story, for Sayers purposely puts the problem of women in the novel and the problem of sin—both of which go beyond the solution to the crime problem in the book. This is true even in the framing plot which involves Dr. Carr's engagement to Nurse Philliter: Dr. Carr does not marry her at the end but goes off with someone else, and the impetus to uprooting the whole mess is not tied up in a nice, comfortable package.

Even the detectives fall in with these discomfiting elements in the novel. Wimsey is, of course, full of facetiousness: Sayers for the first time officially compares him to "the heroes of Mr. P.G. Wodehouse." To the Chesterfield chairs and first editions she adds a Daimler (christened Mrs. Murdle, after a character in *Little Dorrit)* to fluff up the aristocratic ambience. Parker, too, is as decent and common-sensical as in the earlier books. But there is something wrong with the relationship between Wimsey and Parker—it has become a bit more parasitic than in the earlier books. One passage makes this specific:

> When he [Parker] worked with Wimsey on a case, it was an understood thing that anything lengthy, intricate, tedious and soul destroying was done by Parker. He sometimes felt that it was

irritating of Wimsey to take this so much for granted. He felt so now.[15]

The amateur detective takes advantage of the professional who gathers evidence and gives him access. This is hardly an equal proposition. The problem surfaces but never gets solved.

Still, Sayers keeps the unsolvable human problems in the background, carrying us back, again and again, to the detective. She does this by switching from Wimsey to Miss Climpson and back again as a way of closing off problems which are not really solved. Further, she adds Mr. Trigg's story, and two additional murders to keep the detective business in the foreground. There is also the physical danger at the end which Sayers narrates with good, standard thriller technique to slam the door of the detective game and fool us into forgetting the other issues.

The Unpleasantness At the Bellona Club (1928)

This novel begins a new stage in Sayer's works. Up to this point her books were, by and large, anti-detective novels. All of the earlier novels undermine the conventions of the detective story by being more complex and more serious than the novels of her predecessors. Now, however, Sayers had become known as a major detective story writer—the next year she would write a critical introduction for *The Omnibus of Crime.* Perhaps because of this, she wrote a series of novels which are largely like most other well-written, straight, conventional detective books of the 1920's.

Unpleasantness was the first of these. It shows how different Sayers' earlier books were as well as the degree to which Sayers mastered the conventions of the detective story. Perhaps the most notable divergence from her old mode in *Unpleasantness* is the metaphor with which Sayers describes detection. In all of the earlier books she had insisted on the serious moral ambiguity which surrounds the whole business of detection. Here, however, the book runs on the metaphor of the game. Wimsey has no crushing doubts about the justice of his actions but blithely detects along. Perhaps the key indicator of the new spirit in this book is that the chapter titles describe a bridge game, beginning with "The Queen is Out," and ending with "Cards on the Table." The inward and visible sign of this attitude lies in the fact that now Sayers emphasizes the standard writer-reader game which was becoming part of detective fiction conventions in the late twenties. Certainly Sayers drops clues in her earlier books, but she does not come right out and challenge the readers as she does here. Consider Wimsey's statement to Mr. Pritchard in this novel:

> I have been requested by Mr. Murbles to ascertain the facts. They are rather difficult to ascertain, but I have learned one very important thing from you this afternoon. I am obliged to you for your assistance.[16]

In *Unnatural Death*, Sayers provides the clue of the malfunctioning motorcycle without comment: we, like Wimsey, need to work out the solution with intuition and inspiration—if we try to work it out at all. The conversation with Mr. Pritchard, however, directly and specifically challenges the reader since it is tantalizingly enigmatic. Mr. Pritchard has been a louse and has not told Wimsey anything. What, we then ask, is the "one very important thing?" It is part of the game.

One other part of Sayers' unconventional approach in the earlier stories is her presentation of a complex hero instead of the super efficient Great Detective who is the simplified hero of romance. Here, of course, Wimsey is as bumptious as ever. However, not only does Sayers eliminate any bouts with conscience in *Unpleasantness,* but she also directly connects Wimsey with the tradition of the romance hero which she had undercut in the earlier books. Thus she writes that

> Wimsey was the Roland of the combination—quick, impulsive, careless and an artistic jack-of-all trades. Parker was Oliver.[17]

One cannot get more heroic than that; it is just the sort of thing which Edgar Wallace might have written if his fiction were a bit more highbrow.

This is not to deny that there are some serious concerns in *Unpleasantness.* George Fentiman's shell-shock, his economic failures, and domestic troubles culminating in temporary insanity convey some concern with contemporary problems: so do Anne Dorland's repression and constriction produced by the confining and artificial role foisted on women by society. But these problems are neatly tied up in the novel. George gets his health back along with some money to get him back on his feet, and Anne has a husband in the offing, which will be just what the doctor, in this case Wimsey, ordered. It is jackpot fiction. Sayers ties everything up and nothing goes beyond the confines of the novel—as the social and spiritual issues do in the earlier books.

Unpleasantness is also Sayers' first novel which approaches the conventional detective problem of who committed the crime in the conventional way of providing a group of suspects whom one can really suspect. *Whose Body?* and *Unnatural Death* are really single suspect books, and so too is *Clouds of Witness*. Here, however, Sayers gives us several *bona fide* suspects in Robert Fentiman, George Fentiman, Anne Dorland, and Dr. Penderby. Then, through the course of the novel, attention and suspicion shift among them.

For all of this, perhaps because of it, *Unpleasantness* is a flawed work in which Sayers seems only to be going through the paces. First of all, it is not really a novel in its conception. Sayers made it by jamming two short story ideas together: the story of determining the time of the murder, and the story of discovering the identity of the murderer. This breaks the novel in half, the solution to the first problem coming too early to be a radical surprise tied in with the climax, and too late to be part of an organic, developing plot. Further, Sayers does little in the way of characterization here, but simply repeats characterizing material from her earlier books. Dr. Penderby, for instance, simply repeats Sir Julian Freke from *Whose Body?* One researches the physiological basis of conscience and the other claims to have found it in the ductless glands. Anne Dorland, too, is in many ways a repeat of an earlier character. Her distorted sexuality is in many ways like that shown in Vera Findlater and Mary Whittaker, only in this novel Sayers ties Anne's problem to reading too much D.H. Lawrence, which serves to warp her further, like the habitues of the Soviet Club in *Clouds of Witness*.

The Documents In the Case (1930)

Between *The Unpleasantness at the Bellona Club* and *The Documents in the Case,* Sayers wrote an introductory essay for the anthology, *The Omnibus of Crime.* In it she explores several ways to make detective stories work—among them is the author's manipulation of point of view. *Documents in the Case* is an exercise in point of view: instead of writing a continuous narrative as had been her practice, Sayers put together a number of letters and statements which cover the events leading up to and following the death of George Harrison. The book, however, never descends into being "found evidence" like that in the murder-game books like *Murder off Miami,* but remains pretty much a standard detective story. Sayers probably got the idea for the format of this novel by thinking about *The Moonstone*—a novel in the epistolary tradition if not exactly epistolary form—and by carrying Collins' technique to its logical conclusion, a collection of documents and statements. She may have also borrowed Collins' device of concluding the action with a scientific experiment, but the evidence here is too general to be decisive. What is decisive is that Sayers borrowed some of her organizing principle from R. Austin Freeman. In all of Sayers' earlier novels, the death to be investigated occurs at the beginning or before the beginning of the narrative. Here George Harrison does not die until half way through the book. What Sayers does is to organize this book the same way that Freeman organized his inverted detective stories—stories in which the readers first see the crime committed and then see its solution. Accordingly, she divides this work into two sections, "synthesis" and "analysis," in which we see the events moving toward the crime and then moving toward the detection. It is like Freeman, only Sayers improved on his techniques for the inverted story. In Freeman's inverted Dr. Thorndyke tales the readers know the criminal's identity in the first half of the story and are propelled along by the question of when the crime will happen. In the second part the readers see how Dr. Thorndyke discovers the truth which they already know. Like Freeman, Sayers emphasizes when in part one of *Documents in the Case* and how in part two, but she adds the question of who by using the documents to describe the motivating action and the events surrounding the crime itself while keeping the identity of the murderer veiled.

Because this is, in large measure, a story told through letters from various people, Sayers has the opportunity to include a good deal more character study than she had in the previous novel. Perhaps the simplest character in the cast is Miss Milsom. In Miss Milsom Sayers redrew Miss Clack (one of her favorite characters it seems) from *The Moonstone,* only instead of making her character's world turn on evangelical christianity, she makes Miss Milsom an evangelist for the new religion (actually heresy to Sayers) of Freudian psychology. Miss Milsom's mentor, one Dr. Trevor, is thus a repetition of Godfrey Ablewhite, someone who bilks helpless and empty-headed women. There is also a Collinsesque air to Paul Harrison, the collector of the documents, whose literal outlook colors his interpretation of the truths which more imaginative people tell. He has a touch of Betteredge about him. Margaret Harrison, who is naively and sloppily romantic, cunning, and egotistical, reminds one of P.G. Wodehouse's Madeline Bassett tossed into the real world instead of Wodehouse's Arcadia. The most complex personality in the whole book resides in John Munting. In many ways Munting has the same personality as Wimsey—he is given to limericks, and to going off on flights of facetious rhetoric. More important, Munting has the same delicate sensibility that Wimsey does: he constantly questions the propriety of his actions. Munting is, however, not an aristocrat but a struggling writer; the title of his first novel, *I to Hercules,* signifies that his area of concern, like Hamlet's, is complex questions of morals and metaphysics. Sayers, in fact, fills this novel with non-detective issues' going back to her old habits.

Documents in the Case is really a microcosm containing a number of important intellectual issues of the twenties. Sayers presents the problem of women in the letters about Margaret Harrison's aimless life at home and her yearning to do something—if not office work then an affair. The business about Miss Milsom and Dr. Trevor satirizes the fashion for Freudian psychology. But Sayers' first concern is with theology. Metaphysical speculation and argument about science and religion dominate the novel from Munting's speculations *a la* Hamlet, to the pivotal account of an evening's conversation between Munting, two priests, and several scientists. It is, as Munting suggests, like *Point Counterpoint* without the wit—and with the palm going to religion. The whole metaphysical issue in the novel ultimately turns on the concept of creation or cause, and the argument attempts to demonstrate that science and religion are not inimical. This argument is also useful for the detective plot, because while it goes on Munting realizes the key to the whole question of how the crime was committed.

Unlike the earlier books, however, the key to the detective

plot depends on very specialized, abstruse science. For this, and perhaps for the entire scientific argument in the book, Sayers turned to Robert Eustace (Eustace Robert Barton M.D.) to whom she gave credit as her coauthor. She knew, though, that one cannot make a career out of very abstruse, scientific detective stories, and from then on made her methods of murder and science more available to the layman.

Strong Poison (1930)

Strong Poison introduces Harriet Vane, who will subsequently appear in *Have His Carcase, Gaudy Night,* and *Busman's Honeymoon.* Since she appears so often, it would be well to dispose of one part of her character right here—that part of her which is a detective story writer. In the late twenties, several detective story writers toyed around with making up fictional detective novelists whom they introduced into their books: in the year before *Strong Poison* Anthony Berkeley Cox, one of Sayers' fellows in the Detective Writers' Club, introduced a fictional detective novelist in his *Poisoned Chocolates Case.* Sayers, perhaps following this lead, made Harriet Vane a detective novelist so that she could make ironic as well as serious observations about the theory and practice of detective fiction through Harriet Vane's role. To add realism and to give impetus to discussion of detective literature, Sayers created a short bibliography of Harriet's novels: in *Strong Poison* comes Harriet's *Death in the Pot,* in *Have His Carcase* comes her *Murder by Degrees* and *The Fountain Pen Mystery,* and in *Gaudy Night* Sayers shows her working on *Death 'twixt Wind and Water.* In these made-up novels, presumably, Harriet's detective hero is Robert Templeton (apparently Sayers forgot that she had given this as Wimsey's pseudonym in *Unnatural Death).* Templeton is a good example of the old, masterful, Great Detective: he

> was a gentleman of extraordinary scientific skill combined with
> almost fabulous muscular development.[18]

He is a parody figure through whom Sayers drives home the essential unreality of the Great Detective and the detective story. Thus irony virtually drips from this description of his *sang froid:*

He was, indeed, notorious for his *sang froid* with which he examined bodies of the most repulsive description. Bodies reduced to jelly by falling out of aeroplanes; bodies charred to unrecognizable lumps by fire; bodies run over by heavy vehicles, and needing to be scraped from the road with shovels—Robert Templeton was accustomed to examining them all without turning a hair.[19]

This burlesque is a restatement of points which Sayers had made earlier in her career through the characterization of Wimsey.

Another point which Harriet's books made for Sayers is the need for verifiable accuracy. Of course it is the drive for accuracy in her novel about arsenic, *Death in the Pot,* which almost gets Harriet in the soup in *Strong Poison.* She had been too conscientious in her research.

Sayers, moreover, portrays most of Harriet's novels as complicated and ingenious constructions. The narrator of *Have His Carcase* describes *The Fountain Pen Mystery* as a "complicated and interesting problem," in which

the villain was at the moment engaged in committing a crime in Edinburgh, which involved constructing an ingenious alibi involving a steam-yacht, a wireless time signal, five clocks and the change from summer to winter time.[20]

In *Gaudy Night,* Harriet's projected new book, *Death 'twixt Wind and Water,* is different in a few details—it involves people and not things—but there is the same complexity and ingenuity:

she had five suspects, neatly confined in an old water-mill with no means of entrance or egress except by a plank bridge, and all provided with motives and alibis for a pleasantly original kind of murder.[21]

Neither of these Harriet Vane novels resembles anything that Sayers wrote before 1930—although they may resemble *The Five Red Herrings.* The one thing which ties Sayers' descriptions of Harriet's books is the fact that although she works on them conscientiously, Harriet finds this sort of detective fiction unrewarding and sterile. Wimsey puts his finger on the problem later in *Gaudy Night.* The moral aridity of detective fiction, of course, was Sayers' chief objection to the form; she tried to correct this in most of her books by making human problems impinge upon the problems of detection. Harriet Vane's earliest works had in them some human potential: in the first Harriet Vane novel which Sayers mentions, *Death in the Pot,* the subject is

> two artists who lived in Bloomsbury and led an ideal existence together, full of love and laughter and poverty, 'till somebody poisoned the young man and left the young woman inconsolable and passionately resolved to revenge him.[22]

This may be a trite story, but it is about human beings, just as through 1930 most of Sayers' detective works had more thematic interest in them than logic and problems. It is only later that Harriet's books become mechanical constructs, and this period corresponds with the time that Sayers had her gravest doubts about the detective story and was about to give it up for good.

When Sayers wrote *Strong Poison,* however, she had not yet given up on the detective story as a vehicle for voicing serious concerns; there are plenty of them in this novel. For example, when Wimsey drives down the Embankment he is hit with the sledgehammer of his own mortality; he realizes that he, too, will die and that

> from now on, every hour of light-heartedness would be not a prerogative but an achievement—one more axe or case-bottle or fowling piece, rescued, Crusoe-fashion, from a sinking ship.[23]

Mortality is not the sort of neat problem which detectives solve, and this sort of issue pervades the novel. Sayers again brings in the difficult problems of the lives of unattached women— this time not with Miss Climpson, but with her younger colleague, Miss Murchison. Miss Climpson in this book introduces the subject of spiritualism in the scenes in Westmoreland. Once again we get criticism of the lack of direction and general silliness of the *avant garde* in Wimsey's visit to Kropotky's party where the music is all discord and the people read D.H. Lawrence. There also appears the spectre of Philip Boyes who, like the villains before him, stood for atheism, anarchy, and free-love. All of these things probably amount to more diverse, non-detective concern than in any of the previous novels, and they are probably there because of the

most important non-detective concern in *Strong Poison*—
Wimsey's love for Harriet Vane. Their love affair, of course,
goes beyond the scope of this novel because Sayers wanted to
show the complexity of a real, human relationship which
cannot be neatly tied up with the solution to an artificial
puzzle. To do so would have been to make the book back into the
cliche which Sayers had tried so hard to avoid. Further, Sayers'
problem of balance in this book was a delicate one; she had
written in the *Omnibus* of the discomfiting effects of
improperly joining love plots with detective plots. She knew
that disaster would follow if she focused too much on the minds
and psyches of the lovers. Everything would be colored by
sentiment. Consequently, Sayers handles the Vane-Wimsey
relationship with economy, and it gains some of its effect in
framing the other human issues of the novel.

Sayers follows this principle in her plotting—she does not
emphasize Wimsey's or Harriet's emotions. She brings in a
number of subsidiary detectives who do much of the detection.
Bunter snoops understairs at Urquhart's house, Miss
Climpson has four chapters at the most exciting part of the
book, and Miss Murchison has several important scenes rifling
her employer's office. They have most of the action, in order to
keep the spotlight off of Wimsey and to add credit to his
emotions. By keeping Wimsey off-stage, he can be ga-ga in love
and still coolly intelligent at the same time.

If her composition of the introduction to the *Omnibus*
clarified or suggested ways to use love in this detective story, it
certainly also contributed to another area of *Strong Poison*. As
the *Omnibus* discussed how to read and write detective stories,
so, in a way, does *Strong Poison*. In chapter five Wimsey and
Miss Climpson review for themselves and the reader the range
of motives which murderers may have. These include: murder
for the fun of it, for power or control, for passion, for money
(including the motives of inheritance, insurance, and robbery),
and for blackmail. Like all of the previous critical discussions
of motives (Christie's and Van Dine's for instance), Wimsey
specifically dismisses homicidal mania as an allowable
motive. This discussion focuses the readers' intellectual
attention in the novel and moves it toward the puzzle story
which in the earlier novels Sayers had largely avoided. The
composition of the *Omnibus* introduction also clarified Sayers'
thinking about the detective story to the extent that she was

able to return to her old plotting pattern wherein the guilty party is fairly apparent to the readers from the first. This, no doubt, was due to her examination of the subject of scientific detection in the *Omnibus,* where, in a section on "The Unexpected Means," she writes that

> ..."How" is at present the one [question] which offers the most scope for surprise and ingenuity and is capable of sustaining an entire book on its own.[24]

Sayers, therefore, makes the detective plot of *Strong Poison* run on the same two questions which *Unnatural Death* uses: how and why. As in the earlier book it is the *why* which takes up the most space, initiating much of Miss Murchison's and Miss Climpson's work. The answer to how Philip Boyes was killed was supposed to be the radical surprise, but it does not come off as well as the surprise in *Unnatural Death.* The scientific and medical clues are all there, but the revelation lacks punch, probably because the same means had been used earlier by several other writers including Cox and Hammett.

The Five Red Herrings (1931)
Sayers wrote to Victor Gollancz that

> I quite appreciate the point you make about the decline of the "pure puzzle" story but I wanted to try my hand at just one of that kind. I am always afraid of getting into a rut, and like each book to have a significantly different idea behind it.[25]

So it was either Sayers' desire to make her books different from one another—based on the problem endemic to detective writers of readers knowing the plots because they have read the writer's previous books—or her desire to write a "pure puzzle" story which lead to *The Five Red Herrings,* and it is too bad.

Of course there is no such thing as a pure puzzle novel; because of the length of the novel, there must be elements which are important to the characters or atmosphere but which are irrelevant to the problem under consideration. Sayers, however, comes as close in this book to the pure puzzle story as she or most other writers ever came. The puzzle element comes into this novel in Sayers' shift from the questions of how and why to the question of who killed Campbell. Thus she strings the book on portraits and inquisitions of six suspects, all of whom had equal motive and opportunity to murder the noxious Campbell. Since the puzzle story traditionally provides orderly means for the reader to think through the facts of the crime, Sayers here provides lists and timetables for the readers to ponder. She also purposely leaves a piece of the puzzle out—in the initial investigation Wimsey notices that an item is missing from Campbell's painting kit, and calls the readers' attention to this without identifying the object:

> (Here Lord Peter Wimsey told the Sergeant what he was to look for and why, but as the intelligent reader will readily supply these details for himself, they are omitted from this page).[26]

This device was, in all probability, the inspiration for the whole book. Sayers wanted Gollancz to print the missing descriptive paragraph on a sealed page at the end of the novel, and two of her working titles were "The Missing Object" and "There's One Thing Missing."[27] The publisher, apparently, did not want her to base the book on a gimmick and persuaded Sayers to let the puzzle of the characters stand without too many fancy frills.

To enliven up the interviews and deductions inevitable in any puzzle story, Sayers adopted Anthony Berkeley Cox's patent technique of the multiple solution. She went to novels like *The Poisoned Chocolates Case,* which recounts eight credible solutions to a murder mystery, and she plugged in this device three quarters of the way through the novel in the series of conference scenes. In these scenes each of the investigators outlines a probable case against each of the suspects, ending with the correct interpretation—or at least the interpretation which Sayers chose to verify in the closing action of the book. What she did not realize, though, was that the multiple solution gambit usually only works when the writer is willing to have the detective proven wrong. But this is the least of the flaws in the book.

In spirit, *Five Red Herrings* steps backward in time. I suppose that if the facts of its publication date were lost, many people would see this novel as among the first of Sayers' Wimsey novels because of its lack of non-detective concern, and the general bumptiousness of Wimsey's character: I have, in fact, met people who could not believe that *Five Red Herrings* was written after *Strong Poison.* One would never suspect from the way in which he acts in this novel that in the previous book the consciousness of his mortality drove an ice pick into Wimsey's consciousness, or that he is in the midst of a rather painful love affair. Not once in this book does Wimsey mention Harriet Vane. Instead he sings silly songs, much like the "Body in the bath" number from *Whose Body?* and continuously comes out with Sam Wellerisms like "Well, now, Dalziel, I also, as the lady said, have not been idle." It is almost as if *Strong Poison* had not been written.

Five Red Herrings is probably Sayers' worst novel. She leaves the readers with no lasting impressions of any of the characters—except for Wimsey and the victim. The conduct of the murder is actually a replay of the murder in *Whose Body?* in that fundamental to both plots is the murderer masquerading as the victim to throw off pursuit and suspicion. With the exception of the last few chapters in which Wimsey reenacts the crime, one gets the impression that this novel was something which Sayers felt that she had to do rather than something that she wanted to do. In fact, it resembles *Death 'twixt Wind and Water,* the book which Harriet Vane projects while she is up at Oxford during *Gaudy Night,* the book which irritates Harriet because it has no human beings in it and because it revolves around a barren puzzle.

Have His Carcase (1932)

In *Pickwick Papers,* when Mr. Pickwick is about to be committed to the Fleet, this interchange occurs:

> "Well, Sam," said Mr. Pickwick, "I suppose they are getting the *habeas corpus* ready."
> "Yes, " said Sam, "and I vist they'd bring out the have—his—carcase. It's wery unpleasant keeping' us vaitin' here. I'd ha' got half a dozen have—his—carcases ready, pack'd up and all, by this time."[28]

This novel with the Pickwickean title is fully fifty pages longer than any of Sayers' previous detective books; it is the most complex detective story that she wrote. In it we find few excursions into personal, social or moral problems—just as in *Five Red Herrings,* the focus is almost entirely on solving the detective problem. Sayers put into this novel most of her most baffling and complicated detective story ideas. A list shows this best:

1. There is a criminal who uses disguise and establishes a double identity as in *Unnatural Death.*
2. There is an alibi puzzle which turns on a disabled automobile and which is solved in part through the use of lists and time-tables as in *Five Red Herrings.*
3. There is a complex problem concerning the time of death as in *Unpleasantness at the Bellona Club.*
4. There is an unusual medical fact with diagnosable symptoms at the heart of the mystery as in *Strong Poison.*
5. There is the fact that the circumstances of the body and the evidence which they present have been scrambled as in most of the novels—only here the false appearances are caused by natural instead of human agencies.
6. The identity of the murderer is clear long before the end of the novel as in *Unnatural Death,* etc.

To these devices, in order to make things more complicated still, Sayers adds a new one (for her), cryptography: this novel, like the two succeeding books, *Murder Must Advertise* and *The Nine Tailors,* depends in part for its solution on the cracking of a code. As if this were not enough, Sayers fortifies the plot by using the thriller devices of disguised accomplices (one of whom, ironically, reads Edgar Wallace) and international intrigue of the most exotic, Ruritanian sort. In short, the book is a complex construct in which discoveries and hypotheses need to be constantly reevaluated.

But why make it so complex, especially when she must go to the lengths of introducing thriller elements which by the thirties had been marked off as taboo by most serious writers of detective fiction? There is a clear and obvious answer; the same one which lies under the motive to compose *Five Red Herrings.* When Sayers crystallized her thinking about the detective story in the *Omnibus,* she realized that the main weakness of detective writers lay in their tendency to use the same basic plot over and over, so that readers could read the writer instead of the story and predict pretty accurately what would happen at the end without reference to the text. Her preoccupation with this problem comes out here in Harriet Vane's search for an answer to the problems in this case:

> "I don't know," said Harriet. "I can only suggest a few methods and precedents. There's the Roger Sherringham method, for instance. You prove elaborately and in detail that A did the murder; then you give the story one final shake, twist it round a fresh corner, and find the real murderer is B—the person you

suspected from the first and lost sight of....

"No; well there's the Philo Vance method. You shake your head and say 'There's worse to come,' and then the murderer kills five more people, and that thins out the suspects a bit and you spot who it is.[29]

Sayers simply did not want her plots to be as predictable as Cox's or Van Dine's, so she mixed up elements which she had already used and added a few new ones to knock her readers off stride and to keep them interested and guessing.

This still leaves the thriller elements in the plot—which also pop into the plot of *Murder Must Advertise.* The thriller comes into *Have His Carcase* on two levels: Sayers uses the thriller readers' desire for romance (in all of the ramifications of that word) by introducing certain plot elements like the accomplices. At the same time Sayers has her characters self-consciously allude to thriller heroes and devices thereby implying certain critical concepts. Using thriller devices in her detective story plots was nothing new for Sayers, she did this from the start, but here they are more numerous and more pronounced. This is especially so because Sayers' characters call the readers' attention to them here. Therefore the allusions to the thriller claim a special place in this novel. In *Have His Carcase* there are numerous allusions to thrillers and detective stories. On one hand we have a detailed introduction to Harriet's detective hero, Robert Templeton, who is a thriller hero—strong, silent, handsome, informed. He is precisely the sort of character summoned up by the dancer, Leila Garland's summary of the thriller which she has been reading, *The Tail of the Purple Python.* On the other hand we have numerous allusions to the detective story coming from Wimsey and Harriet as they play at being Holmes and Watson. Here Sayers does what she had done all along, burlesques the cliches of the thriller and the detective story. This burlesque, however, connects the two. What it means is that detective conventions and thriller conventions are essentially the same in their remoteness from life. Only the readership and the degree of escape are different: lower class readers, like Leila Garland, read thrillers and become emotionally transported while upper class readers, like Harriet and Wimsey, read detective stories for the fun of it.

That is one comment; there is a deeper one too. After *Have His Carcase,* Sayers' novels change substantially, moving away from the puzzle story which had dominated her attention for the past few years and toward the novel of manners. In some respects this novel can be seen as a summation of the previous puzzle books; one which she wrote in order to clear the way for a new kind of novel. It is, moreover, something else; it is a dismissal. This becomes apparent at the end of the novel. The earlier Wimsey books usually ended with the hero's distress or depression caused by the human outcome of the detective story. Here, however, the story ends with a rejection:

> "Well," said Wimsey, "isn't that a damned, awful, bitter, bloody farce? The old fool who wanted a lover and the young fool who wanted an empire...God! What a jape! King Death has asses' ears with a vengeance."
>
> ...
>
> "Let's clear out of this," he said. "Get your things packed and leave your address with the police and come up to town. I'm fed to the back teeth...."[30]

This is what Sayers felt about the detective story in this form, and she went up to town for the next novel which is different indeed. The detective story for her was becoming less of a romp and less of a game. Human life began to once again move into the foreground of Sayers' attention.

Murder Must Advertise (1933)

There are, remarkably, some similarities between this novel and *Five Red Herrings*. In both books the victim was a worthless grub while the murderer is seen in a reasonably sympathetic light. Once more Sayers serves up multiple suspects—all of the employees of Pym's Publicity. Likewise, except for the fact that Parker and Lady Mary are married, one could place this novel as an early book—Wimsey is full of Wodehousean high spirits and self parody, Harriet Vane is forgotten. Superficially, *Murder Must Advertise* seems to have all of the marks of the puzzle story. There are lists of things and suspects, interviews with suspects and tests for them to pass.

But this is not a puzzle book. The detection in the novel, when examined, is muddy, routine, and not well handled. To begin, the book relies on thriller obsessions. Back in 1927 Wimsey twitted Parker about Scotland Yard's preoccupation with nasty social crimes

> ...Scotland Yard have two maggots which crop up whenever
> anything happens to a young woman. Either it's White Slavery or
> Dope Dens—sometimes both.[31]

One of the things which Wimsey suggests in *Unnatural Death*
when he alludes to prostitution and narcotics and excluding
them from consideration merely echoes what prescriptive
critics had been saying about eliminating organized crime
from the detective story. If one were to complete the aesthetic of
the detective story, it is easy to see why writers should
eliminate gangs: being what they are, gangs complicate the
issues of individual motivation and detection to an extent that
they cannot be worked out in a novel in a satisfying and
complete manner. In spite of these dangers, however, *Murder
Must Advertise* turns on thriller devices. It revolves around a
gang which procures and distributes cocaine, and as a
consequence of this the detective part of the novel becomes a
muddle. At the end of the book a *deus ex machina* is necessary
to dispose of the gang, in this case it is one Mr. Smith and a
shadowy Harley Street physician. We know virtually nothing
of these men, and placing them at the core of the crime violates
much of what the "fair play," puzzle detective story had been
trying to achieve. If this were not problem enough, Sayers
never quite finishes up the dope plot. When we get to Wimsey's
unravelling, he bogs down in vagueness. He explains to Parker
that

> I don't know the details, but I imagine it's done this way.... Then
> he informs the head distributing agents. I don't know how....
> There must be some code or other.[32]

Not quite the clarity which one expects from the detective
story. Perhaps Sayers grew tired of the narcotics plot, or
perhaps she reacted against the excrutiating exactness of
building a puzzle story.

Not many people, however, would read this novel if it were
only for the detection. The book succeeds because Sayers here
experiments with a new sort of detective novel. In the *Omnibus*
Sayers made various predictions about the future of the genre.
Among these comes the suggestion that

> There certainly does seem a possibility that the detective story will
> some time come to an end, simply because the public will have
> learned all the tricks. But it probably has many years to go yet,

and in the meantime a new and less rigid formula will probably
have developed, linking it more closely to the novel of manners
and separating it more widely from the novel of adventure.[33]

Sayers uses this formula, moving toward the novel of manners,
for all of her novels after *Have His Carcase,* and it begins here.
She loosens up the detection and treats manners more fully.
The subsequent novels work both as detective stories and
novels of manners.

The comedy of manners, going as far back as Jonson, or
Congreve, or Thackeray, depends for its effects upon witty
dialogue, particular characters and a specific atmosphere in
which and from which these things grow. All of these things
can be found in *Murder Must Advertise.* Take the dialogue.
Wimsey is nothing if not a witty man. In the earlier books,
however, he really has no one in the same class (except Harriet)
and he cannot sparkle. Here he has Miss Meteyard, late of
Somerville College, and Mr. Ingleby, late of Trinity. Both of
them can banter with Wimsey at his most facetious—they are
witty people. It comes out in their work of writing ads, and it
blossoms in halls at Pym's.

As far as Wimsey goes, I recall reading somewhere that
Sayers once said that he acted like an eighteenth century
gentleman. Here he fills the role of a character in an eighteenth
century, neo-jonsonian comedy of manners. Most comedies of
manners have in them a character who moves from group to
group pretending to be something which he is not in order to
stimulate action in the form of reactions to him. This is the part
which Wimsey plays here. In earlier novels, Wimsey briefly
disguised himself in order to get information, but here he is
disguised more variously and consistently than ever before: he
plays the parts of Bredon, the harlequin, and even that of Lord
Peter Wimsey. At the end of the book, in fact, he goes to
Scotland Yard as Wimsey to visit himself as Bredon. This is the
sort of situation which one might find in Congreve or Oscar
Wilde.

The minor characters in the novel fall into clearly defined
types, the collision of which produces either fireworks or
explosions. There are the higher public school types, the lower
public school types, like Tallboy, and the Council school types,
like Smayle. There is Helen, Duchess of Denver, a caricature of
snooty aristocracy, and Dian DeMomerie, the bored, sensation-
seeking vamp. Enthusiasms of some characters, like humours,

make them function in the novel: Ginger Joe's amateur
detection, old Mr. Brotherhood's cricket mania, Mr. Copley's
fastidiousness. All Sayers has to do is to bring these types
together to produce collisions which move things forward.

Exploiting manners almost always means creating a
special milieu which affects the way in which the characters
act. Sayers' backdrop in *Murder Must Advertise* may be the
most important thing in the novel. It is, of course, a distillation
and presentation of all of the years which she spent as an
advertising copy writer. Advertising not only gives the people
at Pym's jobs and a place to work, thereby coloring their
characters, but it becomes an independent force in the novel
which is more powerful and enduring than anyone in the book.
It taints most characters' speech and also (like the cliche about
Frankenstein's monster) has a life of its own. Sayers puts two,
striking, telegraphic paragraphs in the novel which flash ads
at the readers:

> SOPO SAVES SCRUBBING—NUTRAX FOR NERVES—
> CRUNCHLETS ARE CRISPIER—EAT PIPER PARRITCH—
> DRINK POMPAYNE—ONE WHOOSH AND IT'S CLEAN—OH
> BOY! IT'S TOMBOY TOFFEE...[34]

The novel ends in advertising. It is fake, crass, noxious, silly,
and stupid; it announces the loss of dignity, privacy, and taste;
it shapes people's lives and they are powerless to stop or even
ignore it. It causes the success of this novel, and it also causes
the novel's soft spots which come when Sayers tries to push the
obvious relationship between the ad business and the narcotic
trade, and this gums up the credibility of the detective story.

The Nine Tailors (1934)

Two years earlier, in *Have His Carcase,* Harriet Vane
mused about her work in progress, *The Fountain Pen Mystery.*
She considers the alibi of the murderer when the idea of using
the ringing of a church clock strikes her:

> But church-clocks and bodies in belfries had been rather overdone
> lately.

Whether they had been overdone or not, a body in a belfry is the
basis of the mystery in *Nine Tailors.* As in most of Sayers'
works, once she has thought of the cause of death, constructing
the rest of the mystery plot is simply a matter of fitting in

devices which she has already perfected. Here we get the problem of identifying the corpse, solving a cypher, and determining the cause of death, all of which Sayers had done before. These problems are solved by running about to find dispersed bits of information (rather like a scavenger hunt), by inspiration (when Wimsey looks up at the church ceiling), and by accident. Naturally Sayers camouflages these things and complicates them by altering the condition and situation of the body. She had done this before in books in which 1) the criminal alters the situation and condition of the body, or 2) nature alters the condition of the body. Here there is a new wrinkle: two innocent men, acting separately, alter the condition and situation of the body. All of this presents a nice mystery plot, but scarcely a great one; it may have been great if this were Sayers' first novel, but it is her ninth. It is not the mystery plot which makes many readers select this as Sayers' best book.

It may well be the locale. In her previous novel, Sayers decided to write about a place which she really knew—an advertising office—and readers remember the atmosphere of Pym's long after they have forgotten the young quat Victor Dean and the person who killed him. Sayers does the same thing here. The portraits of the Fen country of East Anglia, of Fenchurch St. Paul, and especially of the eight bells in the church tower remain vivid long after Deacon, Will Thoday, and the rest are dust. Sayers depicts the atmosphere with great care. The technical material about the bells is merely the most obvious example of this. She includes a drawing of the church and a map of the district—the only other one of her novels to contain a map is *Five Red Herrings* which, in part, Sayers wrote to celebrate the Scottish village where she and her husband vacationed—which are the literal signs of the importance of the locale in this novel. The spiritual importance of the place, the church and the bells, pervades the novel; it shapes and moves the characters even more powerfully than Pym's shapes and moves people in *Murder Must Advertise.* Some of the vividness comes, no doubt, from the fact that Sayers grew up in the Fen country. But more important than this, Sayers uses the landscape and the church much as an Elizabethan dramatist would use nature. The moral forces in the novel reside in nature which cleanses human folly and crime: the flood in the novel does, after all, have a Biblical parallel. In this book Sayers removes from the detective story the necessity of dealing with human justice; instead of courts or an individual's decision, providential nature—God—deals with the problems which human beings create for themselves through their ignorance or sin while the ark of the church rides safe on the waters.

There is something else which gives this novel body beyond the atmosphere and the mystery plot: Sheridan LeFanu. Joseph Sheridan LeFanu, when he is known, is known as either a writer of ghost stories or as one of a group of Victorian novelists, including Wilkie Collins, called Sensation Novelists. When Harriet Vane goes up to Oxford in *Gaudy Night,* one of the things which keeps her busy is the composition of a study of Sheridan LeFanu. But LeFanu comes in earlier, he comes in here. When Wimsey and Bunter first consider the note which Hilary Thrope finds on the church tower, Bunter says

> I should say that it was written by a person of no inconsiderable literary ability, who had studied the works of Sheridan LeFanu and was, if I may be permitted the expression, bats in the belfry, my Lord.

Sayers, I think, is having a bit of fun with herself, for much of the pseudo-gothic atmosphere of this novel comes from LeFanu. Not only this, one of LeFanu's favorite motifs was the return of the criminal to his home after years of exile and the recognition of the criminal at the catastrophe. This may have been where Sayers got the outlines of the Deacon business—the return of the criminal to his old haunts and its discovery precipitates the catastrophe of *Nine Tailors.*

There are a number of character points in this novel which should be noted. Wimsey acts much as he did in the pre-Vane books; he is just as full of songs and Wellerisms as ever. Surprisingly, Bunter plays a larger part in this book than in any of the previous novels—and he is a slightly different sort of character here. Not only does he allow himself to use the expression "bats in the belfry," but he also does music hall imitations for the people understairs. These are cracks in the solid front of respectability which Sayers had set up for Bunter in the earlier books. More interesting than this is the character of Will Thoday. Ever since *Five Red Herrings,* Sayers began to show increased sympathy for her criminals—in both *Five Red*

Herrings and *Murder Must Advertise,* the reader is intended to pity the criminal as Wimsey does. Here Sayers in her characterization of Will Thoday (who did not murder the man in the belfry) goes much deeper into the individual's consciousness of his own sin and shows a man progressively burdened with troubles.

Nine Tailors shows a departure for Sayers in terms of her style. Sayers in her earlier novels was consciously anti-modern: she specifically rejects in *Clouds of Witness* the sort of experiments in style done by Joyce and Lawrence. Lawrence, because of his thematic obsessions, remained on Sayers' blacklist until the end, but in this novel she uses patches of stream of consciousness. At the funeral, in part three, Sayers shows Wimsey's mind popping from the Service, to reflections on people, to reflections on the text, to the bells, to the rope, and so on. The passage is not as fractured as Joyce's are, but it is stream of consciousness used to characterize as well as to move forward the detective situation.

Gaudy Night (1936)

In the twenties Sayers strained against the confines of the detective novel and generally filled her books with non-detective themes. After she wrote the *Omnibus* introduction she devoted herself to writing standard detective stories with less non-detective material. With *Have His Carcase,* however, she returned to doubting in print the efficacy and morality of the form. *Gaudy Night* carries this movement to its furthest extreme. In it the detective interest is miniscule, Sayers reflects upon the weakness of the form, and she concentrates on what seem to her to be more important themes than those of the standard detective story. It is hardly a detective novel at all.

Gaudy Night, although it does contain several scenes which threaten danger or death to several characters, does not involve murder or mysterious death, which by the 1930's had become one of the accepted criteria for the detective novel. Instead the novel moves on a number of malicious pranks directed at the faculty and students of Shrewsbury College, Oxford. Throughout most of the novel the chief threat comes from the danger of scandal rather than from physical threats directed at individuals. Another heretical element in the detective material is that the perpetrator of the pranks is psychologically warped; her motives do not simply spring from the desire for revenge, but from twisted sexuality. This goes a bit beyond what prescriptive critics considered fitting as motive in a detective story. In fact, Sayers spent relatively little effort on the detective plot in this novel. Harriet Vane pokes and chases about a bit at the college, but does not get very far; Wimsey, who does not appear often in the book, is the god from the machine (in this case a Daimler) who polishes off the problem with a few flourishes, looking into things which should have been investigated at the beginning. The one part of her typical pattern which Sayers does follow here is the demonstration of the sordid nature of the final results. She manages the scene in which the guilty party is judged so as to create the maximum discomfort for everyone involved: no one really comes away from the judgment with any sense of dignity or integrity. But this cannot be construed as a normal part of the detective story. It is the result of Sayers' increasing awareness of the complexity and humanity of criminals and detectives.

Sayers pays a good deal of attention in this book to Harriet's composition of her new novel. While staying at her old college, Harriet works on *Death 'twixt Wind and Water*. This story, as you recall, contains a standard plot concerning five people with motive and no alibis. Throughout *Gaudy Night,* Harriet must face up to the essential nature of the detective story and come to terms with its weaknesses. She acknowledges that the book which she is working on is "significant of nothing in particular," and that the characters are robots instead of human beings. It is conventional, escapist literature which provides relief from the sort of complexity which one confronts in human problems like those at Oxford. Harriet's dilemma is that "human beings were not like that; human problems were not like that."[35] So she has difficulties writing the book because she is bothered with its artificiality. Wimsey, as usual, puts his finger on the problem:

> You have to abandon the jig-saw kind of story and write a book about human beings for a change.[36]

And that is what Sayers does here.

As a novel, *Gaudy Night* discusses a number of interrelated themes which grow from the issues and problems of women and education: these points combine and recombine to form the chief concerns of the book. The education theme starts from the issue of intellectual integrity, and Sayers localizes the theme in a question of scholarly dishonesty which she twines around references to C.P. Snow's novel, *The Search.* Snow's novel recounts the scientific career of one Arthur Miles. Included in Miles' decisions are whether to withhold contradictory evidence about one of his experiments, whether to expose another scientist's faulty research, and whether a researcher is responsible for the accuracy of the work done by his subordinates. Sayers eliminates the last problem, since historical and not scientific research is the basis of her plot, and focuses on the scholar's duty to truth. Thus, a scholar's having withheld a valuable piece of evidence, and another scholar's exposure of this dishonesty lies at the bottom of the mystery in this book, and it motivates some of the characters' actions and a good deal of the discussion in the novel.

The issue of intellectual honesty opens up not only into questions of academic life but also into the questions about women discussed here. This is a women's novel—it discusses the problems of higher education for women who throw it away when they leave the university, it discusses the antagonism of both men and women toward women in positions of authority and respect, and it discusses one particular woman's reticence toward marriage because it threatens to erase her identity. The solution to the last problem—Harriet Vane's problem—contains the solution to all of the problems for women in the book. Possessiveness, the evil which lies at the root of the problems in several early novels, is the key. Just as Harriet finds a man who is unwilling to extinguish her identity with his, so must other men and women not only in their private lives but also in their professional relationships know what they are and respect what other people are. It is the job done which is important, and this is why there is so much stress on work and doing a good job of it.

Busman's Honeymoon (1937)

Probably Sayers intended *Gaudy Night* to be her last detective novel. In it the detective interest is weak and she ties up the relationship between Harriet and Wimsey which she had shifted from burner to burner since 1930. Someone, however, convinced Sayers to write a play about Wimsey. Although she later gained recognition as a lay theologian in part because of her conversion of narrative Biblical materials into drama, Sayers needed help in 1936 to shape her material into a workable play. For this she turned to Muriel St. Clare Byrne—a scholar of Elizabethan drama and editor of Massinger's plays—who helped her to cut and fit her ideas to the stage. *Busman's Honeymoon* as a novel is a narrative adaptation of this play: it is the play with narrative clothes. It revolves around a number of set scenes in the drawing room at Tallboys, which depend for their interest mainly upon dialogue. One can easily see these chapters as scenes from a play. Further, we can see the play through the novel by looking at all of the simple and clear parts for comic, character actors— Puffet, Ma Ruddle, the vicar, etc. When Sayers turned the play into the novel all she really had to do was to add the epistolary opening, the travelling scenes, the scenes out of doors, and she could also restore some of the material which the time restrictions of the stage had caused her to cut.

Sayers subtitled *Busman's Honeymoon* "A Love Story with Detective Interruptions." I do not know whether this is the proper description; somehow "hail wedded love" comes more to mind when one considers the Harriet-Wimsey plot in this novel, for it focuses not on the process of love but upon the happiness of the lovers' wedded state and the adjustments which they make to perpetuate that happiness. The relationship of the Wimseys becomes one based on openness, trust, and freedom—although all of this becomes a bit self-conscious at times, as it must in a book written to make these points. If part of the love story lies in the trust and understanding evolving in the Wimseys, part of it resides with the foils who show the anguish of love when it is based on egotism or avarice. This, in large measure, is why Miss Twitterton and Crutchley enter the novel: each views marriage from selfish and inferior motives. Miss Twitterton, Sayers' final version of Miss Clack, grasps at marriage as simply the thing which women do, and pursues it without any higher or inner motives. Crutchley, on the other hand, sees it as simply a means of getting money, and when the prospect of money disappears so does his desire for marriage.

Parcel but not part of the Wimsey-Vane marriage story is the aristocratic milieu. No novel since *Clouds of Witness* has so much of the high life in it. To start with, the novel is framed with pictures of aristocratic life. It begins with letters describing the Wimsey-Vane alliance and it ends, or almost ends, at Duke's Denver amidst eighteenth century splendor and modern plumbing. The middle of the book shows how Harriet and Wimsey condescend with grace, wit, and style. They have to deal with pesky newspaper men, policemen, rustics, untutored servants, social climbers, well meaning vicars, pushy agents who demand Nokes' furniture, clogged chimneys, and broken crockery. None is really any problem. They cope with ingenuity and good humor, each protecting the other insofar as they can, showing not only the resources of style, but the efficacy of a good marriage.

The "detective interruptions" are really more than interruptions. There is certainly more detection here than in *Gaudy Night*. What Sayers does in this novel deflects some of the detection from Wimsey, for she puts most of the mid-book wondering and theorizing about the crime in the mind and conversations of Superintendent Kirk. Once again, the detective problem grows not from who but from how. The discovery of the method of the crime almost automatically produces the murderer's identity. Further, Sayers runs the detective interest on a medical fact as she had done before: in this case the fact is that a person can receive a mortal wound and move about in a relatively normal fashion. She even goes to the extent of citing passages from Taylor's *Medical Jurisprudence* to substantiate the medical side of the story. There are a few reminiscences of Sayers' first book in *Busman's Honeymoon,* but perhaps the most striking is Wimsey's leap of imagination which solves the problem and is accompanied by a dream. The substance of Wimsey's dream, however, shows how far Sayers had come since 1923. Here Wimsey dreams a scene from T.S. Eliot's "Hollow Men," a modern poem about the spiritual aridity of modern life. This shows not only that Sayers began to accept modernism in literature—the form and substance of Eliot and Joyce—but also that her overriding concerns were turning from the burlesque of the traditional detective story toward active work for the spiritual revivification of modern life.

The novel at the close shows this concern in action. In the earlier books Wimsey constantly has doubts about his avocation as a detective and is often affected by the ending of any case which puts human life in jeopardy. Here these problems are magnified a hundred fold. The end of the novel concentrates on Wimsey's protracted agony at the exposure of human depravity and the taking of a human life. It is something which cannot be glossed over and another book of detective adventures begun. It is the end of Sayers' detective stories. In this book she simply portrays in Wimsey's character what she would later intellectually formulate in essays like "Problem Picture" (1941) which contrast the finite, solvable mathematical nature of the detective story with the insolvable, protean, and transcendental problems of the world, the flesh, and the devil. Sayers felt that she had to move to more practical and honest ways of coping with the world than the detective story offered, so she devoted herself exclusively to theological writing and mainstream literary scholarship. She was, however, I think, wrong about herself and her detective books: the Wimsey stories have more to do with life than any other writer's detective books. They confront problems and do not give easy answers. They may be, in fact, Sayers' best pieces of theology.

Chapter 6

Anthony Berkeley Cox

In many ways Anthony Berkeley Cox was the most important of the Golden Age detective writers. It was Cox who founded the Detection Club to which most of the important writers of the period belonged and which produced the communal detective story books like *Six Against Scotland Yard* (1936). Cox had, perhaps, the most sophisticated understanding of the nature of the detective story of any writer of his generation. He must have been an intelligent, witty, urbane, if somewhat sarcastic, man. But few people read his detective stories today (none is in print in the U.S. at the time I am writing). If he is remembered at all it is usually because of Alfred Hitchcock and Cary Grant and the 1941 film, *Suspicion,* based on Cox's *Before the Fact.* This neglect is in some respects understandable. Even though Cox was a knowledgeable plotter, most of his detective stories have the same plot pattern which Sayers outlined in the following passage from *Have His Carcase:*

> There's the Roger Sherringham method, for instance. You prove elaborately and in detail that A did the murder; then you give the story one final shake, twist it round a fresh corner, and find the real murderer is B—the person you suspected first and lost sight of...[1]

Second, Cox hardly ever drew any sympathetic characters: his people are either weak or vain or stupid, and this sort of person is hardly the sort that will survive in popular fiction. Finally, even though he could sparkle in places, Cox's prose sometimes becomes elephantine, awkward, and dull. Thus his narratives too often bog down in passivity, again, hardly the sort of thing which gains a wide reading public for an author. Except for the occasions of stylistic weakness, however, there are conscious reasons for these features of Cox's works which seem to detract from their popularity and these reasons are based on Cox's attempts to remake the detective novel.

Cox made a specialty out of offensive people: every novel contains at least one, and usually more, obnoxious, offensive, unattractive person—and this does not count the criminal. Cox, in fact, began his career in detective writing by purposely creating the obnoxious detective, Roger Sherringham. Roger Sherringham was to be Cox's bread and butter (he frequently makes remarks, through Roger, about the purely mercenary motivation for writing novels) through ten books: *The Layton Court Mystery* (1925), *The Wychford Poisoning Case* (1926), *Roger Sherringham and the Vane Mystery* (1927), *The Silk Stocking Murders* (1928), *The Poisoned Chocolates Case* (1929), *The Second Shot* (1930), *Top Storey Murder* (1931), *Murder in the Basement* (1932), *Jumping Jenny* (1933), and *Panic Party* (1934). In these novels Roger goes through several metamorphoses, but in spite of these changes Cox's motives for creating him can always be seen. The first of these motives we have already seen in other Golden Age writers; Cox wants to create a detective who is the antithesis of Sherlock Holmes. Thus he announces in the dedication to this first novel, *The Layton Court Mystery,* that

> I have tried to make the gentleman who eventually solves the mystery as nearly as possible as he might be expected to do in real life. That is to say, he is very far removed from a sphinx and he does make a mistake or two occasionally. I have never believed very much in those hawk-eyed, tight-lipped gentry who pursue their silent and inexorable way straight to the heart of things without ever once overbalancing or turning aside after false goals.[2]

In this recognition about the detective hero there are several implications. Obviously Cox follows Bentley's lead in drumming up the fallibility of the detective—there is a good deal of Trent in Roger's make-up. Fallibility, in fact, is one of Roger's basic traits, for he is not only misled to false assumptions in all of the novels, but sometimes, as in *The Vane Mystery, The Poisoned Chocolates Case, The Second Shot, Top Storey Murder* and *Jumping Jenny,* Roger does not solve the mystery at all. It is solved by another character (Morseby or Chitterwick), or by the intervention of the narrator which unravels for the reader what is really an unsolved murder.

Making his detective "as nearly as possible as he might be" in real life holds another implication besides the human possibility of faulty reasoning and failure. Cox, I think, asked himself what kind of man would have the gall to push himself into other people's private affairs, to intrude where he is not wanted, to assume the duties of others, the police, and to have sublime faith in his own perception and acumen. His answer was a very disagreeable one. Cox has, indeed, admitted that he based Roger on "an offensive person I once knew because in my original innocence I thought it would be amusing to have an offensive detective."[3] So he set out in the first few Sherringham books to make Roger into the offensive detective. Roger, of course, is most repulsive in the first novel when Cox's purpose was fresh in his mind. Here the narrator takes pains to remind the reader about what kind of person Roger really is. Thus when he first appears we learn that there was "a spontaneous heartiness about his voice which grated intolerably."[4] There are not only narrative pointers like this one but numerous instances of Roger's officiousness, his desire for praise, his self-satisfaction, which lead him into mistakes and into downright buffoonery—as when he tracks down the villain "Prince" only to discover that he is a particularly nasty bull. In the succeeding novels Roger contrives to be "officious" especially where women are involved, but with time Cox discovered that Roger had become a successful detective character and he had to "tone his offensiveness down and pretend that he never was."[5] The last Sherringham novel, *Panic Party,* in fact, shows Roger to be pretty much of a normal hero, for in this novel he asserts his real intelligence and leadership in order to maintain civilization on an island where he has been stranded with a group of people among whom is a murderer and a host of flighty and unstable characters.

Roger has two other suggestive ingredients which point up several things about Cox's works. First, Roger is a popular novelist—Cox never pins down the exact type of novel that Roger writes but they are certainly not detective stories—who is absolutely truthful about his trade. In spite of the fact that it jars with his self-satisfaction, Roger never claims that his books are important or that they are art. Thus he bridles whenever he is around arty people who discuss the higher functions of literature. He is quite frank about being in it for the money just as he is quite frank about doing detective work for the fun of it. Further, after the second novel Roger becomes something of an expert on historical criminology. By the time of *Silk Stocking Murders* he has a newspaper column about criminology (having been up to this point only a special correspondent), and there are lengthy sections in most of the novels in which he discusses criminology and cites his Crippen chapter and verse. The usual point which Roger makes with his criminology is that history repeats itself, but the inclusion of this material has a more significant purpose for Cox. Studying the ways in which criminals actually behave was one of the first steps that Cox took toward the kind of novels which he would write as Francis Iles in the thirties.

By 1927, after having exploited the grossest parts of Roger's nature, and after having wrung most of the possible jokes out of this kind of character, Cox turned to a new kind of detective hero in *Mr. Priestley's Problem*. Strictly speaking, *Mr. Priestley's Problem* is not a detective novel at all, as it has no crime in it, but a novel about a practical joke in thriller dress. In this book a group of sophisticates decide to hoax Mr. Priestley into believing that he has committed a murder in order to chortle at his reactions. This, in turn, leads to loads of mistakes and uproarious consequences during which the detective story hoax becomes a zany thriller improvisation. Here Cox shows not only his predeliction for joking but he also introduces a new character type in Mr. Priestley which he would later go on to exploit in later novels. Mr. Priestley is the opposite side of Cox's earlier hero: he is the victim of loud, insensitive, hearty souls like Roger. Content to spend his middle age as a bachelor of sedate, scholarly, and reclusive habits, Mr. Priestley is yet another attack on the cliche of the Great Detective. He is timid, demure, and weak-chested: in short, he is everything which Holmes or even Roger was not. In this novel, however, Cox uses the romantic theme of the underdog turning the tables and proving his own wit and resource at the expense of the superficially resourceful characters—a theme common to the schoolboy story. That is, at the end Mr. Priestley wins, is accepted by the gang which had formerly baited him, and his personality changes accordingly. Such would not be the case with Cox's second incarnation of this character type.

Ambrose Chitterwick (note the carefully chosen name) is Cox's second version of the meek hero. Mr. Chitterwick appears in three of Cox's novels: *The Poisoned Chocolates Case* (1929), *Piccadilly Murder* (1930), and *Trial and Error* (1937). With Chitterwick Cox again draws the eternal victim. Everyone ignores or overlooks Chitterwick who lives inconspicuously with his aged and domineering aunt. He is small, insecure, prissy, and when he talks the narrators of the novels note that he "squeaks." Judge him from this passage in *Piccadilly Murder:*

> He took with him, besides the more conventional parts of his outfit, a hot-water bottle (for even in July you never know), a red flannel chest protector (for his dear grandfather was carried off by chest trouble, as he very well knew, and it is tempting providence to be flagrant in one's recklessness), a white cotton nightcap (for if Ambrose's hair went on disappearing at that rate he'd soon be as bald as a coot, and the only way to stop hair disappearing as anybody but a perfect buffin knew, was to wear a nightcap)...[6]

As anyone but a perfect buffin can guess, given the example of Mr. Priestley, Mr. Chitterwick is extremely astute for all of his shyness and obsequiousness. In *The Poisoned Chocolates Case* he bowls over the wits of the "Crimes Circle," in *Piccadilly Murder* he penetrates the murderer's ruse and rattles off the solution, and in *Trial and Error* he knows the facts but purposely withholds them from the police (and the readers). Chitterwick is so acute in his judgments that I suspect that in some of his traits, Cox drew a caricature of himself—a look at George Morrow's drawing of Cox on the frontispiece of *Jugged Journalism* (1925) confirms this, and watching Chitterwick's victory over the "Crimes Circle" in the *Poisoned Chocolates Case* suggests Cox and his friends at the Detection Club. At any rate, Mr. Chitterwick, in spite of his intellect and his string of victories, never changes as Mr. Priestley does. He never becomes the hero, he never gets the girl, but he goes back to his obscure retirement and dowdy respectability every time a case is closed. This in itself was something new in the detective novel: a hero who persistently refuses the limelight.

Cox's other heroes in the Berkeley series (actually there are no heroes in the Iles books, but that is another subject) are all, more or less, like Priestley or Chitterwick. Cyril Pinkerton, who provides the solution to the problem after Roger botches it in *The Second Shot,* is short (five feet six inches), stuffy, squeamish, fastidious, sheltered, and naive, but like Mr.

Priestley he solves the problem (in several senses) and gets the girl. Lawrence Todhunter, who shares the bill with Mr. Chitterwick in *Trial and Error,* is a prissy little man who nevertheless goes out with a romantic bang. Finally, Douglas Sewell, the detective figure in *A Puzzle in Poison* (1938) is an innocuous bungler burdened with an "inferiority complex" which consistently controls his actions and keeps him from exposing the murderer at the close of the novel. Here Cox has served up a whole gallery of physically and psychically weak people who also have first class brains. Sometimes they change character to win romantic kudoes, but sometimes they do not. This more or less corresponds to the fact that in the Sherringham novels sometimes Roger noses out the truth and sometimes he fails. With Cox one can never tell—he is perfectly willing to sacrifice his heroes in order to provide surprises— and it is in the realm of character that Cox surprises readers and does it more efficiently than in the realm of plot which was for many other detective writers the only place where they would put their surprises.

If Cox came to stand for anything in the Golden Age, he came to stand for "psychology." Psychology is a word which has a rather loose definition and it has to be treated gingerly when it is applied to literature. Any story which contains human behavior (and show me one that does not) can be called a picture of human behavior just as a study of characters' manias, libidoes, egoes, ids, and super egoes in fictional form can be called a psychological novel. Cox's fixation on psychology was neither immediate nor consistent and before one can understand it a look into its development must be undertaken. Not all of Cox's novels were intended to be about human psychology, and those which are about it deal with different approaches to and different kinds of human behavior; and they succeed in their aims to different degrees.

When he began to write detective books, psychology was the furtherest thing from Cox's mind. He frankly intended to amuse, as he says in the dedication to *The Layton Court Mystery,* and the early novels are romps in one field or another: jokes about one subject or another. Roger and Alex fool around in the first two novels, and the serious psychological premise of *Mr. Priestley's Problem* is rapidly displaced by ruritanian slapstick. The one element in the early books, however, which leads Cox to bring in arguments about psychology is the heavy anti-

Thorndykean bias which they display; that is, following Milne's advice, Cox does not wish to have the detective story turn on obscure scientific or technological minutiae.

Cox's first, tentative step toward the psychological novel came in *The Wychford Poisoning Case*—which in itself is not a psychological novel. Here there are several passages which reflect on the place of psychology in the detective novel. The first comes in the dedication to E.M. Delafield:

> You will recognize in it [this novel] many of your own ideas, which I have unblushingly annexed; but I hope you will also recognize the attempt I have made to substitute for the materialism of the usual crime-puzzle of fiction those psychological values which are (as we have so often agreed) the basis of the universal interest in the far more absorbing criminological dramas of real life.
>
> In other words I have tried to write what might be described as a psychological detective story.[7]

During the investigations in this novel, Roger reiterates many of these same ideas and expands upon them, as in this passage:

> . . . it's the psychology of the people concerned; the character of the criminal, the character of the victim, their reactions to violence, what they felt and thought and suffered over it all. The circumstances of the case, the methods of the murderer, the steps taken to elude detection—all these arise directly out of character; in themselves they're only secondary. Facts, you might say, depend on psychology. What is it that made the Thompson-Bywaters case so extraordinarily interesting? Not the mere facts. It was the characters of the three protagonists. Take away the psychology of the case and you get just a sordid triangle of the most trite and uninteresting description. Add it, and you get what the film-producers call a drama packed with human interest. Just the same with the Seddon case, Crippen, or, to be very criminologically classical, William Palmer.[8]

There is a lot of important material here: opposition to the materialism of the standard detective story (thirty nine varieties of tobacco ash, for instance), focus on the reaction of the criminal and victim, and the identification with historical crimes. These psychological elements would burgeon in the Francis Iles novels, but they do not burgeon here. Instead of being a psychological study, *The Wychford Poisoning Case* is a game of playing detective with Roger and Alex and Sheila Purefoy. There is no real attention given to the inner natures of detectives, suspects, or victim. Finally, the book depends on a very real, almost Thorndykean, medical fact. In short, here Cox's spirit wills a psychological novel but the flesh is weak— the traditional form of the detective story was made to be unreal and it takes more modification than Cox provides here to give it real psychological interest. He could not change the puzzle game but only the rules, making motive the thing to be guessed instead of a set of material facts—and there was nothing particularly new about this since most good detective novelists before him had relied on motive instead of material clues.

After *The Wychford Poisoning Case,* Cox did little with psychology until *The Second Shot* in 1930. In the dedication to this novel Cox once again takes off on psychology. He repeats and clarifies most of the points which he had made in 1926.

> In my own opinion it is towards this latter [the development of character and atmosphere] that the best of the new detective-writing energies are being directed. I personally am convinced that the days of the old crime-puzzle pure and simple, relying entirely upon plot and without any added attractions of characters, style, or even humour, are, if not numbered, at any rate in the hands of the auditors; and that the detective story is already in the process of developing into the novel with a detective or a crime interest, holding its readers less by mathematical than by psychological ties. The puzzle elements will become a puzzle of character rather than a puzzle of time, place, motive, and opportunity. The question will be not *"who* killed the old man in the bathroom?" but *"what* on earth induced X, of all people, to kill the old man in the bathroom?..."* The detective's solution will only be the prelude to a change of interest; we shall want to know exactly what remarkable combination of circumstances did bring X, of all people, to the decision that nothing short of murder would meet the case. In a word, the detective story must become more sophistocated. *There is a complication of emotion, drama, psychology, and adventure* behind the most ordinary murder in real life, the possibilities of which for fictional purposes the conventional detective story misses completely.[9]   (my italics)

This statement is a reasonably good description of what had already happened to the detective novel after *Trent's Last Case.* Its derivation from Sayers (the allusion to the body in the bath points to *Whose Body?* and some of the other comments sound like points which Sayers made in her introduction to *The Omnibus of Crime)* points to this. The novel which follows this dedication carries out, to some extent, its premises. The

conclusion of the investigation in *The Second Shot* is followed
by a section narrated by the murderer outlining the motives for
the crime. But it is really nothing new—Christie used the
technique almost a decade earlier in *The Man in the Brown
Suit.* Further, the murderer is not a terribly original character
but one upon whom Cox had depended in earlier novels. In this
novel, moreover, there is little place for meaningful
examination of motive, and there is little real drama—given
the wry attitude of the narrator throughout. Finally, the puzzle
apparatus, the "guess who did it" signs, obtrude into the novel
and block any meaningful attention to the consideration of
human beings. Cox, I think, realized this: the puzzle game and
the psychological novel do not mix easily since one drums on
the fact of unreality and the other depends upon the belief that
what goes on in the novel contains the truth about human
actions.

Given the criteria of the detective story developed by Ellery
Queen, particularly considering the points that the hero must
be the detective and that the problem must be centrally
important, it is difficult to write a detective story that is a real
psychological novel. This is not to say, mind you, that people
did not try to write them. Any number of methods were
attempted in the late twenties and early thirties to open the
detective novel into a means of portraying human nature. As
Cox diagnosed the technical problem, there were several
critical hurdles to jump in order to make a psychological
detective story. The first was the detective story's obsession
with physical clues; this he surmounted by replacing physical
with psychological clues. The other problems were how to
study a criminal's psyche when his identity had to be hidden
until the end of the book and how to center on the criminal
when the detective story by nature focused on the detective.
The Second Shot was a failed attempt to solve these problems;
they needed a more radical solution. Cox's different solution
was, he felt, so different that he needed to present it under
another pseudonym so that readers would not compare the new
book with the Anthony Berkeley stories. So he became Francis
Iles.

As Francis Iles, Cox wrote three novels: *Malice
Aforethought* (1931), *Before the Fact* (1932), and *As for the
Woman* (1939). None of these is a detective story. They are
psychological novels about crime which accomplish those

things which Cox had spoken of in his early dedications. *Malice Aforethought* dissects the character and motives of a murder, *As for the Woman* does the same for a would-be murderer, and *Before the Fact* examines the reactions of a victim to her impending death. His formula for this kind of novel in the dedication to *The Second Shot* was that it should consist of a mixture of emotion, drama, psychology, and adventure. In the Iles novels he uses emotion, drama, and psychology, but he substitutes something else for adventure. The substitution was necessary because of the equation by sophistocated detective writers of play and adventure. In its place Cox used suspense (most markedly in *Before the Fact),* perhaps, as I have suggested earlier, because of *The Lodger* and Alfred Hitchcock's film of that novel.

While the Iles books seem substantially different from Cox's other detective novels because of their new approach to the subject of crime, they grow from a number of elements implicit and explicit in the earlier books about Sherringham and Chitterwick. Perhaps the most prominent of these elements is Cox's fascination with puny, little people. Priestley and Chitterwick in the earlier novels are meek, little men into whom Cox pours several romantic themes: the worm turning to show its intelligence and resources is the most prominent of these. As Cox moved from Priestley to Chitterwick he became less romantic in his treatment of this type, and in the Iles novels this movement continues. They are loaded with meek, prissy, petty individuals. In *Malice Aforethought* we see Dr. Bickleigh—as downtrodden a little twirp as Ambrose Chitterwick. Bickleigh is deferential, insecure, and secretly idiosyncratic. The difference in the Iles character lies in the fact that Bickleigh dreams of getting out of his trap—he dreams of power and love—but when he takes steps to achieve his dreams he simply becomes more petty, insignificant, and pathetic; he becomes wicked (evil is too grandiose for him) and more repellent than he was originally. Virtually the same thing happens to Alan Littlewood in *As for the Woman.* Littlewood (again, notice the name) is a young man of modest competence who nurses a sense of inferiority in the company of his more talented family. He is seduced by a married woman and builds their grubby, little affair into a grand passion. But Alan is so petty that he does not even rate a serious recognition of his illusions. He attempts murder in a heated moment only to fail at this too and he is punished in a particularly humiliating way by Dr. Pawle, the cuckolded husband. The third Iles character is somewhat different, partly because she is a woman, and partly because she is the victim of a crime instead of its perpetrator. Lina Aysgarth in *Before the Fact,* however, is like Bickleigh and Littlewood because she is so insecure and mentally limited. Any reasonable reader who experiences *Before the Fact* wants to strangle her for her abysmal stupidity even before she is murdered at the end of the book.

Cox's rendition of these petty, insecure, limited individuals is the hallmark of the Iles novels. Instead of turning out to be heroes, these people never rise above themselves. Part of Cox's motive in these novels was to give a psychological portrait of this type of person which was ruthlessly honest. The books, for this reason, make for very oppressive reading; it may be useful and interesting to know about this kind of people, but reading repeated incidents grounded on stupidity, inflated egotism, and ludicrous fantasies is certainly not the sort of escape which many seek in popular fiction. And this is also part of what Cox aims at. If in the Anthony Berkeley books Cox dances through human affairs giving a jovial, horatian quip to a personality defect here and a social institution there, in the Francis Iles books he wields a juvenalian lash which cuts again and again into the nasty perversity of human behavior.

Writing about this kind of person, moreover, has a very real relationship to the tradition of the detective story. As it evolved in the twenties, the detective novel rested on the premise that the criminal to be uncovered in the novel was a clever, and, no matter what the motives, worthy opponent of the detective hero. Cox brings the light of reality to this propostion. Murderers, he says in the Iles books, are repugnant, petty, unsuccessful, unintelligent people whose motives and acts are squalid if they were not so insignificant and stupid.

This point is made more forceful by the fact that the murders in the Iles novels are not artistic concoctions to serve as the subject for a parlor game. They are real, historical people. Throughout the arguments about psychological realism in the early books, Roger Sherringham insists on connecting his cases with real, historical murder cases. It is in these, he holds, that one finds drama. And this is what Cox did in *Malice Aforethought* and *Before the Fact.* In the first novel he converts into fiction the poisoning career of Herbert Rowse Armstrong. Cox based the second book on the victim's view of William Palmer (d. 1856) who, like Johnnie in *Before the Fact,* embezzled, poisoned friends and polished off his wife in order to maintain his lust for horseracing.

All of this should not suggest that Cox's interest in psychology is limited to the Iles books. During the thirties the Berkeley books increasingly depend upon psychological premises. *Panic Party* shows the disintegrating effects of stress on a party cut off from civilization, and *Trial and Error* examines a dying man's effort to do something good for mankind in the face of circumstances which thwart him. *Panic Party* almost becomes a psychological adventure tale, but the Berkeley novels are substantially different because they are still games and because they are plotted in a uniquely different manner.

Character, or if you will, psychology, plays a large role in Cox's novels—directed in part at the cliche of standard detective fiction practices, and in part existing for its own sake. The same thing holds true of Cox's plotting. While his novels may all end in the same fashion, they all begin in original and interesting ideas which, when examined, say something about detective plot conventions.

It is an undeniable fact that most of Cox's plots work the same way. As Sayers describes them, they prove that A is guilty and then proceed to show that B is really the culprit. This multiple solution plot goes back as far as *Trent's Last Case,* but Cox and John Dickson Carr are its most active advocates. The multiple solution story has its basis in the fact that the reasoning in most detective situations is based on trial and error, searching for the individual who best fits the specifications of the crime. But it is also connected to something which satisfies and entertains readers in a more essential manner. The detective story, pure and simple, satisfies because it unravels an enigma like a puzzle, a problem or a joke. The multiple solution story, of course, does this, but it does something else, too. A basic human trait is that we can make one object serve a multiplicity of functions—a bowl can, for instance, hold fruit, act as a substitute for a compass, serve as a guide for a child's haircut. Call it ingenuity or inventiveness, it satisfies and gratifies us to see an object used to many ends. Thus when Cox takes one set of facts and applies them equally to several people we get satisfaction and amusement beyond that which we would receive if one set of facts were applied to one person only. Further, the multiple solution plot is a fairly unmistakable attack on the seriousness of the detective story, for if one hops from one solution to another there is certainly no guarantee that the final solution is true; it is simply the last in a line of clever fabrications. It is no coincidence that in Cox's *tour de force* multiple solution book, *The Poisoned Chocolates Case,* which has eight solutions to the murder, five of the solutions are given by fiction writers and none of the solutions will ever be put to the test of a judge and a jury.

If the multiple solution story shows that any one of the conventional group of suspects can be proved to be guilty and thereby undermines any pretensions to realism which the detective story claims, Cox, during the course of several novels, makes a point which devastates the basic assumption of the "fair play" detective story. He first states this point in *The Vane Mystery* in the following speech by Inspector Moresby:

> "Anyhow, Mr. Sherringham," he went on the next moment, "you see how it is. It's easy enough to twist the facts, when they're so few, into meaning exactly what you want them to mean, and away from meaning exactly what we don't want them to mean. It's only in those detective stories, where the inspector from Scotland Yard shows up so badly, that there's only one inference drawn from a set of facts (not one fact, I'm meaning; a set) and that's invariably the right one. The fact of the matter is, sir," the inspector added with a burst of confidence, "that what I said about Miss Williamson might just as well apply to anyone. Given motive in this case, *anybody* might have done it!"[10]

Cox reintroduces this same subject in *The Poisoned Chocolates Case* where Percy Robinson (who writes detective novels under the pseudonym Morton Harrogate Bradley) puts it this way:

> I have always thought that murders may be divided into two classes, closed or open. By a closed murder I mean one committed in a certain closed circle of persons, such as a house-party, in which it is known that the murderer is limited to membership of that actual group. An open murder I call one in which the criminal is not limited to any particular group but might be *anyone in the whole world.* This, of course, is almost invariably what happens in real life.[11]   (my italics)

Of course Robinson is wrong about this, as in real life most murders occur among friends or relatives, but this is not Cox's point. He directs us to the "closed" convention of the detective story and shows how its neat little world falls apart when readers consider that anyone in the whole world, anyone *might* be the murderer. What is the use of lists and logic then, he asks.

But this is not the only convention of detective story plotting which Cox hauls out into the light. Before *Trent's Last Case,* and to some extent after it, the detective story typically ended with the hero's solution to the crime and some sort of justice (arrest, punishment, suicide, escape). In *Trent's Last Case* Bentley shattered these conventions by showing Trent to be wrong and in allowing the murderer his carefree liberty. Cox does this too. Roger, like Trent, makes errors in most of the books, and in over half of Cox's books the murderer goes free at the end—free not only from the law but often from conscience as well. Further, Cox sometimes shows that the world of the novel with its police and amateur detectives is incapable of getting at the truth; he makes the first person or the third person narrator intervene at the end of the book to give the readers the truth which the characters in the novel cannot uncover.

In addition to evolving from sets of facts, ingenious methods of murder, and original detective characters, Cox's novels tend to grow from certain premises formed in reaction to standard detective story plotting. This is what Bentley did in *Trent's Last Case* when he built a story around the idea of a fallible detective. As I have hinted above, Cox began writing novels by copying Bentley's premise in *The Layton Court Mystery,* and he quickly learned to make up his own premises. Some of Cox's books rest upon fairly tame but ingenious ideas—for instance, the *what if's* that stand behind *Mr. Priestley's Problem* (what if an innocent man believes that he has committed a murder) and *Panic Party* (what if a murder were committed in a party stranded on an island) are interesting but hardly novel. The premises for the Iles novels are, however, startling and something new to crime fiction. Finally, among the Berkeley novels there are a number of premises which instead of challenging detective tradition, as the Iles books do, stand it on its head. Obviously, *The Poisoned Chocolates Case* falls into this category, but there are others. *Top Storey Murder* makes news out of dog bites man, for, flying in the face of convention, it shows that the simple, routine police answer is the correct one as opposed to Roger's baroque concoction. *Jumping Jenny* rests on the premise of the open detective story since we find out that the murderer is outside of the group of suspects which is presented to us. Finally there is *Trial and Error* which seems to be a story about a man forced to prove that he actually committed a crime (as opposed to the standard plot in which the hero proves his innocence), but turns out to be something else indeed.

Cox was, in many ways, the epitome of the Golden Age detective story writer. He went into the trade because it offered money and a good time. In the Berkeley books and in the playing at the Detection Club he joked and quipped, showing how much fun an intelligent person can have with this crabbed and artificial form. As Francis Iles he showed how the form could be made more serious, but, beyond showing the way, he wanted little to do with it, and in 1939 he left the detective story for good—indeed, in the mid-thirties Cox's output shrivelled up and there were no novels in either 1935 or 1936. He didn't lose his ingenuity or his wit as *Death in the House* (1939) and *As for the Woman* show; he lost his will to write detective stories. Even though few read Cox today, he left his mark on young enthusiasts like Carr who carried on his tradition of wit and ingenuity.

Chapter 7

Margery Allingham

To an even greater extent than most people born in 1904, Margery Allingham grew up with Robin Hood, Sexton Blake, and a bookshelf of other popular heroes. Other children no doubt read just as avidly, but Allingham had the advantage of being born into a family of popular serial writers. Her father, Herbert Allingham, was, to quote Allingham's husband, "one of the great and prolific serialists at the dawn of the Northcliffe era."[1] He wrote mainly for various Amalgamated Press publications, which means that he worked for the house which owned and published Sexton Blake, that heir to Sherlock Holmes who exploited the wild adventure potential in Conan Doyle's stories. The Allingham household was constantly full of writers, not only those in the family, like Allingham's mother and her aunt, Maud Hughes, who ran several papers about the cinema, but friends from the world of serial publishing, like G.R.M. Hearne, who wrote both Robin Hood and Sexton Blake adventures. These were no Shelleys or Brontes but a group of hard-working, commercial adventure story writers who made their jobs pay. They understood and discussed the craft of story building, were conscientious enough to try to be good at it, and worked following Hearne's axiom: "They never mind you putting all you've got into this sort of stuff. They never pay you any more for it, but they don't stop you."[2] They all, no doubt, hoped through hard work to break out of serials into the world of novels, popularity, and artistic respectability, but none achieved it—none but Margery Allingham.

Allingham moved into the family profession quickly and easily. By the mid-1920's she worked for one of her aunt's magazines, *The Girl's Cinema,* turning silent films into prose narratives—which is, after all, pretty good training for anyone who wants to write fiction. She also wrote serials for the

Amalgamated Press; her husband recalls one about "The Society Millgirl and the Eight Wicked Millionaires,"[3] and suggests that she may have written Sexton Blake too.

The only one of these serials to survive in book form is *The White Cottage Mystery* (1928), which has recently been edited by Allingham's sister, Joyce, and published by Chatto and Windus. It is a pretty poor mystery book, but well up to standard when compared with the other serials printed in the *Daily Express,* where it first appeared. Allingham later was to ignore its existence when lists of her mystery novels were compiled. And no wonder. It is precisely the sort of fiction which she lampooned and then transcended in her later books. Based on a reasonably surprising conclusion, *The White Cottage Mystery* plays to all of the stale cliches of second-rate detective fiction of the twenties. Every suspect has a heart-rending "guilty secret," but they go queer all over and eventually spill the beans to the sympathetic detective. This detective, W.T. "Greyhound" Challoner, has a masterful grasp of facts and profound understanding of people, but is hindered by inept colleagues (like Inspector Deadwood, who will crop up later), as well as reluctant witnesses. There is a love plot with W.T.'s manly, handsome son and one of the suspects, and fully half of the story takes place on the Riviera, thus cashing in on the fad for Riviera novels. In fact the story is an odd mix of thriller elements, for there is a secret society, and geographical movement accompanies and sometimes takes the place of plot movement, and detective story interests like motive and alibi. If pressed for a description of *The White Cottage Mystery,* one would have to call it uninspired hack work.

Allingham and her husband both realized that these stories were trite and silly; her second novel, which later she tried to forget, was about Bright Young People, and her husband, fresh from Cambridge and art school, must have known that serial fiction in the twenties was largely hack work and frivolity. They both saw serial writing as a way to make money and to have a few laughs. By 1928, however, Allingham saw the possibility of institutionalizing the silliness of serial fiction in a detective novel; after all, everyone else was doing it, and she had all of the requisite technical equipment to write adventure stories and to spoof them too. So appeared *The Crime at Black Dudley,* which is part spoof, part detective story, and part thriller—a combination which Allingham kept returning to even after she was influenced by the regular detective story of the thirties.

Adventure or thriller writers follow a number of simple formulae in manufacturing their stories: the hero must be good, the villain bad, and the other characters quickly realized and recognized. The plot, as Allingham put it, must contain "as many colourful, exciting or ingenious inventions...[and] incidents...as one [can] lay hands on," and it must contain "a surprise every tenth page and a shock every twentieth."[4] Further, the plot must strike a dim, unrecognized memory in the reader which comforts him because somewhere he has read it or heard it before: in short, it must be archetypal. And one other thing— which Allingham mentions in her introductory essay in her omnibus collection, *The Mysterious Mr. Campion*—the thriller needs to be non-intellectual if not anti-intellectual. If Dr. Johnson is wrong about Donne when he says that poetry should appeal to women with soft thoughts of love instead of perplexing them with metaphysics, this idea certainly does apply to the thriller and, to some extent, to the detective story. It simply must not treat the agonizing problems of the day or else its escape value will be vitiated. In the twenties, when Allingham began writing, the current topic was Freud and men and women haranguing on the "Horrors of Love." Consequently the adventure story needs to studiously avoid this. Allingham would later change her mind, but that would be later. Right now we are dealing with the thrillers.

The first group of Allingham's novels[5] grows directly from her education as a thriller and adventure writer. They begin with *The Crime at Black Dudley* (1929), and include *Mystery Mile* (1929), *The Gyrth Chalice Mystery* (1931), and after an excursion into the regular detective novel, *Sweet Danger* (1933). Although these novels do have elements of the regular detective story in them, in terms of plot and characterization, these books are thrillers: if it weren't for the special Allingham ingredients they could be by Edgar Wallace. And they ignore most of the "rules" laid down by the Main Line detective story writers in the later twenties.

At the heart of each of these books beats the struggle between a titanic villain and his goons who are trying to steal or buy the birthrights of decent people (in the first two books the villains are Master Crooks and in the last two they are international financiers), and a group of good, plucky, charming, innocent people who, under the direction of the hero, triumph in the end. In each case the Foreigner, the Gangster, or the Millionaire invades the idyllic English village— Allingham's villages, containing authentic yokels, a comfortable pub, and a big house which has seen better days what with the Income tax and all, have names like Keepsake, Sweethearting, or Sanctuary—and attempts to pillage the heart of an ancient tradition which insures peace and serenity in the community. This is implicit in the attack on the family's honor and the law personified in *Black Dudley* and *Mystery Mile,* but it is explicit in the attempts on the Gyrth Chalice and on the Fitton's Earldom in the later two books. As traditional in the thriller, regular law enforcement is helpless against this sort of villain; hence the chief Scotland Yard man mentioned in Allingham's thrillers is one Inspector Deadwood, and he is only mentioned and never appears.

In thrillers, and in these books, the single menace of the villain is not enough to provide the requisite chills. There must also be a tie-in with some sort of horror, a carry-over from the gothic tale. In Allingham's books this comes from the introduction of the occult, which she learned to use as the books progressed. The first two novels have relatively mild instances of ancient and supernatural things in the legend of the Black Dudley Dagger and the legend of the Whistlers in *Mystery Mile.* In *The Gyrth Chalice,* however, Allingham introduced a subordinate plot involving witchcraft which blends with the thrill of the major good-bad struggle, and in *Sweet Danger* she brought the witchcraft sub-plot into the frame of the major action by making it genuinely confuse and threaten the heroes and provide the first crescendo which announces the climax of the novel.

But back to the heroes. Adventure stories have two basic hero patterns: there is the isolated hero who fights evil alone, unrecognized and unaided, like Richard Hannay during most of *The Thirty Nine Steps,* and there is the group comprised of the hero and his associates, like Jim Hawkins, Squire Trelawney, the Captain, and the loyal crew members in *Treasure Island.* Both patterns have their origins in the patterns of ancient myths, and each has particular advantages and disadvantages for the story teller. In all of her adventure novels, however, Allingham chose to use the hero and his associates as the protagonist pattern. Using the group has a definite attraction for the writer trained in the serial, in that it provides more opportunity for threat, capture, and escape simply because there are more good people to be threatened, captured, and rescued, thus providing the opportunity for more incidents than in the story with the single protagonist. From the beginning, in *The Crime at Black Dudley,* Allingham uses the group with a leader who solves problems and gets folks out of tight places. In all of these early books, there is a leader accompanied by young men and women who alternately assist and naively hinder the leader's plans, young men and women who also invariably fall in love during the course of the adventures. As a plot pattern Allingham typically includes the kidnapping of one member of the group and one unconsidered act which complicates the action in the course of each of these books.

The crux of this kind of writing lies in finding an attractive or original hero-leader. In her first novel of the series, *The Crime at Black Dudley,* Allingham muddled the issue of the leader but realized this and remedied the situation in *Mystery Mile.* In *Black Dudley* there are actually two heroes. The first, upon whom the book focuses, is Dr. George Abbershaw, who, in spite of being a prominent pathologist, is really the Average Man with whom the reader can safely identify. Abbershaw functions in the story as half of the love interest and as the solver of the murder mystery which frames the action. The hero-leader of the middle of the book, the part filled with threats, is Albert Campion. This dual focus, Allingham realized, really does not work very well, so she sought means to remedy it. As she says in *The Mysterious Mr. Campion,*

> I thought one simply had to have a sleuth who was instantly recognizable, so that the reader could follow him without effort...an opium smoker in a deer-stalker hat, perhaps. Most of the showy types had been bagged by the time I came in and, on looking around, my eye lighted on a minor character called Albert Campion in my own first detective story. True, he was not very suitable and, indeed, had been described as a minor crook, but I did not think anyone would ever read Black Dudley again and so I promoted him.[6]

So, enter Albert Campion.

Campion was to undergo another role change in the

thirties, but as Allingham draws him in the adventure novels, his biography works out something like this:

> K____, Rudolph. Born 20 May 1900. Aliases: Albert Campion, Mornington Dodd, Christopher Twelvetrees, Orlandi, Tootles Ashe. Younger brother of an anonymous peer (presumably a Duke), but disowned by his family and presumed by them to be living in the colonies. Educated at Rugby and St. Ignatius College, Cambridge, and, presumably, Dartmoor prison. Professions: "adventurer and universal uncle;" "coups neatly executed. Nothing sordid, vulgar or plebian. Deserving cases preferred. Police no object." Clubs: Puffins, Junior Greys. Address: 17 Bottle Street, Piccadilly, London, W1: above the Bottle Street Police Station with secret entrance through restaurant. Phone: Regent 01300. Description: "fresh-faced young man with...tow coloured hair...pale blue eyes behind tortoise shell-rimmed spectacles."

The Albert Campion of these books comes from the hero-outlaw tradition of Robin Hood and, especially, Raffles (to whom Allingham punningly refers in *The Gyrth Chalice Mystery* when Campion calls the crooked Societe Anonyme the "pre-Raffle-ite brotherhood"). That is, he is the hero, rejected by his family and society, who turns to unlawful activities and notorious companions, but who, nevertheless, upholds and defends the values of that society which has rejected him. Particularly applicable to this issue is an anecdote from her childhood which Allingham relates in *The Mysterious Mr. Campion.* As she tells it, careless printers introduced a picture of men lolling about in boaters and flannels in the middle of one of G.R.M. Hearne's Robin Hood serials with which he coped by inserting the line "swiftly disguising themselves in modern costume, Robin Hood and his Merry Men took council."[7] More than simply an amusing story, the inserted line captures the essence of modern adventure heroes like Raffles and the Saint—and a bit of Albert Campion too, for he is in many respects Robin Hood in boater and flannels. Campion and his Little John, Friar Tuck manservant, Magersfontein Lugg, with their changing bands of merry young people and shady acquaintances, protect the weak, defend the valuable, and do battle with the usurping modern Prince Johns—the Master Crooks, the Millionaires, and the Foreigners. They save England for its rightful heirs. The modern touches go beyond apparel and speech—Campion has, of course, been disappointed in love—but the basic character conception was an old one and one which was constantly exploited by serial writers and by thriller producers like Oppenheim, Wallace and company.

The trick was to use the popular character and to rise above it at the same time. And Allingham accomplished this in the same way that Christie, Sayers, Bentley, Knox, and all of her predecessors did—by turning to comedy. For Allingham the process of making a novel also involved making comedy. Both she and her husband describe the construction of these novels in the same way:

> They are gay because they reflect the mood of the time and into them she crammed every idea, every joke and every scrap of plot which we had gathered like magpies and hoarded for a year.[8]

Thus the novels are loaded with puns (some good and some groaners), jokes, absurdities, travesties, burlesques, slapstick, and cross-talk acts. No one would call their villainous criminal master-mind "Simister" or Ali Fergusson Barber and expect readers simply to grunt and follow the direct line of the adventure. It is all meant for fun, and the play world of childhood, which is dressed up in the righteousness of the thriller, loses its trousers and becomes the play world again in these books. And this also extends to the hero. Campion is no granite-jawed ex-infantry major but a different sort altogether. Allingham says this about his character:

> He appealed to me because he was the private joke-figure of we smarter youngsters of the period. The Zany or Goon, laughing inanely at danger, who is now beloved and imitated by most young people everywhere [in 1963] was, in those days, considered a very unhealthy and esoteric phenomenon.[9]

Campion is himself a joke and a deliberate comic affront to the tradition of the thriller. Underneath or on the surface (who knows?) he may be as resourceful as Hannay or Drummond or Bond, but, good Lord, he does not act like them.

For one thing, Campion is preoccupied with toys. At *Black Dudley* he fools around with a magician's two-headed penny, in *Mystery Mile* he wanders onstage with a pet mouse named "Haig," and in *Gyrth Chalice* he appears at the door of his Bottle Street flat holding a pink balloon. Instead of packing a service revolver, Albert carries a water pistol. He is forever fooling. The plate on the door of his flat reads "Mr. Albert Campion, Merchant Goods Dept.," and Lugg routinely answers the phone by announcing "Aphrodite Glue Works speaking." Whenever Allingham stops to describe Campion she always notes that he wears a "foolish," "idiotic," or "inane" look behind his specs. Now in the context of adventure fiction, all of this can be seen as the hero's ruse to cover a super subtle brain and to lull the enemy into miscalculation in the tradition of Sir Percy Blakeney and the Scarlet Pimpernel, but in the context of Allingham's novels this is not the case. Campion exists in part to give the pie in the face to "manly" types like Chris Kennedy, the rugger blue in *Black Dudley*, in part to do various music hall turns for the audience, and only in part to keep the adventure going.

Aside from the comedy of a thriller hero acting like a school boy, the chief comic element in Campion comes from the way that he talks. Talking drivel, we have seen, has a long and intimate connection with the Golden Age detective novel, from Philip Trent's speech through Wimsey's Wodehousian drawl. There is nothing particularly original about Allingham's making her hero talk nonsense, but there is also nothing in it that is particularly derivative. Although the full bouquet of Campion's speech fades as Allingham moved into the 1930's and came under the influence of other styles of detective fiction, the early vintage is a heady one. In content, early Campionese combines puns, jokes, comic anecdotes, comic exaggerations, and several other devices with a particular style of delivery. His delivery not only includes sophisticated slang ("beano," "cove," "old bird," "toddle"), but it also brings in two aspects of contemporary culture which Campion himself notes. In *Black Dudley* Campion confesses the first source of his diction: "I learned the language from advertisements."[10] And indeed he has, for he laces his speeches with an unending pitchman's spiel:

> They laughed when I sat down at the piano, but when I began to play they knew at once that I had taken Kennedy's Patent Course.[11]

While many of the pitches are for cliche products, Campion also advertises himself as a vaudeville attraction,

> The time has come...when I think our distinguished visitors

> ought to hear my prize collection of old saws, rustic wise-cracks,
> and gleanings from the soil. I am able to lay before you, ladies and
> gentlemen, one or two little gems.[12]

but more particularly as a magician:

> For my next I shall require two assistants, any live fish, four
> aspidistras, and one small packet of Gold Flake.[13]

The other source of Campion's cliched, telegraphic diction
came from a medium with which Allingham was familiar from
her work on her aunt's paper, *The Girl's Cinema;* for in *Sweet
Danger,* after mouthing a particularly noisome pun, Campion
admits "I'm not blathering...I think like that. I spend so long
at the movies that I've picked up their culture."[14]

The stand-up comedian, like Campion, who entertains his
audience with quips, jokes, anecdotes, and impersonations (in
Sweet Danger Campion does an imitation of the Prime
Minister's speech habits), can be very funny, but this brand of
comedy cannot be sustained throughout an entire novel and
Allingham knew this, so she introduced a second comic
character in *Mystery Mile.* This was Magersfontein Lugg. Two
comic characters can interact in a number of ways, but they
universally have contrasting personalities—Burns and Allen,
Laurel and Hardy, Abbott and Costello. Frequently, too, the
pair is comprised of opposite physical types. With Campion
and Lugg, Allingham built the contrast of a hyper-personality
in Campion's constant blathering and nervous activity to
Lugg's hypo-personality, which is accentuated by the use of
"lugubrious" (which may have given rise to his surname) to
describe Lugg's slow-moving and pessimistic nature.
Allingham institutionalizes the music hall cross-talk act in
these two—the cross-talk act, beloved of Wodehouse, was a
music hall turn in which two people simply abused one another
for the audience's edification. And there is plenty of abuse
between master and man: Campion, for intance, addresses one
letter to Lugg which begins "Dear Cretin," and Lugg responds
in kind. When he is first introduced, Lugg is an
unreconstructed ticket-of-leave man. He putters around Bottle
Street "in what looked remarkably like a convict's tunic," goes
to his "club" which, in *Mystery Mile,* devotes a good deal of
time to discussing the affairs of the underworld, and he

carefully keeps his burglar's kit in good repair. His solicitude for Campion in the early books is squarely based on protecting his own soft job. His criminal background, his abusiveness, and his low-class gangster patois all provide lots of opportunities for laughs, but they do a bit more. In one of the later books, *The Case of the Late Pig* (1937), Colonel Leo Pursuivant asks Campion about Lugg—

> Extraordinary feller, your man.... Keep an eye on him, my dear boy. Save your life in the war?[15]

To which Campion emphatically responds "Dear me, no!" Lugg's position is not one founded on sentimental condescension like that of the cliche valet—like Wimsey's Bunter, for instance. In the beginning, Lugg's position rests on his usefulness to Campion in his illicit activities, and Campion's usefulness to the old burglar who has run to fat. And this is all defiantly stated. Only later would Lugg become a sentimental character as Allingham's style changed in the 1930's.

When one reads, say, *Dancers in Mourning,* it is very difficult at first to believe that it was written by the author of *Mystery Mile.* This is because Allingham's writing underwent a drastic change in the early 1930's. With *Police at the Funeral* (1931) Allingham entered the world of the "regular" detective story, which she explored further in *Death of a Ghost* (1934), *Flowers for the Judge* (1936), *The Case of the Late Pig* (1937), *Dancers in Mourning* (1937), and *Fashion in Shrouds* (1938). Part of the motive for this change no doubt lies in the fact that in the thirties detective stories were more popular and acceptable than the thriller, which by then had become a lower class property and was mocked as such by the Bright Young People who wrote detective stories. Of course, Allingham had written thrillers largely to make fun of the form, but she discovered that the adventure spoof was something which needed to be done but which can only lead to stagnation if done over and over again. Part of her motive for change, moreover, came from Allingham's inclination to tinker with her own creations and to experiment with new forms. This motive can be seen in the early books in the shifts in Campion's role and his speech: he began as a secondary character and became a primary one, and he started out talking like a voluble lunatic and ended speaking pretty much like a normal person. In the early books, Allingham even experimented with the unalterable role of the villain, making the chief villain in *The Gyrth Chalice Mystery* a woman. If she could experiment within the thriller, she could also experiment with new forms, and so in 1931 she tried her hand at the detective story. And the desire to experiment did not stop here, for in each of the detective novels she tries something new, and during the thirties one can observe that the novels before and after *The Case of the Late Pig*, although they have some basic similarities, are very different kinds of books.

With *Police at the Funeral,* then, Allingham moved into the very different world of the detective story, one which has marked differences from that of the thriller. None of her new, detective novels deals with monolithic international conspiracies, but shift to the domestic murder as the central concern—almost as if she had read the "fair play" rules about the absurdity of writing a mystery story about such mythical monsters as Master Crooks and Secret Societies. Therefore much of the exotic, wild action disappears, and there are no kidnappings or extended chases in the detective books. Instead of using the whole of England as the ground for the action, the new novels concentrate on specific locales. *Police at the Funeral, Death of a Ghost,* and *Dancers in Mourning* are pretty much confined in terms of place with an attempt to focus on that mainstay of detective writers, the mansion. The atmosphere, sick and oppressive instead of scary, comes from the house and from an examination of the household's relationships and personalities, rather than from the suggestion of ancient and supernatural horror which colors the thrillers. Perhaps most significantly, Allingham disbands the hero-leader and his group of assistants, leaving the detective noticeably isolated in a world in which fast action, quick wits, and the other virtues of the thriller hero are of no use.

In addition to structuring these novels around one major crime which occurs early on and scrapping many of the accoutrements of the thriller, Allingham uses detective story sources— *Police at the Funeral* is certainly based on Conan Doyle's "The Problem of Thor Bridge"—and she incorporates into her books, especially those in the late thirties, the mechanics of the fair play detective story. She does not do this with much enthusiasm or originality, but she does it nonetheless. Chiefly, Allingham uses the "had he but known" formula to call the reader's attention to specific facts, personalities, or relationships, thus producing the signal for the reader to cudgel his brains—if he is so inclined. The first book in which this technique prominently appears is *The Case of the Late Pig,* in which there are seven instances of it throughout the story. This one is fairly typical:

> I stood looking down at the glass in my hand, twirling the ice round and round in the amber liquid, and it was then that I had the whole case under my nose.
> Unfortunately, I only saw half of it.[16]

There are also prominent, if less pointed, uses of the same technique in *Dancers in Mourning* and *Fashion in Shrouds.* In *The Mysterious Mr. Campion* Allingham recalls being inducted into the Detective Writers' Club and swearing before Dorothy Sayers that "I would never cheat";[17] and in the detective novels she never does, and she provides the required signposts for the curious reader.

A fundamental difference between the thriller and the detective story is the social and moral position of the law and its statutory enforcement. In thrillers, and Allingham's are no exception, the criminal is above or beyond statutory law and the established procedures of law enforcement which protect the community. The police are useless, and in the twenties society had not developed supra-legal police forces like MI5 or the CIA, although a few writers dreamed up comparable agencies. Thus, in the thriller the police are helpless, and the hero must 1) detect the super criminal and 2) represent self-sufficiently the force of good by either destroying the villain or bringing him into the range of the law. In the thrillers, therefore, Campion, Lugg, and the band of friends work without the assistance of Scotland Yard. The very opposite is the case of the detective story, for in it a recognized statute has been broken, and the police work to bring the offender to justice, even if they need the detective's help to do so. Allingham's move into the detective story consequently means an introduction of the police, as the title of her first regular novel, *Police at the Funeral,* indicates. Here Allingham gives the policeman, Stanislaus Oates, who had only been a voice on the phone in *Mystery Mile,* a significant role to play. One of Oates' functions, in fact, cuts the thriller down to size as he emphasizes the real nature of crime and police work. From now on the police will take charge of the body, the material evidence (especially in the bomb squad's work in *Dancers in Mourning*), and of the arrest. The hero now helps the police, instead of the police giving a limp hand to the hero as in the thriller. Consequently the hero becomes subordinate as part of a system, and his role fades when compared to the thriller hero's. Further, this new role, at least for Campion, is both humiliating (in that it involves sordid work), and alienating, for Allingham's detective hero finds that in snooping around, trying to help his friends, he is trusted neither by the police nor by the people he is investigating.

All of this happens to Albert Campion. Beginning with *Police at the Funeral* he moves into the background. He now has only moments of his old facetious role—in the opening chapters of *Police at the Funeral* and *Flowers for the Judge* he pops a few witticisms, and in the former he enters wearing a deer-stalker hat. But, in the main, Campion is pretty sober in these books, Allingham feeling that to have him behave otherwise would be inappropriate to the somber and serious tone of the books. These cases, after all, do take place in the houses of the dead, and there is no place for the cap and bells. So Campion becomes an observer and, for about three-quarters of the plot, a relatively passive one. He does not interrogate or entrap people—the other characters do most of the talking until the second catastrophe, when Campion swings into action. Symptomatic of the change in the detective books is what happens to Lugg. Largely nothing happens to him, for he appears only briefly in *Police at the Funeral* and not at all in *Death of a Ghost*. When he re-emerges in *Flowers for the Judge,* Lugg is a new man. He continues to act the comic part of the surly servant, but he has given up or forgotten his underworld connections and becomes respectable. Now he consorts with other gentlemen's valets, and looks forward to being valet of a Duke when Campion's brother dies. In the later novels of the thirties, Lugg becomes the center of the sentimental theme, as in his care for Sarah in *Dancers in Mourning,* but his role is reduced largely to that of an ex-convict tutoring a gentleman in the ways of respectability. He becomes, and there is, no doubt, the shadow of a parallel, Falstaff who has grown old and who his master or his creator have outgrown.

Instead of depending on movement of people, as she had in

the thrillers, Allingham uses the techniques of the "serious" novelist, description and analysis. Characters are not swiftly described so as to get to the main business of the book—they are the main business of the book. Therefore the key term for these books, especially *Police at the Funeral,* is "psychology." In turning to character examination and psychology, of course, Allingham was following the detective story trend of the early thirties which sought to make the regular detective story more than "a puzzle game." For Allingham at this stage, however, psychology was not synonymous with examining relationships between men and women, and in the first two regular novels she studiously avoided dealing with "the horrors of love." Even when love appears in *Flowers for the Judge,* Allingham makes Lugg speak disapprovingly of "sex rearin' its ugly 'ed," and she does not permit the agony of love to play a prominent role. Rather, in the early thirties, in *Police at the Funeral* and *Death of a Ghost,* she examines families dominated by the widow of a famous man showing not a Freudian analysis but an appreciation of the strong, vital, and valuable influence of an old woman over a group of others who understand neither her nor themselves. This also lies in the background of *Flowers for the Judge,* but there Allingham chooses to exploit the courtroom scene instead of the relationship of the heirs to the personality of Jacoby Barnabas. In each case, and in all of the subsequent books of the thirties (with the possible exception of *The Case of the Late Pig),* the action is subordinate to the passages of character description and analysis, and to the narrative voice which does the description and analysis. Naturally all of this is necessary to a detective story devoted to unmasking a hidden criminal, but it is more important than this—more important than the half-hearted fair play frame. As shown by *Death of a Ghost,* where the identity of the murderer is not in doubt for long, the important thing about Allingham's detective stories was not unmasking the criminal, which is always done with a few quick flourishes, but description of the people. It is there because Allingham wanted to be something other than a detective writer.

In the process of doing this she diminished the role of Albert Campion and radically altered his personality so that he almost functions as a neutral character. Gone are the days when she wished to make her detective hero eccentric and striking in the tradition of Sherlock Holmes. By 1937, however, she wished to resuscitate him, and she moved to do this in *The Case of the Late Pig*. Here, instead of being the unrealized Mr. Campion of the early detective novels—the narrative voice of these novels always refers to him with this formal title, and the effect in the novels of the early thirties is that he is removed from the reader—Allingham makes him the narrator of the book. *The Late Pig* is virtually Wodehousian in tone, it departs from London to take place in the pastoral village of Kepesake, and it revolves around comic characters: Lugg is more prominent, and there are Sir Leo Pursuivant, the frank parody of the military man, Campion's school chum, Whippet, and the bubbly Effie Rowlandson. The whole novel runs on a pun on the initials of a large insurance firm, and not only is psychology shoved into the background, but so is the murder mystery. In this book Allingham got back in touch with a bit of the old Campion, and this renewed attention to the hero helped her to focus the subsequent novels, *Dancers in Mourning* and *Fashion in Shrouds*.

Although in *Police at the Funeral* and the other early detective books Campion stays pretty much in the background, Allingham does develop several parts of this character. The most important one for our purposes here is that of the civilized man. In the thriller Allingham had attacked the cliche hero by making Campion into a comic character, and by avoiding the rough and tumble masculinity so common to the form, but in the detective stories she uses the other technique for criticizing the bully hero by making Campion into the civilized man. One way in which she does this is by giving Campion sensitivity to art, in *Death of a Ghost*, as well as other things not commonly associated with the manly hero: in *Police at the Funeral*, for instance, Campion, "who had an eye for such things," notices that Great Aunt Catherine has a vast collection of lace and never wears the same piece twice. Much of his sensitivity shows in his understanding of other people, but it shows most prominently in his sensitivity to his own feelings. In the thirties Campion is the civilized man to whom both criminal passion and poking one's nose into others' lives are repellent. This role is most apparent at the end of *Death of a Ghost*, when Campion is both enraged by the criminal actions of another and at the same time ashamed of his own anger. The part of the civilized man, moreover, causes the hero to stay in the background, reticent of becoming involved in the ugliness of personal problems and family squabbles. After *The Case of the Late Pig,* which shows Allingham's desire to once again give the hero a prominent role, Campion as the civilized man moves toward the center of attention in the novels; he becomes more intimately involved with the action. This involvement stems from the two forces which will move the civilized man to action—love and family.

   If romance was a minor current in *Flowers for the Judge,* it becomes a major factor in *Dancers in Mourning: Dancers in Mourning, Fashion in Shrouds,* and *Traitor's Purse* (1940) are, in effect, Allingham's romantic trilogy. *Dancers in Mourning* has, on the surface, all of the ingredients of the earlier detective novels: 1) it uses the professional world of the theater as *Death of a Ghost* uses art and *Flowers for the Judge* uses publishing, 2) it uses the oppressive atmosphere of a house and household touched by death, as in *Police at the Funeral* and *Death of a Ghost,* and 3) it uses the group of people to which Campion is attached by friendship—in fact, Uncle William in this novel is a carry-over from *Police at the Funeral.* But although all of these things are present, Allingham does not exploit them, for here she wants to focus on Campion in love, and it is the issue of love which dominates this novel. *Dancers in Mourning* is an experiment in fusing the detective story with the romance. Allingham here triangulates virtually all of the characters, and every one of the major characters, except Lugg, Uncle William, and some of the minor ones, is engaged in the agonizing process of finding and possessing their soulmates. Most are caught up in the stock romance quandary of the hopeless passion for another who has become unattainable because of circumstance. The pains of love cause personal agony, aberrant behavior, social discomfort, and they cloud individuals' judgments and demand quantities of self-abnegation and self-discipline. And all of this can be seen most clearly in Campion who, with his hopeless love for Linda Sutane, acts out on center stage the passions of the others in the background. He is now the civilized man in love with another's wife, and the chief concern of the book is how he deals with this while helping the police solve the murder mysteries in the case. Allingham, with *Dancers in Mourning,* plunged into "the horrors of love" with a vengeance, but the result is not very satisfactory and the book is labored and unwieldy. She tried to do too much in this book (what with the persecution plot, three murders, the neglected child, presentation of the profession, depiction of the atmosphere, etc.) while making love the dominant concern of the hero's thoughts. But it taught her some lessons about character and structure.

The failure of the love business in *Dancers in Mourning* caused Allingham to rethink the combination of the compassionate man, love, and the detective story, and she tried one new combination in *Fashion in Shrouds* and another in *Traitor's Purse,* neither of which falls into the sentimental traps of *Dancers in Mourning* and both of which move her back toward some of the elements of the thriller, which she had neglected. The two later novels also show the diminution of "the horrors of love" which play such a prominent part in *Dancers in Mourning,* for in *Fashion in Shrouds,* Allingham segregates the "horrors of love" plot from the hero by using Campion's sister, Val Ferris, and in *Traitor's Purse* Amanda's infatuation with Lee Aubrey receives only miniscule attention. In fact, in *Fashion in Shrouds,* Allingham introduces a specific contrast and criticism of the love which only causes agony and soul-searching with the development of Campion's love for Amanda Fitton, the peppy, breezy, bright, and independent woman first introduced in *Sweet Danger.* All of this also changes Campion, and there is a happy blend of the old Campion and the new: he is a man who can wisecrack and quip, who can deal with danger but who can also be compassionate towards and involved with others, and be in love too. It is in these last two books that Allingham finally achieved the perfect blend of the thriller, the detective story, and the novel about people—something which she had worked toward throughout the thirties.

In spite of the new clothes of the detective novel in which Allingham dressed her fictions in the thirties, she never quite left the thriller behind. One can see this by looking at her plots. All of Allingham's detective novels have the same basic plot. Albert Campion becomes associated with people who have become involved in the investigation of a murder which occurs early in the book. Among these people are two groups: first, there are those people who appear frequently and who, to some degree or another, are Campion's friends, and second, there are one or two people on the fringes of the first group who appear now and again but are not extensively seen. The murderer always comes from this second set and he is a relative outsider. Further, every one of the murderers in the detective stories is a mental case, someone who murders because of his own bloated ego and inflated opinion of his own power. What this pattern reflects is an adaptation of Allingham's thriller structure. Whereas the thriller uses the International Financier, she here uses the megalomaniac who is in actuality the International Financier on the domestic level, separate from and determined to dominate the other characters. Instead of the group of protagonists, as in the thriller, Allingham uses the observer and suspects in the detective stories; nevertheless, there is a bond between them and she never concedes that Campion's friends—or even their friends—could be murderers. The plots of the detective stories are not romps through spooky castles or idyllic villages in pursuit of the bad guy, but neither are they the "anyone can be the murderer" variety of detective tale. They are examinations of the strengths and weaknesses of Campion's friends, and they vindicate love and spontaneity— with Val and Dell in *Fashion in Shrouds* or with Richie Barnabas in *Flowers for the Judge*. In short, they apply thriller morality to the detective story, showing why the good are good and the bad wicked.

The thriller coexists with the detective story in a number of overt ways in Allingham's novels of the thirties. First there is the gang. Banished by the "fair play rules," the gang is the staple of the thriller which few writers could give up entirely, so they merely changed the gang into the accomplice, which is, incidentally, a way of causing complex crimes without having to box a lot of motive and action into one person. Except for *Police at the Funeral,* which turns on death traps, all of Allingham's detective novels use either an active or passive accomplice. A consequence of this is the fact that in most of the novels the accomplice gets murdered—usually near the end so as to speed up the pace and usher in the climax. And the climax almost always involves action. In most of Allingham's detective novels it is impossible to prove the villain's guilt through ordinary legal means. This can only be accomplished by action and the hero. Thus in all of the novels except *Police at the Funeral* and *Dancers in Mourning,* Campion purposely walks into a trap to get the goods on the bad guy—precisely the same thing he does in *Mystery Mile, The Gyrth Chalice,* and

Sweet Danger. At the end of the detective novels, Allingham gives a fillip of adventure to round the thing off.

Just as the thriller runs through the detective story, so does some of Allingham's sense of the comic. It is overtly seen with Lugg's scenes and in the high spirits of *The Late Pig,* but in some of the detective novels there is a substrata of irony with which Allingham mocks the form itself. *Police at the Funeral,* for instance, is a "psychological" study of crime in the same vein as the other psychological detective stories popping up in the early thirties, but it is also an attack on psychology, for all of the meanness and misery is caused by a man wrapped up in studying psychological analysis and criticism of his fellows. The novel pillories Freudian critics who were engaged in dissecting Eminent Victorians. Quite a different sort of irony crops up in *Flowers for the Judge.* Here a provincial detective story writer appears in court, and the question is raised of the morality of writing detective yarns which others might use as blueprints for crimes. Then Allingham turns the argument on its head when Campion knowingly lets a murderer go free at the end of the book. This is quieter and more sophisticated than the raucous burlesque of the thriller, but Allingham hasn't lost the ability to put out her tongue every now and again.

After the conclusion of the romantic trilogy—before Allingham completed it in fact—the war began and Allingham devoted herself to war work, including *The Oaken Heart.* When she returned to the detective story after the war she gave her workbag another shake and came up with new syntheses for her story elements. Essentially, however, they do not change form but only pattern to confront the new world of violence born in the 1940's. Her best novel, *The Tiger in the Smoke,* was written after the war, but it could have been written before, since Allingham possessed everything she needed to write it by the end of the thirties.

Chapter 8

John Dickson Carr

The Bencolin Novels

Carr's first detective hero, Henri Bencolin, *juge d'instruction* and head of the Paris police, appears in five novels: *It Walks By Night* (1930), *The Lost Gallows* (1931), *Castle Skull* (1931), *The Waxworks Murder* (1932), and, after a five year hiatus, *Four False Weapons* (1937). He does everything that a detective is supposed to do. He uncovers facts, deduces, uses police lab facilities, judges people, and unravels complicated problems. He also comes straight out of several romantic traditions. Bencolin is a tall, slim, middle-aged man with dark hair beginning to gray and twisted up like horns, hooked eyebrows, drooping eyelids, a thin, aquiline nose, a small moustache between lines which run from his nose to his mouth, and a pointed black beard. He is, naturally, the Great Detective. In the first novel Bencolin boasts that "I have never taken more than twenty-four hours in understanding the exact truth of any case,"[1] and this infallibility stays with him in all of the other books. He is also Byronic in the early novels. In *The Lost Gallows* Carr begins to compare his appearance and manner to Mephistopheles. We start to see the weariness and disgust of a man who "knows too much," and who cannot sleep without the aid of drugs.

To this Carr adds the characteristics of the thriller hero. Bencolin is "the most dangerous man in Europe" who, among other things, has "broken a man's back in a frowsy cafe on the rue Brisemiche." By the time of *Castle Skull* he has acquired the background of having been a Master Spy during the war, and he achieves some distance from police work when we learn that he is independently wealthy and chose police work because it coincided with his hobby of criminology. In the last of the early books, *The Waxworks Murder,* he has become "the manhunting dandy" who careens through Paris at 50 mph in

his big Voisin, and whose wardrobe resembles that of
Marlowe's Tamburlaine: when he wears a lounge suit he is out
to relax, when he wears a dinner jacket he is on the prowl, but
when he wears the full evening rig, look out. His opponents are
mostly larger than life supercriminals or supercops (he uses the
term "supercriminal" in *The Lost Gallows* and *The Waxworks
Murder*). In *The Waxworks Murder* he works against Gallant,
the brains behind most of the crime in Paris, and in *Castle
Skull* we find a larger than life detective contest between
Bencolin and Baron von Arnheim. In these early works
Bencolin acts the part of the typical hero of popular fiction: he
is the Western sheriff who will enjoy fighting until "some
quicker bullet or blade drops him....," he is the Master Spy who
plays a suave and deadly game in Constantinople, and he is
the Great Detective who outthinks and outmaneuvers the
Super Criminal.

Bencolin, however, displays at times a contradictory
character whose attitudes undermine his sinister and
sophistocated exterior. Carr allows this to happen because he
is unalterably opposed to artificiality and pretense in its
million incarnations. Bencolin's discordant elements come
mostly from his American connections. We know from the start
that Bencolin went to college in America and that he speaks
fluent American, but we learn little of his American experience
until *Castle Skull* where a boisterious element enters his
makeup. Here Bencolin recounts some of his exploits with the
New York Police:

> Well do I recall the time when Detectives Flynn, O'Shaughnessy,
> and M'Gooan of the New York Homicide Squad rode down Fifth
> Avenue with me in a stream calliope, which was being played by
> Chief Inspector Riley, and we harmonized on "The Minstrels Sing
> of an English King."[2]

Somewhat later in the same book he and two other noisy and
playful characters break out in choruses of that bawdy ditty,
"Mademoiselles from Armentieres." This rowdy boyishness
does not jibe with the suave, intellectual, Byronic, dandified
manhunter which Carr had built into Bencolin's character.

Probably because of this contradiction, Carr dropped
Bencolin and moved to other detective characters. When
Bencolin reappeared in 1937, in *Four False Weapons,* it is an
entirely different sort of man who appears—one in whom the

contradiction between manhunter and fun-loving spontaneous man has been resolved. To see this all one needs to do is to scan his entrance in the 1937 novel:

> Curtis first noticed the smoke of the rankest and worst tobacco he had ever smelled; then the sleeves of the corduroy coat, worn at the elbows, of the man in the doorway. He was a tall, lean, stringy man in the middle fifties, and his appearance was not improved by his hat. He was smoking a pipe. A genial eye was turned on them from under a wrinkled eyelid, and he needed a shave.[3]

This is the new model Bencolin, retired from police work, and who now describes himself as an "old geezer." We learn that he has "always" been fond of alcoholic singing and dirty limericks; he is comfortable now that he is rid of his evening kit and his mephistophelean demeanor: he confesses that "I am tired of playing bogeyman to scare the underworld of Paris." Naturally he has retained his old perception and ability to unravel people and their plots, but here Carr has made him into the sort of man who would warble on a steam calliope. All of this shows a good deal about Carr's development in the mid-thirties, but we will let that wait for Dr. Fell and H.M..

The other character who appears in all of the early books, and in *Poison in Jest* (1932), is Jeff Marle. Jeff is a young American of no certain employment who appears in Paris to look up Bencolin (who had gone to school with his father) and who winds up staying there for several years. In the first few books Jeff has an English valet, Thomas, who hardly ever appears, and he has moments of flippancy—for instance in *It Walks By Night* Jeff says to his mentor "The Alibi Baby... I don't see how you're going to shake it." Both the valet and the slang, however, quickly disappear. Jeff Marle narrates all of the early novels, providing Carr and Bencolin with a Watson who sees but does not understand the facts and who enables the narrative to shift away from examining the detective's every move. But he is more than a Watson and has to be more since Carr envisioned his detectives novels as puzzle stories plus—plus love story, plus adventure story, plus gothic horror story. Romantic love centers on Jeff; he falls for the mysterious Sharon Grey whom he pursues through the first two books, then he falls for Sally Reine in *Castle Skull* and for Mlle. Augustine in *The Waxworks Murder*. There is even an old flame in *Poison in Jest*. His success rate is low, perhaps because Carr has yet to fully develop the peppy female characters who appear in the later books.

Carr also uses Jeff as the adventure surrogate for the readers. This is why he gets mixed up with Bencolin—to find adventure. Of course he gets it. People get killed in his presence, he chases murderers in dark attics, he breaks into an illicit sex club and is chased by French Apaches with guns and knives, and he tags along when Bencolin goes hunting. Carr pays a good deal of attention to these adventure episodes; not only does he render Jeff's sensations but he also alters the tempo of the prose in order to involve the readers in vicarious excitement. Jeff is a particularly apt adventure character because he imaginatively grasps the possibilities of his situation; after all it is suspense, fear, and other extra-physical reactions which generate excitement, not simply the fact of being chased or threatened. At the slightest provocation Carr triggers Jeff's imaginative responses to people, places, and atmospheres, and this goes a long way toward creating the gothic climate for which Carr was known. In *The Lost Gallows,* for instance, Jeff sees an Egyptian artifact and then imaginatively walks the streets of ancient Thebes. There are similar imaginative experiences about every fifty pages in the novels in which he appears. Jeff is exactly the sort of person who can be and who likes to be scared by ghost stories.

The ghost story plays a major part in all of the early books—in fact the term "ghost story" is frequently invoked in them. Part of the gothic feeling of these books comes from following Jeff's imagination through which Carr attempts to evoke the feeling of "tensity" (another one of Carr's key words). There is also a good deal of standard gothic atmosphere-making—gloomy, rainy nights, secret passages and rooms, old mansions, and a castle built to resemble a skull: all of which gain impact by the contrast to the jazz filled cafe life. Carr also knows that the atmosphere of terror can be heightened by allusions to the dark, horrific past. Thus in *It Walks By Night* there is a quote from Archbishop Batogonolles on werewolves, there are ancient Egyptian artifacts and the eighteenth century Brimstone (Hellfire) Club in *Lost Gallows,* a sorcerer's castle in *Castle Skull,* and effigies of ancient criminals in *The Waxworks Murder.* Things which are dead yet alive form a central image in Carr's imagination of horror, and so the images of the waxworks and the puppets of the Punch and

Judy show recur in the novels until whole novels are eventually built around them. The ultimate in gothic horror is, of course, the intrusion of the supernatural—demons, werewolves, vampires, and witches. But Carr lets them enter only one book, *The Burning Court,* published in 1937. They do not and cannot enter any of the other novels because the presence of the supernatural vitiates all of the logic and reason upon which Carr's detective stories rest. So the gothic elements exist for atmosphere which, ultimately, radiates from the grotesque and grisly crimes which occur in the books: a surgeon's head grins from one of his specimen jars, a corpse is walled up *a la* "The Cask of Amontillado," a dead man drives a car through London, a burning man runs across the battlements of a medieval castle. None is the standard, cliché corpse on the library floor. All of the horror which Carr brings in has one final effect in these early novels. And there are two ways in which the detective hero can deal with horror. In the early works Carr employs the first of these with Bencolin: Bencolin can function in this gothic world and master its horror because he participates in it. Thus the satanic, mephistophelean images attached to him make him master of the nightmare world. But this is not the only way to deal with horror. Carr showed the other way with Dr. Fell and H.M.. They will be discussed later.

Rossiter and Gaunt

Between the early Bencolin books and the first appearances of Dr. Fell and Henry Merrivale, Carr wrote two transitional novels which clear away some old ideas and techniques and introduce new ones which would shortly change the essence of Carr's detective novels. They are *Poison in Jest* (1932), and *The Bowstring Murders* (1933).

Poison in Jest follows Jeff Marle back to his home in Western Pennsylvania where he is present in a household in which a poisoner kills two people and tries to kill several others. The mood of the book is Eugene O'Neill gothic, and Carr examines the psychological problems of the Quayle household, mainly through Jeff's thoughts and imaginings. If it were only this, however, the book would be stuffy and lack-luster. The most significant part of the novel, other than its departure from Europe in setting, comes in the character of the detective hero, Pat Rossiter. Rossiter enters the plot rather

late—another departure from standard practice—but he brings
with him traits which will come in again and again in later
works and later characters. Far from being the suave man
hunter, Rossiter is a zany. He is a tall, awkward Englishman
who does things like travelling from California to
Pennsylvania to apply for a job as a hotel detective. He has a
naive air, he bumbles and bungles most things, he rolls his
cigarettes so badly that they flame like torches when lit, he
uses "picturesque profanity" (including the interjection "My
Hat!" which Dr. Fell will later use and modify), and he "can't
stay away from anything that's childish." Yet he is also adept,
intelligent, imaginative, and sensitive. He is a long way from
Carr's early detective and a long way toward his later ones in
the fusion of humor, childlike spontaneity, and keen
intelligence.

The detective in *The Bowstring Murders,* John Gaunt,
never achieves the success of Rossiter as a character, but he
shows Carr's as yet unfulfilled desire to fuse the Great
Detective with the anti-detective. In John Gaunt there is too
much of the romantic side of the Great Detective and too little
of the anti-detective. Gaunt fulfills most of the criteria of the
Great Detective: he is "the greatest criminological genius in
England," he is a "throwback to more perilous days," he is an
aristocrat, and he knows the identity of the murderer after one
hour at Bowstring Castle. In these things he is simply another
version of Bencolin or, if you will, Sherlock Holmes. But here
the Byronic element has gone haywire, for in his grief for the
loss of his wife Gaunt has become an alcoholic. His alcoholism
no doubt does puncture some of the cliches of the Great
Detective, but Carr realized, I think, that it was not a very
fitting way to undercut convention.

Aside from Gaunt, the only new character in *Bowstring
Murders* is Dr. Michael Tairlaine. Tairlaine begins in the same
pattern as Jeff Marle, but instead of romantic or imaginative
flights, Dr. Tairlaine pursues analytical speculations, and he
probes the physiological and psychological ways in which he
reacts to adventure—including taking his own pulse and
temperature during the adventure episode so that he can write
a technical article about it later. Here Carr has a chuckle at
someone's expense. More important, though, is the fact that
Tairlaine is a middle-aged Professor of English from Harvard
on sabbatical in England. This is Carr's first use of an

academic in his fiction, and thoughts about academe would later help to reshape his fiction and provide him with new kinds of characters.

In spite of the fact that *Bowstring Murders* is a turgid and uninspired affair, it does mark a technical turning point for Carr. All of his previous novels had been cast in the first person and took the form of the Watson character's memoirs. Here Carr switches to third person narration in which the narrative focuses on Tairlaine but does not come from him. Switching points of view may have come from Carr's use of the pseudonym Carr Dickson for this novel, but it really has no particular advantage as far as this book goes. It would, however, prove very useful to Carr later on.

The Dr. Fell Novels

In 1933, after exorcizing Bencolin and making two false starts with Rossiter and Gaunt, Carr introduced a new detective hero who was to become one of his standard characters and one of the most renowned heroes in detective fiction. He introduced Dr. Gideon Fell. From 1933 to 1939 Dr. Fell appeared in eleven novels: *Hag's Nook* (1933), *The Mad Hatter Mystery* (1933), *The Eight of Swords* (1934), *The Blind Barber* (1934), *Death Watch* (1935), *The Three Coffins* (1935), *The Arabian Nights Murder* (1936), *To Wake the Dead* (1938), *The Crooked Hinge* (1938), *The Problem of the Green Capsule* (1939), and *The Problem of the Wire Cage* (1939).

Carr describes Dr. Fell as looking like a fat bandit, Old King Cole, Father Christmas, and the Ghost of Christmas Present. He is, there is no getting around it, fat, monstrously fat, so fat that he has to walk with two canes. In spite of his bandit's moustache, though, his face radiates geniality from his dark hair with its white plume, down to his several chins. His small eyes twinkle behind his eyeglasses which he wears on a broad, black ribbon. In *Hag's Nook* he wears a slouch hat and regular, if large, clothes, but by the next book, *The Mad Hatter Mystery* (perhaps because of it), he wears his standard costume of shovel hat and box-pleated cape. When he speaks his voice booms and his diction is filled with interjections like "Wow!" "My Ancient Hat!" "Bacchus!" and "Achrons of Athens!" Dr. Fell also burbles and wheezes; his speech is punctuated with "M'm," "H'mf" and "Burpf." The latter are perhaps due to his asthma, but are more probably caused by his trying to talk with a cigar or pipe in his mouth or by improperly consumed beer making its presence felt—Dr. Fell is devoted to alcohol. The first time he appears in *Hag's Nook* he drinks, in quick succession, and much to Rampole's dismay, quantities of stout followed by wine followed by pints of beer.

Carr never quite pins down Dr. Fell's early history or professional field. Of course he worked in Intelligence during the war as did every other self-respecting detective hero. In the later books he mentions having been a school-master, but the first time that Dr. Fell appears the narrator calls him a lexicographer and mentions that he has spent time lecturing at an American college on English history. We learn from the novels that he has written several books, including one on the supernatural in English fiction (Tairlaine's specialty in *Bowstring Murders)*, and that he is working on a massive volume entitled *The Drinking Customs of England from the Earliest Days*—which even contains footnotes on tea, cocktails, and the ice cream soda. But these works display only one corner of Dr. Fell's erudition, for he can "talk interminably on any subject whatever" according to Professor Melson, who also tells young Rampole that Dr. Fell's bulk is crammed full of "more obscure, useless and fascinating information than any man I've ever met." Dr. Fell is large enough to contain all.

When Carr decided to build a new detective hero he tucked a good deal into the package. The name, Dr. Fell, Carr got from Dr. John Fell (1625-1686), Dean of Christ Church College, Bishop of Oxford, and patron of the Oxford Unversity Press. He may have seen Dr. Fell's statue in the quad at Christ Church, and he most certainly knew the name from that ultimate example of undergraduate ingratitude, Thomas Brown's epigram on the original Dr. Fell:

> I do not love thee, Dr. Fell
> The reason why I cannot tell.

Characters repeat these verses to Gideon Fell in *Hag's Nook* and *The Problem of the Green Capsule.* The original Dr. Fell was, however, a lean, ascetic-looking man and certainly not a tun of man like his namesake.

Physically Carr modeled Dr. Fell's appearance and bulk on the big, moustachioed Edwardian essayist, talker, and detective story writer, G.K. Chesterton. Carr, at his best, catches some of Chesterton's demeanor in Dr. Fell. James Gunn's painting, "Conversation Piece," included in Chesterton's *Autobiography,* showing Chesterton, Belloc, and Maurice Baring, gives some idea of the man Carr no doubt saw waddling down Fleet Street. All of Dr. Fell's traits are there: the unruly hair, the inner-tube upon inner-tube around the waist, the "bandit's moustache," and the cape. The only thing missing from the painting is the Chesterton/Fell strong cheroot and the pocket bulging with sensational fiction. Not only did Carr model Dr. Fell's reading habits on G.K.C., but he transformed Chesterton's collection of drinking songs, *Wine Water and Song,* into Dr. Fell's *magnus opus.* And he made his detective a lexicographer because of Chesterton's conscious imitation of Samuel Johnson. There are a number of deeper influences too. Reading G.K.C's *Autobiography* one of the most striking facts is his insistence on childhood and also the thoughts about spiritualism which led him to write his first play, *Magic.* Both of these will come in later. Frank Swinnerton, in *The Georgian Scene,* recounts several things about Chesterton which are also apt for Dr. Fell. The first is a small boy's reaction to having tea with Chesterton; instead of being awed by the great man, the boy exclaimed

> ...but oh! you should see Mr. Chesterton catch buns with his mouth.[4]

Swinnerton also gives several descriptions of Chesterton's platform style:

> Upon the public platform he sways his large bulk from side to side.... His speech is prefaced and accompanied by a curious sort of humming
>
> ...
>
> As he talks, and as he makes amusing fancies, he punctuates his talk with little breathless grunts or gasps of laughter.[5]

M'mf, H'mf, Burpf. It does sound like Dr. Fell, and if he were capable of drinking tea, he would surely catch buns in his mouth.

But practically everbody knows of Dr. Fell's Chestertonian background. Less obvious is Arthur Conan Doyle's contribution to Dr. Fell's character. Naturally, as a detective he is linked to Sherlock Holmes—specifically linked in *Hag's Nook* when Dr. Fell spots young Rampole on the train and greets him. Here the narrator adds that

> If the stranger had added, "You come from Afghanistan, I perceive," Rampole could not have been more startled.[6]

Carr, however, does more than this. The controlling thesis of Carr's biography, *The Life of Sir Arthur Conan Doyle* (1948), is that Conan Doyle built Holmes out of his own background and character—not a startling thesis. As early as 1934 Carr must have begun to dig into Conan Doyle's life. In terms of his own detective novels, Carr came up with the notion that if Conan Doyle put himself into Holmes, why not eliminate the middleman and instead of copying Sherlock in a detective hero, copy his creator. A general similarity between Dr. Fell and Conan Doyle can be adduced from the fact that both men are addicted to "the glories and sports of Old time England." But there is better proof than this. In *The Eight of Swords* Chief Inspector Hadley's assistant brings in the card of DR. SIGISMUND VON HORNSWOGGLE which is followed by an "enormously stout" individual, wearing "almost to his cheek bones, the most luxuriant set of black whiskers Hadley had ever seen." Von Hornswoggle starts to spout German to Hadley, but Hadley sees through the whole disguise almost immediately—it is, of course, Dr. Fell. Now, Carr modeled this episode pretty closely on one of Conan Doyle's unfortunate jokes. As he relates it in the *The Life* Conan Doyle's favorite character was Professor Challenger, the hero of *The Lost World*. For an advertising photograph Conan Doyle put on false eyebrows and an immense, black beard. The photographer, however, was not sufficiently convinced that the disguise was good enough, so Conan Doyle and the beard went to see whether they could fool E.W. Hornung, Conan Doyle's brother-in-law. According to Carr this is what happened:

> This caused trouble. Announcing that he was der Herr Doktor von Somebody, this hirsute apparition towered in the doorway. He said he was a friendt of Herr Doktor Conan Doyle, who was from home, und would Herr Hornung receive him?[7]

The borrowing is obvious. Carr also used some of his Conan

Doyle material to build his other major detective character, Sir Henry Merrivale. In *A Graveyard to Let* (1949) some American baseball players get the shock of their lives when H.M. belts one out of the park. This was a fictional recounting of the old cricketer, Conan Doyle's actual experience with baseball during one of his North American tours.

There is, perhaps, another Sherlock Holmes connection in Dr. Fell, for, as Carr knew, Conan Doyle not only based his character upon himself but also on his old teacher, Dr. Bell. It does not take much to make Bell into Fell. But, in any case, whatever else Dr. Fell is, he is a teacher. Using the relationship between teacher and student as the connection between the detective and the narrator or focal character has unique advantages for the detective writer, and it had been on Carr's mind since *Castle Skull* when Jeff Marle alludes to it. With Dr. Fell Carr crystallized the relationship, making Dr. Fell an academic and Hugh Rampole a student. This has a number of advantages for the detective story over the usual detective-stooge relationship: 1) the teacher is supposed to know more and be more astute in his judgments than the student, and there is nothing socially wrong about showing this, 2) the teacher is licensed to give quizzes and ask questions which he does not answer immediately, and 3) the teacher is supposed to lecture. Those things which give readers pain when done by prissy aristos like Philo Vance are entirely acceptable when viewed as pedagogical devices. Dr. Fell certainly employs a number of pedagogical devices, including the Socratic one to which Hadley takes such exception, but he always lectures. In *Hag's Nook* Dr. Fell lectures on death traps and cryptography, on the Spanish Inquisition in *Death Watch,* where there is a non-Fell lecture on the history of time-keeping, on ghost stories and locked room mysteries in *The Three Coffins,* and on the history and psychology of poisoners in *The Problem of the Green Capsule.* The lecture on locked rooms is a gem and it has been extracted from the novel and anthologized by Haycraft. Then also, Dr. Fell lectures at the close of every book. Two of the books, *The Blind Barber* and *The Arabian Nights Murder,* resemble thesis defenses in which others present the entire narration while Dr. Fell occasionally prods them with questions and then presents a better interpretation of the facts at the close. In almost every case Dr. Fell, like a teacher, tries to direct the nominal detective—usually Hadley or Elliot—to the right answer to the problem and only steps in when they are manifestly wrong. It is of some interest that Dr. Fell on his early American visit lectured at Haverford College where Rampole (the focal character in *Hag's Nook, The Mad Hatter Mystery,* and *The Three Coffins)* presumably studied, and where Dr. Walter Melson (the focal character in *Death Watch)* presumably teaches. In *The Burning Court,* which takes place in eastern Pennsylvania, a number of references are made to Dr. Weldon, another fictional faculty member at Haverford. Apparently the experience stuck with him—John Dickson Carr attended Haverford College.

Late in the thirties Carr shifted the emphasis of Dr. Fell's profession. Instead of stressing his heavy academic background, Carr introduces the fact that Dr. Fell had been a schoolmaster, teaching young boys instead of young men. In *The Problem of the Green Capsule* he reminds Inspector Elliot that

> You must remember that I started life as a schoolmaster. Every minute of the day the lads were attempting to tell me some weird story or other, smoothly, plausibly, and with a dexterity I have not since heard matched at the Old Bailey. Therefore I started with an unfair advantage over the police. I have much more experience with habitual liars.[8]

Now, I'd like to suggest that this shift came from Carr's experience as a parent, but I know nothing about it. At any rate, in the books one finds that there is a growing recognition that anti-social behavior as well as emotions like jealousy, hatred, and fear take root in childhood. In *The Crooked Hinge* Carr makes the following psychological formulation:

> What was the origin of that obsession or kink, even in a child of seven?
> It's not difficult. That's the age at which our essential tastes begin to be stamped on us by outside impressions. They are never eradicated, even if we have forgotten them.[9]

Thus, if the detective or schoolmaster understands the child in the adult—his jealousies, hatreds, fears, drives, and obsessions—he will understand the criminal. It is not sophisticated psychology, but seeing criminals as big children with all of the nasty side of childhood showing works well in the detective story.

But not everyone is a criminal and not all of childhood is full of snares, pits, and traps for the personality. Childhood also provides spontaneity, joy, freedom, and love. The difference lies in the vast distance between the words "childish" and "childlike." If Carr's criminals tend to be childish in their inability to control their selfish impulses, Carr's heroes are childlike. As we have seen, this part of Rossiter's nature and Dr. Fell's is frequently described as "childlike." In lots of ways, Dr. Fell is still a boy living in an unfettered world. His rooms always have odd and interesting things littered about—his wife apparently has neither the desire nor the persistence to pick up after him (Mrs. Fell only appears in the first novel and afterward is mentioned only in passing). And he loves toys: in *The Mad Hatter Mystery* he buys a toy mouse at a novelty shop and it scoots across the table at an inopportune moment, in *The Three Coffins* his "scientific experiments" remind Rampole and us of a boy with his first chemistry set. Like a child Dr. Fell loves to act parts— in *Hag's Nook* he makes himself look like a "burlesque villain on the stage," he plays the part of Hadley with a toy badge in *The Mad Hatter Mystery,* and in *The Problem of the Wire Cage* he tries to look like a cinema version of a tough newspaper editor. He even gets to pose for a picture in a fire chief's hat in *The Eight of Swords.* What child could ask for more?

Perhaps Dr. Fell's chief childlike attribute is his "absolute absence of affectation." One thing that shouts out in Carr's books is his hatred of and declaration of war on pomp, aloofness, and artificiality. He is always armed with a metaphoric custard pie or soda siphon. And this has its beginnings in childhood. The child makes no distinction between a Prime Minister and a tramp—adults do it, and for doing it often deserve a joy buzzer or whoopie cushion. Therefore Dr. Fell, to puncture artificiality, turns a stuffy history lecture into a laugh riot or walks into Scotland Yard as Doktor von Hornswoggle. In *The Blind Barber,* the most slapstick of all of Carr's books, the ship captain gets punched in the nose, accused of drunkenness, and squirted with an electric bugspray flashlight gun—all for being pompous. Puncturing becomes one of the new tools which Carr developed in the early 1930's after he dropped Bencolin. In the Bencolin books Carr's hero wins out against evil and terror because he participates in it through the metaphors of Satan; after Dr.

Fell, Carr's heroes will win against evil and terror by puncturing it—by throwing a custard pie or exposing it with its pants down.

Just as Carr shifts Dr. Fell's residence from Chatterham in Lincolnshire (*Hag's Nook*) to rooms in Great Russell Street (*Death Watch*) to Adelphi Terrace (*The Blind Barber*) to a house in Hampstead (*The Problem of the Wire Cage*), he also shifts emphasis on the kind of intelligence which Dr. Fell applies to the solution of crimes. In the opening books he insists to Rampole and the police that facts are of the utmost importance, and that all one needs to do to see the truth is to logically analyze the facts. By the time of *To Wake the Dead,* however, the insistence on facts and logic gives way to Dr. Fell's emphasis on the fact that he is "scatterbrained"— presumably suggesting that his mind is open and eclectic enough to see through problems which stymie normal intelligences. Finally, "scatterbrained" gives way to the importance of the imagination. In *The Problem of the Wire Cage* he specifically rejects facts and logic in favor of imaginative apprehension, returning to the "in the mind's eye" approach used by Rossiter in *Poison in Jest.* He is large and can contain all.

Dr. Fell slowly diminishes in importance as the 1930's progress. He dominates the early books, but his presence is felt less as the decade closes. In spite of Fell's comic potential, Carr switches chief attention from Dr. Fell to others in the comic novels, *The Eight of Swords, The Blind Barber,* and *The Arabian Nights Murder,* perhaps because he wants to make Fell comic but not absurd like the Wodehousean zanies of these novels. How would Dr. Fell handle Dr. Illingworth, who believes that thrillers about Dr. Chianti are manuals of police work? Even in the regular detective stories Dr. Fell progressively moves into the background. In fact, in 1937, the year that Carr brought Bencolin back, there was no Dr. Fell novel. There are, I suppose, a number of reasons for this. One is that the form of his later plots made Carr keep Fell in the background and other, less astute, observers in the foreground. Perhaps the diminution of Dr. Fell is also due to the fact that Carr happened to create another character who, for the time being, was more fun than Dr. Fell.

Before leaving the Dr. Fell books, a word or two about the subsidiary characters in them. With the creation of Dr. Fell,

Carr moved away from the first person narrator—even though a few of the Fell books do have first person sections. Instead he uses third person narration with what I have been calling a focal character: a character other than Dr. Fell whom the narrative follows. This character serves the same function in the Dr. Fell books that Jeff Marle serves in the Bencolin novels, only without giving the readers direct versions of emotional or imaginative states. He does the things in the Fell stories which Dr. Fell cannot do, like being the romantic lead or rushing around in adventure episodes. Hugh Rampole serves this function in three books, Hugh Donnovan fills it in *The Eight of Swords,* Chris Kent in *To Wake the Dead,* Brian Page in *The Crooked Hinge,* Inspector Elliot in *The Problem of the Green Capsule,* and Hugh Rowland in *The Problem of the Wire Cage.* Each of these young men gets a taste of adventure and falls in love. In the earlier books they are also Dr. Fell's students. Later, however, they act more independently. The reason for this shift lies in the changes in Carr's other standard character, the nominal detective.

The nominal detective is the character who is supposed to be doing the investigating but who cannot arrive at the full solution without Dr. Fell's assistance. Chief Inspector Hadley is usually the nominal detective—he appears in six of the eleven books beginning with *The Mad Hatter Mystery.* Through *To Wake the Dead,* the nominal detective concocts a solution to the problem which brings him into conflict with Dr. Fell because his solution is invariably wrong. With the shift from Hadley to Elliot in *The Crooked Hinge,* however, the nominal detective changes to acting as an ally of Dr. Fell and their solutions agree: only Dr. Fell does the summation. The same thing happens in the Carter Dickson books at about the same date. As a consequence of this, the focal character tends to become more independent of Dr. Fell when the detective takes over one of his functions. Another consequence is that the focal character receives more attention in order to keep the detectives' thoughts hidden.

Aside from Dr. Fell and Hadley, the one other character from the Dr. Fell books who deserves particular notice is Henry Morgan: he appears in *The Eight of Swords* and *The Blind Barber.* Henry Morgan writes detective stories and is named after a famous pirate, which may say something about swashbuckling or about detective writing as a trade. He is an energetic, intelligent, sociable young man who, like Dr. Fell, has a fondness for alcohol. Among his works are *Aconite in the Admiralty, Murder on the Woolsack, Who Shot the Prime Minister?, The Inland Revenue Murders*, and *Played, Partner!* These novels feature John Zed, who is a sort of double figure: he is a "diplomatist-detective," sort of like someone out of Oppenheim, and he is connected with the puncturing humor of *The Eight of Swords*. His name connects him with the humor in the plot as well because of its connection with the country police official's use of the dialect "zed" for "said" (incidentally also tying him with Gideon Fell in that both men's names join a noun and a verb to form a rudimentary sentence—Gideon fell and John zed). Henry Morgan not only writes detective novels under his own name but he also writes psychologically realistic crime stories under the pseudonym William Block Tournedos. This is clearly a joke about Anthony Berkeley Cox and his switch from Roger Sherringham books to psychological novels written under the name Francis Iles. The importance, however, goes further than this. Morgan's William Block Tournedos stories are ."his graft"; they are no fun. His zany detective stories, like *Murder on the Woolsack,* are the real thing because they are full of "improbabilities and wild situations." The issue of probability is a central one to Carr's theory of the detective story and I will discuss it later. It should suffice here to say that Dr. Fell and the novels in which he appears succeed best when they are full of improbabilities and wild situations.

The Henry Merrivale Novels

Between 1934 and 1939 Carr produced ten books using the pseudonym of Carter Dickson. They were *The Plague Court Murders* (1934), *The White Priory Murders* (1934), *The Red Widow Murders* (1935), *The Unicorn Murders* (1935), *The Punch and Judy Murders* (1936), *The Ten Teacups* (1937), *The Judas Window* (1938), *Death in Five Boxes* (1938), *The Reader is Warned* (1939), and, with John Rhode, *Fatal Descent* (1939). Through 1951 the identity of Carter Dickson was, officially at least, a secret. Thus on the back cover of Penguin's 1951 reissue of ten Carter Dickson books the publisher announces that

> The back cover of a Penguin usually carries a photograph of the author and a short biographical note. Carter Dickson, however, prefers to conceal his identity behind the mystery of not only one but two pseudonyms; and it is therefore not possible to satisfy the

reader's curiosity about a person who to all intents and purposes does not exist.

It was not, however, a profound mystery; or if it was a mystery it was like the pseudonym Irving Washington for Washington Irving. Carr had used the name Carr Dickson for *The Bowstring Murders* in 1933. In the year that Carter Dickson was invented, Carr played around with pseudonyms in *The Eight of Swords* in which Henry Morgan writes under two names. With Carter Dickson he has it both ways—he has a pseudonym with the market advantages of being two writers and the pseudonym is pretty closely connected to his real name so Carr can retain the audience which his work had already attracted.

If all records were lost it would not be difficult to demonstrate that Carr wrote the Carter Dickson books. The style, tone, atmosphere, plotting, attitudes, minor characters, and even major characters in all of the books are consistent and identifiable.

The only difference lies in the fact that Sir Henry Merrivale animates the Carter Dickson novels a bit more than Dr. Fell animates the John Dickson Carr books. In 1934 Carr discovered that he could make his new character, H.M., do things which he had tried to build into Dr. Fell but could not quite pull off, so in the later thirties we see a gradual withdrawal of Dr. Fell and a gradual building of Henry Merrivale. It seems clear, though, that both detectives began from the same point. Carr created Dr. Fell by combining within a humorous frame several personalities from the history of detective fiction (Chesterton and Conan Doyle) in order to break from the cliche of the redrawn character of Sherlock Holmes but still to retain the working parts of the tradition of the Great Detective. He does precisely the same thing with H.M., only here he picks up the hint for his character from the Sherlock Holmes stories themselves. There is no coyness about this either, for from the first H.M. novel Carr proclaims that his second major detective character comes directly from Sherlock Holmes' smarter brother, Mycroft. H.M.'s nickname is Mycroft, and in *The Plague Court Murders* Ken Blake relates that Johnny Ireton came up with the name:

> The most interesting figure in the stories about that hawk-faced gentleman from Baker Street...isn't Sherlock Holmes at all; it's

his brother Mycroft.... He's the one with as big or bigger
deductive-hat than S.H., but is too lazy to use it; he's big and
sluggish and won't move out of his chair; he's a big pot in some
mysterious department of the government, with a card-index
memory, and moves only in his orbit of lodgings-club-Whitehall. I
think he comes into two stories...I tell you, if our H.M. had a little
more dignity...he wouldn't make a bad Mycroft.[10]

Now, Johnny Ireton is not quite right: Mycroft Holmes comes
into three of Conan Doyle's stories. He appears first in "The
Greek Interpreter," plays a walk-on part in "The Final
Problem" and finally appears in "The Adventure of the Bruce-
Partington Plans." In the first of these stories Conan Doyle
describes Mycroft as an auditor for various government
departments who "would be the greatest criminal agent that
ever lived. But he has no ambition, and no energy." He and
Sherlock astonish both Watson and the readers by putting on a
deduction duel in the first story, and Carr reports this in *The
Plague Court Murders*. By the time Conan Doyle wrote "The
Adventure of the Bruce-Partington Plans" he had brought a
good deal of political business to Holmes and he modified
Mycroft accordingly:

> ...his position is unique. He has made it for himself. There has
> never been anything like it....He has the tidiest and most orderly
> brain, with the greatest capacity for storing facts, of any man
> living....The conclusions of every government department are
> passed to him, and he is the central exchange....All other men
> are specialists, but his specialism is omniscience.[11]

Conan Doyle does not describe Mycroft in much detail, but
he does say that he is "absolutely corpulent," his hands are
"like the flipper of a seal," he has a "masterful brow," and his
eyes are grey. He is also wondrous lazy: "His Pall Mall
lodgings, the Diogenes Club, Whitehall—that was his cycle."
Carr took Conan Doyle's sketch of Mycroft and filled in
new parts to make his second important detective hero. Like
Mycroft, H.M. is big of belly—he uses the slang term
"corporation" to refer to it—and in spite of one attempt to
reduce it, it remains his most prominent part. He has big feet
and, again like Mycroft, hands which Carr describes as
flippers. H.M. has a big, bald head, a wrinkled, impassive face
with small eyes behind tortoise-shell glasses which slide down
his thick nose. His mouth is broad and he wears the expression

of one "smelling a bad breakfast egg." Probably because of his baldness and belly Carr describes him as looking like Buddha. But he does not dress like Buddha—he dresses with unconcern and abandon, wearing white socks, refusing to wear a tie, and sporting a battered top hat (which H.M. claims was a gift from Queen Victoria), and an overcoat with a moth-eaten fur collar. When the first book opens he is sixty-three years old, having been born in 1871, and he insists that he is "the old man" which he does not use to suggest senility but others do. Carr also tells us that he is a barrister and a physician—making him a grotesque parody of Dr. Thorndyke. Neither of these professions comes in for much play—except in *The Judas Window* which shows H.M. defending a man in court. His more important profession is something in Whitehall.

Like Mycroft, H.M. works for the government, but instead of being a clearing house, Carr connects him with espionage just as he gave Dr. Fell a wartime history of counter-espionage work. But the spy stuff is more important to H.M. since he is variously described as the Chief of Intelligence and the former head of espionage. In *The Unicorn Murder*, which has a good deal of secret service adventure in the background to the detective plot, he is still in charge of the department. The spy profession accounts also for one of the portraits in H.M.'s Whitehall lair—that of Joseph Fouche, Duke of Otranto (1763-1820), the French politician and head of Napoleon's Ministry of Police who held power through the dizzying shifts of power from the Revolution through the reign of Louis XVIII.

Because of his position, H.M. knows everybody—including "Squiffy," the Home Secretary, and someone in the background of every murder case. In spite of his position in government, H.M. makes his first entrance identified as a life-long, fighting socialist. This political identification makes his constant squabbles with other politicians almost inevitable; he is firmly convinced that everyone in government (or out of it for that matter) is trying "to do him in the eye." Later in the 1930's Carr dropped the socialist connection and brought H.M.'s politics closer to orthodoxy. In *The Reader is Warned* we find that he subs for cabinet officers at speaking engagements, launches ships, and is in imminent danger of being kicked upstairs into the House of Lords. Something else comes into H.M.'s government position in the late thirties: starting with *The Reader is Warned* he becomes Churchillian. At the close of this novel H.M. gives a speech which begins

> Don't let the outside alarmists scare you. The Trident's still on the
> coin. They don't speak Esperanto in Billingsgate yet.

and ends in this description

> Pulling himself to his feet, he snorted once, lumbered over to the
> window, and, with the growing daylight on his bald head and
> square jaw, he stared out across the river and the mighty curve of
> London.[12]

By 1939 England had entered the war, and Churchill became another part of H.M.'s character which was ready for the addition since it already had plenty of external similarities of appearance and style to the Prime Minister.

At his introduction, however, H.M. did not have many internal similarities to Churchill. In most of the earlier novels H.M. is dominated by the notion that people do not take him seriously, that people consider him slightly cracked and a senile old man—and many of the people in the books do treat him this way, from the practical jokers who send him a Chinese diplomat whose name really is Dr. Fu Manchu, to Gasquet the French super-cop who pointedly refers to rumors of H.M.'s senility. Along with this goes H.M.'s paranoia, his belief that everyone is trying to "do him in the eye." And naturally they are trying to do just that: the Home Secretary in *The Unicorn Murders* and Masters in the other books constantly try to shut him up and prove him wrong. He even has a viper in his own bosom, or rather vipers, in the form of his wife and daughters. Fortunately for H.M. they spend most of their time in the South of France, but when they are at home in Brook Street they force the Old Man to accompany them to levees and fancy restaurants and subsequently, because Carr never brings the family into the action, readers hear long and bitter complaints about the way that girls treat their fathers.

It is not his daughters as daughters which bothers H.M. but it is getting dressed up and being subjected to social ritual that burns him. "Don't," Jim Bennett is warned in *The White Priory Murders*, "under any circumstances, use any ceremony with him." As with Dr. Fell, Carr tries to make H.M. the spontanteous man opposed to affectation and artificiality. H.M. calls the Prime Minister "Horseface," and has tangy nicknames for the other Cabinet ministers—a lack of respect which can be expected from the very young and the very old. Instead of decent, respectable associates, H.M.'s friends include people like Shrimp Calloway the burglar (who burgles the police station in *The Judas Window*) and Giovanni the gymnasium proprietor. As a sign of his whole campaign against affectation in all of the books Carr places a picture of Mark Twain in H.M.'s office; Mark Twain whom Dr. Fell uses as the antidote to the stultifying Russian novelists in *The Eight of Swords*. Carr is attracted to Twain, who showed that spontaneousness and honesty are superior to pomposity and cunning, and whose adult heroes like Puddin' Head Wilson carry with them the best parts of their childhood, because these are the traits with which he wished to endow both Dr. Fell and H.M.

Under his sixty-odd years Henry Merrivale is really a boy. Surrounding the discreet name-plate on his office door in Whitehall, H.M. has painted "in enormous staggering letters: 'BUSY!!! NO ADMITTANCE!!! KEEP OUT!!!' and below the plate...'THIS MEANS YOU!' " I find the same sort of notations in books given to me when I was a child. Instead of keeping his liquor in a sideboard or cabinet, H.M. keeps his whiskey and syphon in a safe on which he has painted "in the same staggering white letters, 'IMPORTANT STATE DOCUMENTS! DO NOT TOUCH!!' " Plenty of deep psychology could be brought to bear on this but it is not really necessary beyond recognizing that H.M. has made his office into something like the clubhouse of the Black Spot gang or some similar childhood society. H.M. has retained his boyishness into his sixties and still feels the pull of boyish fantasies which as an adult he can now fulfill; thus he actually gets a chance to be an engine driver in *The Reader is Warned* with the same wonderful and disastrous results that would come from letting an eight year old run a train. Like a boy, too, H.M. is devoted to two kinds of reading which in turn affect his imagination. He reads sensational fiction, especially detective stories, which in the end helps him to figure out the weird events into which he is dragged by Masters. And he also reads lewd books and loves salacious movies; and he is frank enough to admit it. Thus when H.M. meets Marion Latimer in *The Plague Court Murders* he tells her flat out that she reminds him of a girl who he had seen taking her clothes off in a movie. He has absolutely no inhibitions about this sort of thing.

All of this background of childhood in H.M.'s character serves a number of purposes: it digs at Carr's enemy, pretense, it provides humor, and it opens up the most important part of H.M.'s detective nature. H.M. is a great player of games. He litters his office with chess boards, and sets of tin soldiers (in the first two books), and he takes the exhausted Dr. Tairlaine home to Brook Street to play a game of Battleship in *The Red Widow Murders*, and in all of the books we learn that he is an obsessive and successful poker player. Carr solidly and specifically connects H.M.'s attachment to games with his abilities as a detective. At the end of *The White Priory Murders* we get this description,

> H.M. peered at the glasses. He looked round at the ancient room with its stuffings of crazy books and crooked pictures; of dust and the trophies of one man's deadly brain. He glanced down at the scattered lead soldiers on the table where a problem of human beings was being worked out.[13]

The game of manipulating lead soldiers or chess pieces to solve an abstract problem becomes the game of manipulating human beings to solve a problem of murder. There is, however, danger for the writer here. The gamester, the manipulator of people like pawns, can quickly become an inhuman monster— like Control in John LeCarre's spy novels. Listening to the stories and motives of a group of people in order to send one of them to the gallows becomes, in the final analysis, repugnant. Of course this is a problem endemic to the detective story, solved in different ways by different writers. Carr solves it by frequent reminders of the conventional nature of the stories— these are stories, he says, and don't forget it—and by connecting the game playing of his detectives to other innocent and amusing aspects of childhood.

Another defusing part of Sir Henry's character is his language. Carr creates a special language for H.M. which sticks with readers as long as they remember the character. First of all, we are told H.M. is profane and uses slovenly grammar. What we see boils down to an occasional "goddamn," plenty of "ain't's," and a series of dropped g's, for Carr (or his publishers) was unwilling to make H.M. truly profane, and in writing speeches which describe human actions and point out logical relationships a writer must choose between clarity or really sloppy speech, and the detective story being what it is, Carr had to choose clarity. An easier way of creating a distinctive language for a character is to invent unique diction, so Carr concocts a special diction for H.M.. H.M.'s choice of words falls into two categories: interjections and special words or phrases. Carr loves interjections—in *The Blind Barber* (a Dr. Fell novel) we get these interjections: Brubublubluoooo–bl-oo! Coroo! Ah! Bah! Ha-ho! Whee! Coroosh! Haaa! Wha-keeeee! All Right! Rubbish! Whoooo! Ho! Haah! Eeeeee! H.M. has his own set of interjections. They range from Burn Me! to Honk Honk! to Gobble Gobble! to Phooey! He uses these, especially the first and the last, with frequency and vigor. Also Carr invents special words and phrases for H.M.; he calls people "fatheads," and also "son," and he repeats that people are trying to "do me in the eye."

Carr, it seems, is also one of those determined to do H.M. in the eye, for he makes him a slapstick character. In *The Judas Window* H.M.'s gown rips with the sound of a raspberry when he first rises to address the court, in *Death in Five Boxes* he is struck by a car while pushing a fruit barrow up a hill, and in *The Reader is Warned* we learn that while launching a ship he accidentally conked the mayor with a bottle of champagne. He even gets sent a box of exploding cigars in *The Plague Court Murders*. Some of this, no doubt, comes from Carr's love of slapstick films—he refers often to films in general—but it also comes from his attempt to divert attention from the human dilemmas in the detective story and to make it into a form of pure entertainment. Thus the Old Man—a term which refers both to a leader and one who is senile—becomes Carr's ultimate character, in that, in spite of the sobering experiences of a life-time, he shows that protecting and entertaining folks is more important than condemning and lecturing them.

When Carr began the Carter Dickson books in 1934 he changed to the first person for the first novel but changed back to third person narration with *The White Priory Murders*. Thereafter he moved back and forth in point of view, using Kenwood Blake as the narrator of the first person novels. Blake is in the same mold as Jeff Marle and Hugh Rampole, the only difference being that he served under H.M. in Intelligence during the war. Carr used first person narration in the early H.M. books not primarily to convey sensations to the reader but to describe H.M.'s zaniness. He realized later that this was not really necessary and by 1938, *The Judas Window,* which Blake ostensibly narrates, really depends very little for its most important effects on the first person narrative.

The other characters in the Carter Dickson books are identical to the secondary characters in Carr's other novels, and they fall into several clearly defined classes. First comes the character of the nominal detective—the police detective who follows the main detective and arrests the criminal at the end. In the Dr. Fell books this is Hadley or Elliot, and Chief Inspector Humphrey Masters takes their place in most of the H.M. adventures. The difference lies in the fact that Masters argues a bit more vehemently and has a background of exposing fake spiritualists. Aside from the focal character and the nominal detective, Carr often introduces the authority, someone who observes and collects facts in order to propose a theory to solve the problem; this character appears in most of the multiple solution books in order to help to make them work. Finally, in every book there is the girl—the romantic focus in the novel. In every case the girl is a bright young woman with plenty of sex appeal who knows her place: the passage on "ginches" in *The Eight of Swords* could apply to all of Carr's characters of this type:

> She was not cool-headed or strong-minded. She could no more have accompanied the detectives with a gun than she could have brought down the villain with a flying tackle. Quite to the contrary. She was content to leave that sort of thing to the proper people; to beam up at you as though she were saying "What a man!".... Nor, in her case, were there all those persistent attempts to freeze or embarrass the hero up until the very last. She tumbled into Hugh Donnovan's arms from the start, and stayed there, and a very good thing too.[14]

No flappers need apply. Carr wanted good, old-fashioned women of fiction. As for the other characters in the books, they are the usual collection: eccentric noblemen or millionaires, lawyers old and young, a retired colonel or two, a wealthy spinster or two, a brace of physicians, some clergymen, a variety of wives, some newspaper men, an odd engineer or scientist, film stars, several scholars, a few art dealers, and a writer or two. It is the same crowd that one meets in most of the detective books of the period. The uniqueness, however, comes from the fact that, besides the character types which make the detective and love plots work, Carr does not repeatedly make the same sort or type of person commit the crime. This is not due to any particular subtlety of characterization; it comes from Carr's devilishly clever methods of plotting his novels.

Carr's Detective Plots

Hocus-Pocus: a juggler's trick; sleight of hand; hence nonsense to cloak deception.
Jiggery-Pokery: humbug; underhand work.
Flummox: to perplex; to confound.

John Dickson Carr did not begin to write detective stories until the 1930's, after the genre had been established and "rules" for it had been set. In the late twenties everyone from detective writers like Van Dine, Sayers, and Christie to reviewers in newspapers and magazines said that the essence of the detective novel lay in the intellectual problems of who, how, and why, set out for the readers to solve, and that the art of the detective writer lay in the ingenuity and novelty of the puzzle in the book. Essential to the whole procedure was that the writer must at the same time "play fair" with the readers by including in the text the clues necessary for solution and must delight the reader with an unexpected yet consistent solution. So Carr set to work to make himself the best of a generation of ingenious puzzle setters.

All of Carr's novels (with the exception of *The Burning Court*) were constructed as puzzles, and as such he includes the conventional machinery which had become part of the detective story—in fact he includes more of this machinery than many of his contemporaries. First he makes clear to the readers that the narrative is a puzzle game, realizing that it is dirty work to expect readers to attempt to solve a problem when you have not told them that there is a problem to be solved. So Carr includes in his books advertisements like this one which appears early in *The Plague Court Murders* announcing the nature of the game and the readers' obligations:

> And since the ringing of that bell began one of the most astounding and baffling murder cases of modern times, it is well to be careful of what I say; not to exaggerate or mislead—at least, any more than *we* were mislead—so that you may have a fair opportunity to put your wits to work on a puzzle apparently impossible of solution.[15]

This is a contract between the writer and the readers

guaranteeing a problem for the readers to pursue. Naturally, the puzzles in Carr's books revolve around the questions of how, who, and why (almost always in that order with that emphasis) applied to a mysterious death, but Carr wholeheartedly jumps into the puzzle game and fills the books with different kinds of external and internal puzzles. One of his favorites is the game of disparate objects—four watches, a rusty alarm clock, phosphorous and lime—which asks about their similarities. He also peppers the narrative with riddle questions (like Holmes' question about the barking dog) for the readers to puzzle over before they can come to the larger puzzles of who, how, and why.

At any rate, Carr provides the puzzle and the contract warning the readers that the novel is a puzzle. He is more helpful than that. Like most puzzle writers he includes aids for the readers to help to direct them through the exercise; so there are floor plans in several books, time tables in others, and almost always a list of questions which the detective rattles off for our guidance in the middle of the book. Carr even goes further than this. From the very first Bencolin book, there are asides or footnotes telling the readers that certain people can be trusted in their testimony and that certain facts are true. Nailing up these signposts became one of Carr's favorite techniques. He eventually built it into the framework of *The Reader is Warned* in which the reader is warned in footnotes that 1) there is no death trap, 2) there are no accomplices, and 3) the motive is real but not obvious. Giving the readers these aids serves a dual purpose for Carr. First it works in the puzzle framework to direct the readers' thoughts and give them a fair chance at observation. However, at the same time it takes away the readers' options. In *It Walks by Night* Bencolin makes very specific comments about the windows of the murder room, eliminating the possibility that someone entered the room through the window. The only trouble is that Carr eliminates the easy options, leaving the readers with an impossible situation. This can be seen best in *The Three Coffins* in which Carr leads Hadley and the readers to believe that the third brother is the murderer and to look for him lurking about in disguise when, wham, conclusive proof appears that the third brother is dead—so another possibility in which the readers have an investment goes west. As a puzzle setter, Carr is so ingenious and so sure of his craft that he in effect challenges the readers to come up with a solution and then flummoxes them. And experience is no help: unlike Marsh or Sayers or Christie or Cox or many of the others, he never uses exactly the same plot twice—he juggles his devices with dexterity.

Carr employs a fairly lengthy list of plot devices to bamboozle his readers. Like all prolific writers he naturally uses the same devices a number of times, but even when he reuses an old device, Carr changes it so that it becomes unrecognizable. It is, perhaps, best simply to list Carr's plot devices with a few brief comments:

Stage Setting: murderers in Carr's books often arrange the scene of the crime so that the detectives and witnesses are misled.

a. Purpose
   1. Sometimes stage setting is done on purpose.
   2. Sometimes it happens accidentally.

b. The Props
   1. Articles are removed.
   2. Articles are added.
   3. Articles are rearranged.

c. The Actors
   1. The murderer creates an illusion for the witnesses; thus the black-out clothes in *Death Watch* or the mirror in *The Three Coffins.*
   2. The witness does not correctly perceive events, as with the nearsighted man in *The Crooked Hinge.*
   3. The victims are moved, making the apparent scene of the crime enigmatic and hiding the real scene.
   (a) They are moved by the killers.
   (b) They are moved by innocent parties.
   (c) They move themselves.

Disguise: Characters not being who they seem to be is probably the oldest detective story ploy, but Carr, although he uses it frequently, uses disguise with wit and dexterity so that readers forget its hackneyed background.

a. The disguised killer
   1. The long term impersonation where an individual has assumed another's identity long ago for purposes

other than murder.
2. The short term impersonation where the murderer briefly assumes a disguise in order to deceive witnesses.

b. The disguised victim: in a few cases the victim lives in a disguise which must be stripped off before the answer will come.

c. The hidden relationship: disguised husbands or wives or lovers hover in the backgrounds of a number of books.

d. The hidden detective: in *The Unicorn Murders* Carr creates a complete disguise plot in which the murderer, victim, and nominal detective are all disguised—some under two false identities.

Accomplices: in the majority of Carr's novels the effects created by the murderer are so complex that they require an accomplice. Carr, however, twists and turns his accomplices so much that their presence is difficult to spot when combined with other devices in the books.

a. There is the straight accomplice plot in which two people work together to murder a third.

b. There is the silent witness plot in which a witness to a crime holds back testimony out of loyalty, love, or hate.

c. There is the unwitting accomplice plot in which through ignorance or fear an innocent party muddles the facts or assists in covering up the crime.

d. There is the reverse accomplice plot, or the Sorcerer's Apprentice plot, in which the accomplice murders the plotter before he or she can execute the original design. This can work in two ways.
1. With the murderer's intervention in the victim's plot against a third party.
2. With the connivance of the victim, where the victim literally puts the noose around his own neck.

The Series of Crimes: typically there is more than one murder in Carr's novels of the thirties. Obviously more complexities enter with more crimes, but at the same time there is more chance for the intellectual operations of comparison and contrast.

a. The series of apparently random crimes is used to mask the motives for one of them.

b. The series of crimes to eliminate the victim in addition to accomplices. This is the standard multiple murder plot which Carr uses to set up the variations.
c. The series of crimes which is not a series: crimes which the characters in the novel believe to be related but turn out to unrelated occur in several novels. One of these crimes usually receives little attention as the detective story cannot easily hold two full puzzles.
d. The series of crimes which is not a series to begin with but becomes a series. Having learned of an ingenious method of murdering or a puzzling set of circumstances an individual becomes a murderer, making crimes which are not related. The police term for this is copycat crimes.

Special Means of Murder: This is one of Carr's hobby horses; particularly in the Carter Dickson books he introduces special means of murder to baffle and mislead.
a. The disappearing means: among others one finds such fancy creations as the rock salt bullet which melts in the wound, and poison frozen into ice cubes.
b. The misleading means: *The Four False Weapons* title suggests this. Perhaps the best instance is the prefired bullet shot through an unrifled barrel.
c. The death trap: among others one finds a gun fired by a barometer.
d. The changing means: Carr often uses means which are ordinarily innocuous but which become lethal under certain conditions like a poison which is harmless when ingested but lethal if introduced directly into the blood stream.
e. The machine which enables one to commit a murder which is beyond his normal, physical capacity, including a way for a one armed man to strangle his victim.

Intellectual exercise, Bah! Study will do no good; even knowing Carr's standard devices before beginning a book hardly ever helps to figure out the culprit and means before the end. Carr mixes and combines his ingredients so readily and rapidly that it is difficult to untangle them. Further, every item in the list contains an anti-device to consider: is it a series, a series which is not a series, or a set of separate crimes which becomes a series? Finally, detective novels are about people and as such lead the average reader to try to work out the human motivations—the psychology; Carr, although he writes about amusing types, does not really use psychology. Almost all of his books turn on how and glance over why. Consequently while the reader looks at the hand which is guiding the characters, the other hand pulls a fast one and manipulates the physical environment for our mystification and delight.

One of Carr's favorite images is the world turned upside down or topsy-turvy: it comes in most vividly in *The Unicorn Murders* in which H.M. tells of a friend who built an upside-down room with a rug nailed to the ceiling and a chandelier bolted to the floor. This is exactly what Carr seeks to do in his plots—take the readers on a roller coaster ride which turns them upside down. The embodiment of this can be seen in Carr's employment of what can be called the is-isn't-is technique. Consider the following case. In *The Eight of Swords*, Dr. Fell deduces and assures everyone that the gangster, Spinetti, is dead—shot by Depping whom he was trying to blackmail. Shortly after this assertion, Spinetti turns up very much alive. Still later we learn that he should have and would have been dead if he hadn't worn a bullet-proof vest (after all, he is a New York gangster). To round things off, he is shot dead at the end by a person whom he is trying to blackmail. So it becomes is-isn't-is. Carr extends the pattern to several entire plots including that in *Fatal Descent*. In these novels, one of the theories which is advanced early in the book and subsequently discounted turns out in the end to be the real solution. Of course Carr does the opposite too, demonstrating theories and conclusively demolishing them. Sometimes things which seem to be true are true—but not always. You can't tell.

To these plot devices Carr adds several things which color and augment the devices but which are really too large to be classed as plot devices. Among the most important of these is magic. Carr began his work in detective fiction by combining gothic atmosphere with the detective plot in the early Bencolin books. Here werewolves, haunted castles and other spooky effects lurk on the fringes of the novels—as they do in some of the Dr. Fell and H.M. books. One novel, *The Burning Court*, actually goes beyond the detective story with its supernatural ending. The detective story, however, cannot be supernatural; it works through rational means to explain an apparently inexplicable problem. To ring in a ghost in a detective story is to change the rules and to violate the contract. Carr realized this very early, but found that he could have it both ways—supernatural and rational—by using magic. He knew that, as Nevil Maskelyne puts it in *Our Magic* (1911), "Magic consists in creating, by misdirection of the senses, the mental impression of a supernatural agency at work."[16]

The twenties and thirties were boom years for magic. Houdini, Maskelyne, the Great Raymond, Dunninger, Kellar, Thurston, and Hardeen are all names of the period to conjure with. The magician's primary purpose, of course, has always been to entertain people by producing illusions. In the twenties, though, two subsidiary functions preoccupied many magicians. First they made it their business to expose the illusions of bogus spiritualists who bilked innocents like Conan Doyle. Maskelyne first achieved prominence by exposing spiritualists in England, and Houdini lectured on fake mediums in the twenties. Magicians were also occupied with giving away other magicians' secrets in books about magic. This has been a tradition beginning in the nineteenth century with Robert-Houdin, but with the advent of pulp magazines like Houdini's *Conjuror's Magazine* and Dunninger's *Dunninger's Popular Magic* (published by Hugo Gernsback, the science fiction king) it became institutionalized in the 1920's.

Magic plays a major role on almost every level of Carr's novels. There are allusions to Houdini and Maskelyne in several books. There is an epigraph from "Professor" Hoffman's (an important and prolific magic writer) *Modern Magic* in *The Crooked Hinge;* a footnote to the *Encyclopaedia Brittanica* article on "Conjuring" (written by Maskelyne's son, John Nevil Maskelyne) in the same book; a footnote to "the admirable and startling book by Mr. J.C. Cannell" (who wrote several books on magic) and mention of *Hocus Pocus Junior, or the Anatomy of Legerdemain* on the floor of Dr. Fell's study in *The Problem of the Green Capsule.* Superficial coincidence? More important is the fact that Carr peppers every one of his books with the terms "conjuring" and "sleight of hand," and his favorite way of describing the business in the books is to call it "hocus pocus." The next step in the demonstration is that several of the novels contain characters who are professional magicians, beginning with Maleger in

Castle Skull, and including Roger Darworth in *The Plague Court Murders* and Pierre Fley in *The Three Coffins.* Not only are there magicians, but Carr mentions plenty of specific magic routines in the novels: the floating face, the talking head, the disappearing tiger, the disembodied hand, the "shoplifter's suitcase," ventriloquism, mind reading, the indian rope trick, the sealed sack, the man in the automaton, the conjuror's chair, and the paper costume disappearing trick. He explains how most of them work, too. It could almost be John Dickson Carr's books of magic. But more importantly, here, is that Carr combines these tricks with various plot devices to make them work.

In fact, Carr is pretty clear about the relationship between magic and murder from his first novel. Jeff, in *It Walks by Night,* quotes a section of the murdered Edouard Vautrelle's play which makes the connection between magic and murder:

> The art of murder, my dear Maurot, is the same as the art of the magician. And the art of the magician does not lie in any such nonsense as "the hand is quicker than the eye," but consists simply in directing your attention to the wrong place. He will cause you to be watching one hand while with the other hand, unseen though in full view, he produces his effect.[17]

Not a bad description of puzzle writing either, since the detective writer, like the magician, gives clues but distracts the readers' attention so that they will not see them. Magic is, thus, central to Carr's detective writing; it is the reason that stage setting is so important in the novels. Not only stage setting, but also accomplices. When a magician saws a woman in two there is an accomplice hidden in the box to provide the legs for the illusion. In *The Problem of the Green Capsule* Carr points to "the accomplice, as is usual in conjuring entertainments, sitting in the audience" as being essential to the commission of the crime. Carr's accomplices act in precisely the same fashion as magicians' assistants. Think through the plot of *The Three Coffins* and it becomes clear how the illusionist and accomplice work together. Not only stage setting and accomplices come into the books from magic, but so too do most of the devices which make the plots work. Using Maskelyne and Devant's categories of 1) manipulative magic, 2) mental magic—mind-reading—and 3) physical magic—unusual effects caused by basic chemistry or physics—it would be possible to strip each of the novels down to its origins.[18] But that would spoil too much fun.

There is yet one more step to Carr's magic formula. The murderers in Carr's books act as the conjuror setting the stage, making illusions, creating props, and forming an atmosphere of terror and horror against which to work their tricks. In the middle ages this sort of thing would have been called black magic—the illegitimate manipulation of nature for illicit or satanic ends. Carr frequently connects the villains with this background. Thus the backgrounds of werewolves, ghoulish legends like the Imp of Lincoln Cathedral, Louis Plague, the Satyr of the Seine, and witch cults. Not only this, Carr makes the black magician into the modern spiritualist who uses conjuring tricks for his own, selfish ends and dupes the unwary with his mumbo-jumbo. Significantly, H.M.'s friend, Chief Inspector Humphrey Masters is

> ...the ghost breaker; the big, stout, urbane man who was pleasant as a card-sharper and as cynical as Houdini. During the spiritualistic craze that took England after the war, he was a detective-sergeant whose chief business was the exposing of bogus mediums. Since then his interest had increased (apologetically) into a hobby. In the workshop of his little house at Hampstead, surrounded by approving children, he tinkered with ingenious devices of parlor magic.[19]

Masters, Houdini, spiritualism, parlor magic—the equation is meaningful. The detective acts, much in the mold of Maskelyne or Houdini, in a double fashion: as the unmasker of phony, evil illusionists, and as the entertainer. Carr knew about this before Masters, for Pat Rossiter, the detective in *Poison in Jest,* is billed as an amateur magician and his discoveries include exposing how the disembodied hand trick works. Dr. Fell and H.M. do exactly the same thing—they expose and entertain. And Carr at times makes them talk like magicians; witness Dr. Fell's comment after a partial explanation in *To Wake the Dead:* "the conjuring entertainment is over: ladies and gentlemen I thank you." All of Carr's detectives unmask illusionists, they make the impossible happen by explaining inexplicable events, and they entertain the readers with their patter. Behind them stands Carr the magician practicing his sleight of hand with the narrative.

The other area of interest which interacts with many of

Carr's devices and makes plots work is the past. Plainly Carr is interested in history and he includes his interest in many of the books. The character of Dr. Pilgrim in *The Lost Gallows* objectifies this historical interest and points to some ways in which it will develop in the later books. Dr. Pilgrim is a physician turned amateur historian who has written a book entitled *The Detective of History* in which he presents solutions to historical crimes. Carr himself did not immediately become Dr. Pilgrim, but he started off on a route which would eventually make him the detective of history. The first leg of the journey comes in the same book, *The Lost Gallows*, where, in one of his imaginative flights Jeff walks the streets of ancient Thebes: this was vitally important for Carr, as the imaginative apprehension and translation into fiction of historical facts and monuments lie at the core of what he was to do. Soon the process spread further, in that in many of the books Carr takes historical facts and uses them to recreate fictional memoirs of historical characters—thus there are prison diaries from the eighteenth century in *Hag's Nook*, Louis Plague's letters in *The Plague Court Murders*, the journal about revolutionary France in *The Red Widow Murders*, etc. This tendency toward recreating history from fictional memoirs reaches its logical conclusion with *The Murder of Sir Edmund Godfrey* (1937) where Carr really becomes the detective of history by reconstructing an actual, historical murder which took place in the seventeenth century.

It is no coincidence that the particular bits of history that Carr uses are gloomy and spooky, for one of their chief purposes is to help to build gothic atmosphere which always gains from contact with the past. But the past exerts a stronger influence on Carr's novels than simply providing a few atmospheric flourishes. In almost all of Carr's books something vital to the unravelling has happened in the past, usually long before the narrative begins. Most often this is a murder which has gone unsolved. Typically the murder which occurs after the narrative begins effaces interest in the earlier crime and the readers forget about the historical crime when thrust into the welter of details about the murder here and now. But this is another device to voodoo the readers. The crime in the narrative cannot be solved until the earlier crime is understood. Thus the detective acts as the historian to unravel the past and to apply its relevance to the present. This is also the key to Carr's rough and ready psychology, for Carr spurns complex psychological formulations of libido and fifty-four varieties of mania in favor of the traditional understanding that one's past actions determine his future actions. As usual, however, Carr is aware that dependence on the past as a plot device can become predictable, so in some of the novels he creates past events which are interesting but which are not helpful in solving the problem. Further, Carr uses historical events in almost the same way in which he uses the series of crimes, for in several cases the historical background is not directly relevant to the crime but indirectly connected because it provides the murderer with inspiration on how to commit the crime.

All of these things which I have discussed are devices or motifs which Carr fits into the overall pattern of his novels. Reviewing his output in the thirties it is fairly easy to see that Carr was fond of several overall patterns for his novels. The most typical Carr pattern for a novel goes something like this: an observer, usually not one of the main characters but an astute witness, will demonstrate in irrefutable terms that A. is the only person who could have committed the murder; shortly afterwards A. will either be killed or proved to be innocent; then another character, usually Hadley or Masters, will take over and present an air-tight case against B.; and at this point the chief detective, usually exclaiming "that tears it" intervenes and gives the third solution, demonstrating that C. committed the crime, and here the book ends. This pattern probably came from Carr's gift for concocting endless explanations for impossible situations. He is like Dr. Glass in *Fatal Descent* who "supplied the police with sixteen separate explanations of the mystery—every one of 'em convincing...." The multiple solution pattern also has some ties with Carr's attachment for magic. In fact, in *The Eight of Swords,* the narrator specifically connects the way the novel works to a routine in a magic show:

> Again they were all locked up with their own thoughts, because each new development seemed to lead the case in a different direction; and each box opened up like a magician's casket, to show only another box inside of the last.[20]

That is, the evidence and presentation convince the reader that A. is guilty until the conjuror taps his wand and A. vanishes and B. appears, and so on. Loud applause. Magic may have lead Carr to this procedure—or Anthony Berkeley Cox may have, since he worked long and hard on the multiple solution story in the late twenties—but the real importance lies in the light which the multiple solution story sheds on the detective story and its readers.

First, the multiple solution story is another of Carr's fiendish devices for taking away the readers' options. Through arranging clues and providing explanations, the narrative cons the reader into believing that A. must be guilty and then takes away that option. By taking away options Carr prepares the readers so that he can evoke wonder by the final solution, so that he can make the readers say "okay, I give up, give me the surprise." Beside taking away options the multiple solution story is designed to feed to fullness one of the detective story readers' chief appetites. Carr perceived that the heart of the detective story lies in the unravelling at the end when the detective reveals all of the enigmas of the story. If one is good, he reasoned, why not two or three unravellings? What he tries to do is to send the readers away satisfied in their desire for explanations and surprised at the unravelling at the close of the novel. Like any other plot, however, the built-in problem of the multiple solution story resides in the fact that if it is used too often it becomes predictable and the readers know full well that neither A. nor B. can be guilty since such strong cases are being built up against them. Writers can vary the plot by accusing A., giving him up and going to B. and C. only to return to A. in the end, and Carr does this, but he knew that in the interests of freshness he had to get away from the multiple solution pattern. So at the close of the thirties one finds that Fell and Hadley do not argue and even H.M. and Masters consult and tend to agree. These books get away from the multiple solution formula which Carr only used once in the late thirties in *Fatal Descent* which he wrote with John Rhode and which probably had its origins in a game or a joke between the two writers.

I do not particularly want to tangle with the locked room murder, but one cannot avoid it when discussing Carr, since reviewers and blurb writers see him as the master of that form. He may well be the master of the locked room mystery but one must remember that he did other things too, and that the majority of his books in the thirties are not locked room murders. Anyway, eleven, more or less, of Carr's novels written between 1930 and 1939 are locked room mysteries. The "more or less" is there for two reasons. First, because Carr knew from the start that even in the thirties the locked room murder was becoming old hat, and so he created situations for some books which are like locked rooms but are not technically locked rooms because the murders do not take place in them—for instance the tennis court in *The Problem of the Wire Cage* is like a locked room in the apparent inaccessibility of the body, but it is not, obviously, a locked room. Second, the term "more or less" is there because Carr takes advantage of the ambiguity of the term "locked room," which can, but does not necessarily, mean "hermetically sealed chamber," and he writes some novels which seem as if they present "hermetically sealed chamber" situations but which turn out not to be, for the murderer has fired through an open window, etc. But this is quibbling.

Carr tends to put most of the locked room situations in the Carter Dickson novels, but not all of H.M.'s cases are locked rooms and one of the best of Carr's locked room plots, *The Three Coffins,* is a Dr. Fell book. Even though Carr began his career with a locked room plot in *It Walks by Night,* he did not really begin to pay attention to the form until 1934 when he created Henry Merrivale. In 1934 and 1935 most of Carr's novels are locked room plots. There are even three analytical discussions of the sub-genre in the books of this period: the first in *The White Priory Murders,* the second in *The Ten Teacups,* and the third in *The Three Coffins.* These discussions cover, respectively, the criminal's motives for creating a locked room, and the techniques which can be used to create locked rooms.

There are only a few, basic ways in which a locked room plot can work: 1) the victim is killed before the room is locked, 2) the victim is killed after the room is unlocked, 3) the victim is killed by a death-trap which operates independently of the murderer, and 4) the room is not hermetically sealed and the victim is killed through an inconspicuous or unexpected opening. These are the only ways in which locked room murders can work, but possibilities also exist for locked room plots which are not murders but suicides or accidents which, intentionally or unintentionally, happen to look like murder. Carr touches on all of these techniques in the locked room lecture in *The Three Coffins,* but he divides them into different categories in order to blur the essential simplicity of the form. In his novels Carr exploits the locked room situation, but he does not use all of the possibilities: for instance he does not use suicide or accident, feeling, no doubt, that they were cheats which denied the readers the pleasure of a murder problem in a book so advertised. Neither does he use the gambit in which the victim is killed after the unsealing of the room; this, after all, makes dupes out of the witnesses and Carr, through footnotes and other apparatus, insists on the reliability of some witnesses. This leaves only three choices—the victim dead before sealing the room, the secret aperture, and the death trap. Carr prefers the first option although he does use the other two fairly frequently.

In *The White Priory Murders* H.M. tackles the problem of why any murderer would want to create a locked room puzzle for the police to deal with. He lists three possibilities: 1) it is accidentally created and the murderer did not intend to create a locked room, 2) it is an attempt to fake suicide so that no one will look for a murderer, and 3) it is an attempt to suggest supernatural agencies at work. Until 1937 Carr stuck fairly closely to these motives using, because of his predilection for the gothic, the supernatural agency motive most often. In 1937 he exorcized this by writing *The Burning Court,* where he reverses the normal ending by suggesting first that the monkey business in the crypt occurred before it was sealed and then ending the novel with the assertion that supernatural agencies were, in fact, responsible for the disappearance of the body from the sealed crypt. After writing this book Carr loosened up a good deal on motives for creating a zany locked room, and he introduced the motives of 4) framing an innocent party, and 5) creating a situation with a built-in alibi because of the absence of the murderer in the murder room.

Finally, one of the most attractive things about the locked room mystery for Carr was its connection with magic. Fundamentally, it is impossible for someone to be murdered when he is alone in a locked room. Period. It can only be done through some sort of trick or illusion. Magicians, of course, do all sort of escapes and disappearing acts in which they make their assistants disappear from locked cabinets—this reached epic proportions in the twenties with Raymond's making an elephant disappear—and they themselves escape from straight jackets, locked trunks, and even milk cans. Every trick seems impossible until one reads the secret of the illusion. And the secrets parallel those of the locked room mystery: the magician uses twin assistants, the locks are fakes, etc.. Carr does the same thing that the magician does in making the impossible happen through an illusion and by misdirecting our attention by narrative technique, and then, presto, he explains how he did it. As H.M. says in *The Plague Court Murders,* "The fundamental trouble with the locked room situation is that it generally ain't reasonable. I don't mean that it can't be worked, any more than you'd deny one of Houdini's escapes."

Although in *The Three Coffins* Dr. Fell comes close to despair over the evil in human beings, Carr never pretends that his detective stories are about the real world or about real people. His feeling toward the readers who look for reality in the detective story is portrayed in Dr. Illingworth, the Scottish clergyman and Arabic scholar in *The Arabian Nights Murder.* Dr. Illingworth finds a thriller, *The Dagger of Doom,* on the train and after reading it becomes convinced that it is a manual of police work, and thereafter interprets all of the zany events in the novel in the light of adventures of the villainous Dr. Chianti in *The Dagger of Doom* and *The Return of Dr. Chianti.* This becomes wildly absurd. Carr does not pretend that his books are slices of life but frankly identifies them as detective stories full of detective story conventions. Thus in the last chapter of *The Eight of Swords* we get these comments:

> After all, this is only a detective story.
> . . .
> You don't know what you're talking about. And besides, get back to the subject. This is the last chapter, and we want to get it over with.[22]

And at the end of *To Wake the Dead* Dr. Fell is asked how he would describe events like those in the novel. He replies

> I call it a detective story.

It is a wild, improbable, fictional entertainment.

The word "probable" sends Carr's characters off into angry paroxisms. Carr upholds the banner of improbability from the beginning of his career by giving Bencolin a long literary lecture on detective fiction in *The Lost Gallows.* The key part of this lecture is that

> We think it very bad, by some twisted process of logic, that fiction

should fulfill its manifest purpose. By the use of the word
"improbable" we try to scare writers from any dangerous use of
their imaginations.... And yet, of course, truth will always be
inferior to fiction. When we want to pay any tale of fact a
particularly high compliment, we say "It is as thrilling as a
novel."[23]

Carr fights the same fight every time literature comes up in the
novels. It eventually becomes reduced to the formula that one
branch of literature, exemplified by the Russians (i.e.
Dostoevsky), is probable, but humorless, and obsessively
unhealthy and that "the only adequate answer to one who
begins rhapsodizing about the Russians is a swift uppercut to
the jaw." On the other hand there is the branch of literature full
of excitement and humor, like Twain and Dickens, but which is
improbable and often sentimental. It is in this camp that Carr
prefers to fight; he prefers being a detective story writer
searching for the cussedest illusion and the perfect set of
slightly balmy characters. He wants to write the perfect
entertainment and call it a detective story.

Chapter 9

Ngaio Marsh

Ngaio Marsh, the last of the Big Four female detective writers, entered the trade considerably later than Christie, Sayers and Allingham—her first novel, *A Man Lay Dead,* appeared in 1934—and she did not really hit her stride until the 1940's. Nevertheless, she wrote eight novels before the war, and in these books she invented and experimented with characters and patterns which she would exploit more successfully after the war. World War II, in fact, provided a needed hiatus for Marsh to absorb and reassess what she had been doing and to alter some of the directions which she had taken in the late thirties.

Most "classical" detective story writers began to write detective stories because they thought they could create a more engaging detective character or a more original murder situation than those currently used by popular writers. Thus we find fat detectives, witty detectives, boorish detectives, amoral detectives, deaf detectives, foreign detectives, romantic detectives, comic detectives, and so on. And the books of the twenties and thirties show people beaned with flower pots, shot with rock salt, stabbed with icicles, left in locked rooms, keeling over at card games, dying in rodeo rings, and so on. Marsh began precisely the same way: the method of murder in *A Man Lay Dead* is original and zany—just the sort of thing which a writer would use because it had never been done before. She also tried to create an original detective hero who both fulfilled the traditional role of the infallible detective and appealed to readers the same way that Poirot, Wimsey, Campion, Dr. Fell and all the rest did, as well as being a bit original. To fill this order Marsh introduced Roderick Alleyn, who is the central character in all of her novels of the thirties and with whom she tinkered a good deal throughout the period so that she could get him performing exactly the way that she wanted him to run and exactly the way the mood of the times directed.

Marsh got Alleyn's surname from Edward Alleyn (1566-1626), the Elizabethan actor who played Tamburlaine and Faustus, who inherited Philip Henslowe's theaters, acting company and fortune, who married John Donne's daughter, and who founded the College of God's Gift at Dulwich (incidentally the *alma mater* of Wodehouse and Raymond Chandler). The name comes from Marsh's devotion to the theater but it has little effect on the character or actions of her detective. In the first novel Marsh did not really have a clear, unique perception of her detective's character; instead he is a potpourri of attributes, some of which Marsh used in spite of the fact that they must have embarrassed her. Thus, in *A Man Lay Dead* Alleyn pops out of a fireplace and gets the drop on a gang of bolshies who have been running pins under the fingernails of his pals. He even says, "No funny business...you're covered...Put 'em up."[1] It's Hugh Drummond stuff, straight out of the thriller, and Marsh knew it. After her first book she left the adventure hero to other writers. Instead she developed the high class sensibility in Alleyn which was implicit from the start, and turned him into the aristocratic sleuth. As the books progress he acquires all of the outward and inward signs of the fictional type: he has a cozy flat with an exotic servant (a Russian named Vassily acquired in *A Man Lay Dead*), he has had the typical gentleman's training at Oxford and in the diplomatic service, and his class increasingly causes him to feel the degradation of police work which he has entered because of romantically mysterious "private reasons." In these things Marsh follows a whole generation of detective writers who portrayed aristocratic detectives with varying amounts of romanticism in order to attract readers who wished to experience the High Life if only second hand. But there is more to it than this. In the mid-thirties Dorothy Sayers was probably the most influential detective story writer in England. As Marsh developed the character of Alleyn in the earlier novels, she experimented with borrowing and adapting some of Wimsey's attributes: some of these she liked and kept, and some she found to be unsuccessful or stale and dropped.

Perhaps the most obvious attribute of Lord Peter which Marsh tried out on Alleyn is his unique diction. When Alleyn enters the first novel he uses fairly normal diction, except in the episode where he springs out of the fireplace to get the drop on the bad guys—showing that Marsh was really a bit embarrassed by making him act like a thriller character and she papered this over by giving him a consciously mocking speech. Gradually Marsh built up Alleyn's diction so that by the time of *Death in Ecstasy* (1937) he acquired a markedly Wimseyean diction. In his speech he uses advertising tags, like "the best butter" for whisky, inverted cliches, like "put that on your needles and knit it," constant literary allusion, as in this passage from *Death in Ecstasy:*

> Oh Garnette, my jewel, my gem above price, you will need your lovely legacy before we have done with you.... Oh excellent priest! Perdition catch my soul, but I do love thee.... Oh Jasper, my dear, my better half, have I caught my heavenly jewel?[2]

and baldly facetious rejoinders, like this interchange:

> "Ah," said Alleyn.
> "Ah-ha," said Nigel.
> "No, not quite 'Ah-ha' I fancy."[3]

Alleyn even talks about being facetious and dropping a few "facetiae" on people. But after *Death in Ecstasy* Marsh clipped Alleyn's tongue, and his diction becomes more normal in the subsequent novels; she even draws attention to his new, plain style in *Death in a White Tie* (1938) by having Alleyn say

> You are quite right, Fox. Never quote, and, if you do, certainly not from *Macbeth*.[4]

She had tried to make Alleyn talk like Wimsey, wit cracking and making fun of things, and then decided that it would not wash. It would not wash because it was too obviously borrowing from Sayers and because it did not fit either the kind of novels which Marsh was trying to write or with the more sober side of Alleyn which she emphasized more consistently beginning in *Vintage Murder* (1937).

Almost the opposite is true of Marsh's depiction of Alleyn's background and family. Instead of neglecting it, she focuses on the aristocratic background. Before *Artists in Crime* (1938) Marsh provides little information about Alleyn's family or background and makes her character reluctant to discuss it the few times that it comes up in the earlier novels. We know in a general way that he is well educated and a gentleman, but Marsh purposely keeps out details in order to convey a romantic sense of mystery and aristocratic reserve. In *Artists in Crime* and *Death in a White Tie,* however, Marsh makes up for lost time and brings in the detail which has been missing—and most of it is at least parallel to Sayers. Like Wimsey, Alleyn is the second son of an aristocratic family, his brother (the heir) like Denver is a blockhead, and his widowed mother is a sprightly and bright old gal who raises Alsatians at her country house and is alive to both compassion and absurdity. She is Marsh's version of the Dowager Duchess of Denver. The reason for the addition of these details probably stems from the fact that births, deaths, and weddings almost universally provoke family feeling. Here it is the wedding that is important for Marsh and causes her to work up Alleyn's family, for in *Artists in Crime* he falls in love with Agatha Troy whom he marries between *Death in a White Tie* and *Overture to Death* (1939). As it works out, Alleyn's Sayersean family fits in with his Sayersean wife: Agatha Troy is Harriet Vane in a painter's smock. Both women begin as suspects in murder cases who refuse to love the heroes because of the strain and confusion caused by love mixed with the artificiality of imposed gratitude and because of the genuine need for independence and the fear that it will be expunged in marriage. Both women decide on love and marriage after the completion of a succeeding case in which they have been involved. Because of their situations, both women cause the heroes to whine and pine a bit. Troy and Vane come from the same mold. Nevertheless, as much as she depends on Sayers, Marsh copies the externals only; in Marsh readers do not find the sustained insights into characters or the attention to non-detective themes which they find in Sayers. Thus Agatha Troy is a version of Harriet Vane from whom consideration of most serious themes has been distilled until only the stereotyped romantic elements remain. I do not intend this as disparagement. Sayers and Marsh had different views of the detective novel. Marsh simply wanted to write detective stories and so, although she may introduce aristocratic ambience or a spot of romance, she keeps them subordinate to the major part of the detective's work. The major part of Alleyn's character is his job: he is a copper.

Alleyn is no dabbler or dilettante whose hobby is

criminology and who nosey parkers around and chases ambulances to break the grip of boredom with a spot of adventure. He is a professional policeman, a Chief Detective Inspector, C.I.D., Scotland Yard. In this Marsh felt that she was making a departure from the standard practice of picturing Scotland Yard men as middle-class stooges for the private investigator. She makes the point in *A Man Lay Dead* where Nigel and Angela discuss the stereotype:

> "I must say, he [Alleyn] doesn't conform to my mental pictures of a sleuth-hound. I had an idea that they lived privately amidst inlaid linoleums, aspidistras, and enlarged pictures of constabulary groups."
> "Taking a strong cuppa at six-thirty in their shirt sleeves."[5]

Alleyn is certainly not this sort of policeman; he is an aristocrat, but he is, nevertheless, a policeman, and the glamour of his upper class background is subordinated to his police work. Marsh goes to some pains to show this and to thoroughly convey a more real picture of the policeman's job than one finds in most crime fiction of the time. Being a policeman, as Alleyn remarks to Fox in *Death in Ecstasy,* is "in many ways a degrading job-of-work." Marsh makes this impression even more vivid in *Death in a White Tie* where Alleyn says that he is "a filthy crime dentist!" suggesting that the policeman probes at the placque, decay, and infected abcesses of society suffering the foul breath of even his nicest patients.

But then Alleyn does not have many nice patients. The people whom he meets in the novels are a collection of creeps, cruds, moral weaklings, degenerates, cowards, fakes, and phonies. They turn the stomachs of the people who must lift the bandage of respectability from them. Here is a selection of observations from Alleyn, Fox, and Nigel about characters in the novels:

> A pig of a man (*Enter a Murderer*)
> ...He's a horrid man (*Enter a Murderer*)
> What a loathy, what a nauseating, what an unspeakable little dollop. (*Death in Ecstasy*)
> She's a nice fool, and he's unspeakably unpleasant. (*Death in Ecstasy*)
> My God, what a stupid woman. (*Death in a White Tie*)
> Besotted young ninny (*Death in a White Tie*)

None of these remarks refers to the murderers in these books. In each novel the job of police work brings Alleyn into contact with lots of weak, corrupt, degenerate, mean, stupid, little people. Marsh shows Alleyn dealing with them and she also shows the disgust which they and his job provoke in him. This is clear in Marsh's description of Alleyn in *Enter a Murderer:*

> It was an attractive face...and when nobody watched him, a very expressive one. At the moment it suggested extreme distaste. One might have guessed that he had just done something that was repugnant to him, or that he was about to undertake a task which displeased him.[6]

He is about to catch a woman lying and stealing. It is not a pleasant job, especially for a fine-tuned aristocrat, but it is still a job which, once undertaken, must be done with precision.

As Inspector Fox points out about Alleyn, "his job has to come before anything else." To do his work efficiently Alleyn must not only ignore his own personal feelings, but he must use every resource to identify the criminal. Thus he becomes the complete, aloof gamester, indifferent to friendships, feelings, or socially correct behavior. Alleyn feels the pressures of this role, and Marsh does things to soften it (like giving him a wife), but nevertheless he uses people to spy and fink on their friends and takes advantage of others' weaknesses to checkmate the murderer. Nigel Bathgate, whom Alleyn uses in *Enter a Murderer,* upbraids the detective for his callous manipulation of people, but Alleyn goes on in subsequent books to extort confessions and to use other characters' flaws and guilty secrets in order to get to the truth. It is part of playing the serious game of detection; it is part of his job as Marsh shows it.

The other part of doing the policeman's job successfully is thoroughness: this means that the policeman must wade through a mire of facts most of which turn out to be irrelevant or to have only marginal bearing on the case at hand. At the conclusion of the evidence-gathering phase of *Death in a White Tie* Alleyn calls it the "damnable, dreary, involved, addling business...." To stress the routine side of policework, Marsh in the thirties never introduces Alleyn alone; he arrives on the scene with Bailey, his fingerprint man, a couple of constables, and, beginning with *Enter a Murderer,* Inspector Fox, who patiently takes down all of the testimony in shorthand. After the first novel which hinges on "fingerprints," Bailey becomes pretty much a third wheel who says little but is always there. This comes from Marsh's unwillingness to base her novels on bits of scientific fluff or physical evidence: when these things appear in the books they are quickly disposed of. Alleyn, in fact, calls minute examination of physical evidence "Thorndyke stuff," and tends to dismiss it. Increasingly in the thirties Marsh centered on the series of interviews as the essence of routine and made them the heart of her detective plots. By the time of *Vintage Murder,* formal or informal interrogation takes up well over two thirds of the novel. These long and tedious interviews with marginally interesting characters (to put a charitable construction on them) represent for Marsh the awful, boring routine of police work. And we must put a charitable construction on them rather than assuming that Marsh simply could not create engaging characters or write interesting dialogue, because she does, after all, make Alleyn aware of the tedium of these interviews. It is a phase in her writing which Marsh had to go through, a phase which she passed through by 1940 when in *Death at the Bar,* in a chapter labeled "Routine," she discusses the problem of handling drudgery:

> Your novelist too has now passed the halcyon days when he could ignore routine.... He knows that routine is deadly dull and hopelessly poor material for a thriller; so, like a wise pot-boiler, he compromises. He heads one chapter "Routine," dismisses six weeks of drudgery in as many phrases, cuts the cackle and gets to the 'osses.[7]

Like Alleyn's facetious diction, the concentrated doses of interviews in the novels of the thirties were an experiment which Marsh worked out of her system by 1940.

Marsh could create interesting characters, but most of them fall into one of two classes. There are the unpleasant people among the suspects who have some overriding flaw: jealousy, egotism, homosexuality, social pretense, money-grubbing, and so on. There are also dialect characters whom Marsh introduces into almost every novel. These people, who Marsh probably saw as the character actors in her dramas, range from Dr. Tokareff with his Russian accent coupled with the application of an English dictionary to goose up his vocabulary in *A Man Lay Dead,* to Ogden's aggressive New World diction in *Death in Ecstasy,* to the Antipodean characters in *Vintage Murder* and *Artists in Crime,* to the parodies of overly cultivated English (like Mr. Sage's "Aye thot Aye heeard somewon teeking may neem in veen") in *The Nursing Home Murder* (1936), and *Death in Ecstasy.*

All of these people appear in only one book, but Marsh developed a group of characters who became continuing fixtures: the assistant detectives. In the earliest novels Marsh singled out Nigel Bathgate for a good deal of attention. Nigel acts as the Watson character, but not the narrator, in *A Man Lay Dead, Enter a Murderer, The Nursing Home Murder, Death in Ecstasy, Artists in Crime* and *Overture to Death.* Marsh uses Nigel as the traditional detective's stooge: he is a young newspaper reporter who, as we see in the various lists which he produces in the books, has learned to classify but has not learned to synthesize. He also performs as the adventure surrogate in the novels, especially the early ones, seeking situations which will replace boredom with novelty, and chasing Alleyn not only to get the scoop for his paper but also to find excitement. In this respect, Nigel serves as Marsh's comment on the ethics of detection. He wants the puzzle and the thrill without doing the dirty work or taking the responsibility. She makes this clear in *Enter a Murderer* when Alleyn dresses Nigel down on this very topic. It became clear to Marsh after *A Man Lay Dead* that the detective novel could not also be an adventure story, and she made the point through Nigel. In addition to this she made Nigel the repository of wit cracking and facetiae when Alleyn gave it up. Through *Death in Ecstasy* Nigel is the straight man; afterward he becomes the wit cracker. But he is an adolescent one, popping jokes when everyone else has grown beyond it. Nigel was a creature of Marsh's earliest imaginings—when she thought that the detective story could still be all play—away from which she grew until she dropped him entirely in the 1940's.

As Nigel Bathgate's role decreases in the novels, Inspector Edward Fox's grows more prominent, underlining Marsh's growing emphasis on policework and the developing sensitivity of Roderick Alleyn. Fox appears for the first time in *Enter a Murderer,* and he accompanies Alleyn in all of the other novels of the period except *Vintage Murder* which takes place while Alleyn is on holiday in New Zealand. He literally takes over for Nigel, since in the earliest novels one of Nigel's jobs is to take shorthand notes of the interviews with suspects, and this becomes one of Fox's responsibilities. Marsh also uses Fox as a comic character showing his awkward respect for the upper classes and using his attempts to learn French from the B.B.C. and sets of recordings as a standing joke in many of the books. Like Nigel, Fox also performs a structural role in a number of novels: he presents the mid-book recapitulation of facts and suspects which Marsh uses to focus the puzzle strain in the novels. Marsh also uses Fox to direct suspicions since in a couple of stories he decides to suspect one particular character while Alleyn stays uncommitted. By creating Fox as a solid, lower middle-class policeman Marsh is able to make him do things which Nigel as Alleyn's social equal cannot. In this respect he acts more like Sayers' Bunter: Fox saves Alleyn, and Marsh, from the social awkwardness of interviewing servants, which he takes on himself—off stage. Fox is also the one who protests when suspects assume that Alleyn is just another lowerclass policeman, and he watches over his boss' well-being, making sure tht he eats regularly and tactfully consoling him when he sees that the effects of crime are distressing Alleyn.

Marsh can mix up her character types fairly well, presenting different kinds of people in various novels; her murderers, however, fall into a few clearly definable classes. With the exception of *The Nursing Home Murder,* all of Marsh's villains in the thirties commit crimes because of either the need for protection from accusation for a lesser crime or because of sexual jealousy. Four of the novels of the thirties turn upon a criminal who, to cover-up forgery, blackmail, embezzling, or robbery, decides to commit a murder. This means, for the articulation of the detective plot, that the investigators must wade through a subsidiary investigation of the lesser crime, with all of the additional detail which this involves, in order to get to the material of the greater crime. Of course Marsh also uses it as an occasion to emphasize the dirty background of any crime. Connected with this is the fact that the most discomfiting motive for any crime is sexual jealousy, and Marsh places this too in the background of her crimes. In every book there is a romantic triangle with its attendant rivalries, hatreds, and jealousies. Typically two men vie for one woman, but Marsh varies the pattern by having two women struggle for one man in *Artists in Crime* and *Overture to Death.* The constant presence of sexual rivalry and jealousy, whether as the motive or the red herring, adds significantly to the degradations of criminal investigation. It complicates issues by providing an excuse for false testimony and it shows people at their worst, dripping with egotism, deception, self-pity, fear, and hatred masked as love. These are disturbing things to read about; the world that Marsh slowly evolved for her detective books is not a sweet smelling one. It was to create this world and to make characters who could function in it that caused Marsh to work on and alter her main characters. She found that facetiae could not sweeten the world of the books and so she tried to tailor her people to fit it more realistically.

By creating unsavory situations and portraying people with credible motives for committing crimes Marsh, like other detective writers in the thirties, created problems for herself which she could not completely solve. By its very nature the Golden Age detective novel was an entertainment; it was a puzzle, a game, with certain specific conventions designed to engage readers in a guessing contest and to give them a surprise at the close of the narrative. Within this framework it is difficult and often undesirable to treat serious themes or to show a picture of the real world of crime. A number of writers in the thirties, notably Sayers, Allingham, and Cox as Francis Iles, tried to fuse the puzzle story with more serious concerns. In each case this meant making certain adaptations of the conventional patterns. The same thing is true of Marsh: she wants to combine the crime game with realism and needs to make certain adjustments. Marsh knew, as Sayers did, that the chief impediment to making the puzzle story into a realistic picture, or even a traditional narrative, was the convention that the antagonist must be concealed in the detective story in order to make the guessing game work. Without an identifiable antagonist, the writer needs to modify the traditional way stories develop and has no character upon whom to focus the negative side of the conflict of detective hero and murderer-villain. Sayers solved this problem of making the identity of the antagonists clear from the beginning of the plot, never cloaking them very heavily, in order to communicate the various manifestations of evil. Marsh's treatment of the antagonist, which is in some ways like Sayers', does not, however, come from a pressing need to examine the nature of sin, but has its beginnings in Marsh's grounding in the theater: it is important in a good play to show a good deal of the antagonist. Consequently, Marsh does not use plot devices like the least-likely-character or the character who is guilty but only has a minimal role. Quite the opposite. In two of her novels of the period she employs what can be called the most likely suspect formula: that is, the person who is suspected of the murder actually is guilty. She is most interested in showing murderers in all of their commonplace nastiness. Even if Marsh gives in to convention in rigging up fancy ways of killing people—like the gun in the piano trick in *Overture to Death*—the technical means of murder is not as important as the people, not as important as the time honored drama of confronting people with others and with themselves.

Dramatists of course have been doing this for centuries, and a significant portion of Marsh's work depends on the theater and the art of the dramatist. Even without knowing about Marsh's theatrical aspirations and background one could infer them from the novels. Two of her eight books in the thirties (*Enter a Murderer* and *Vintage Murder*) take place in theaters, use the scenes and machines of the playhouse to give atmosphere, and examine the peculiar, often childish, characters of actors who strut and perform on stage and off. Even the novels not specifically set on the stage summon up the theater. In most of the books, for instance, murder is committed in front of an audience: the personnel of an operating theater, the congregation of a church during a service, artists in front of a model's stage, and the audience at a church charity entertainment. Each is a big, dramatic scene and the results of the investigation depend on the perception of the audience and the sagacity of the detective-critic who sees most clearly. If every action begins with a big scene, action in every book ends with another big scene. In many cases—*A Man Lay Dead, Enter a Murderer, The Nursing Home Murder, Vintage Murder,* and *Overture to Death*—this means a reenactment of the crime in order to provoke a confession (a technique which Marsh ties to the play-within-a-play in *Hamlet*), demonstrate a theory, provide a startling way of arresting the criminal, or all three. In the other novels the action ends with a dynamic confrontation of all of the suspects during which Alleyn stage manages personalities to provoke the exposure of hitherto hidden testimony or information. Thus the character is forced out of his or her fear into truth which exposes the malefactor.

Marsh invariably constructs her plots following one specific formula. None of her novels begins with the crime but they start with several chapters which provide atmosphere and introduce the characters who will later become suspects and victim. Then comes the murder. Following the murder the police take over and perform tests and conduct extensive interviews with the suspects. Near the end of the interviews there is a recapitulation scene in which one of the subsidiary detectives sums up the known information and presents it as a list of suspects with notations on motive and opportunity. Then Marsh often, but not always, adds an adventure sequence, like the communist business in *A Man Lay Dead*, or a second murder, as in *Enter a Murderer* and *Artists in Crime*. This is followed by the confrontation scene or reenactment where the murderer is exposed, and the book closes with a very short—atypically short for a detective novelist—summary which ties up and explains events which have not been explained before. The formula, then, is: introduction, murder, interviews, recapitulation, action, reenactment, and summary. It always happens this way. What is so unusual about this pattern? Most detective novelists follow it. That is true, but Marsh varies from the norm in the atypically short summary and in the tenacity with which she sticks to the pattern. With Marsh the murder cannot occur on the first page and the summary cannot take more than a few pages. This is because she constructs her detective novels following the traditional structure of the drama which every beginning student of the drama knows either from Aristotle or from Freytag. Let us take Aristotle. According to ancient dramatic criticism, every play has three structural parts: the prostasis, the epistasis, and the catastrophe. The prostasis introduces characters, sets the scene, provides background material, and incites the subsequent action of the drama. For Marsh the application is obvious: she sets the scene, gives background, introduces characters, and then brings in the murder which incites the rest of the action in the first stage of her plots. Epistasis: the epistasis according to classical theory is the actual action of the play during which there is an increase in tribulations for the hero and the writer confronts the audience with surprises and crises. For Marsh, the middle of the book contains the characters' (the detective and his assistants) collection of a mass of testimony which gives various surprises to the detectives and the readers, it complicates what seemed to be clear-cut issues, and it gives rise to various crises for suspects and detectives alike. When the mid-book recapitulation comes there should be a ready and easy solution to the problem (and there is one since the detective, but not his friends or the readers, knows the answer) but it is not apparent. Finally comes the catastrophe, the last part, in which the problem is solved through action, the threads tied up, and the stage emptied. This is the place where Marsh's books are most obviously made on the pattern of the drama. If one wants to insult or attack a drama—or at least a traditional one—all that has to be done is to whisper the word "anti-climax." Try to find a critic who believes that act five of *Henry V* is structurally fitting and you will see the point. Drama is supposed to stop soon after the most important action has been performed. Marsh knows this and she also knows that the detective's summation can be and is a long, boring lump on the end of many detective novels which makes them anti-climatic. Therefore, she never includes windy summary chapters in her books but sticks to the reenactment because it is structurally more fitting—more dramatic.

Coming as she does at the end of the Golden Age, Marsh was better able to fit her fictions to the post war world than her fellow writers. In part this was because she was not infected so strongly with the spirit of play and in part because she did not have to work at breaking down cliches of the thriller—this had already been done for her by others. She also came to the detective novel just as others were trying to make it into regular, mainstream fiction: as Cox was pulling for the psychological detective story, and as Sayers and Allingham were moving toward the novel of manners. She had no past to live down and could start at the point at which the others finished. Consequently, her realistic view of police and crime, her sensitive detective hero, and her perceptive drawing of subsidiary characters fit in with the new mold. Her books were not as frank or disturbing as much post war detective fiction in both America and Britain, but they were still realistic and used techniques which readers had become accustomed to through their years of reading the other detective writers. Marsh survived the break in cultural continuity brought about by the Second World War because she put both worlds into her books—the old, comfortable arcadia, and the new and disturbing country without a name.

Chapter 10

The End

Detective novels written on Golden Age patterns still, of course, come into print, and some of the original writers cranked out books until the 1970's: Christie continued writing until her death in 1976 and two posthumous works came out in 1977, and a new Marsh novel appeared in 1977. Nevertheless, in the late 1930's for many important novelists of the twenties and thirties the form died. For one thing, a number of them completely quit writing detective novels. Sayers stopped in 1936; Knox gave it up, under pressure, in the same year; Philip MacDonald laid off from 1938 to 1952, and Cox stopped writing detective novels in 1939. Not even the postwar critical boom in America which brought essays on the detective story to *The New Yorker, Harper's, Nation,* and other journals brought them back to writing detective novels. Not even the promise of more money—the motive which moved many of them to take up the form in the first place—could get many of them back. Even before the pressures of the approaching war, these writers stopped writing, sensing that the form had achieved all it possibly could and that fresh surprises could not breathe new life into the old bones. The gang that got together to turn out books like *Six Against Scotland Yard* was simply tired of the game.

For those writers who did not stop, the war added a new factor to the formula of their novels. According to the rules, the old thriller devices like death rays and megalomaniac Master Criminals could not be used in detective novels beause they were too silly. They were not quite so silly in the early 1940's when Hitler was on the loose, buzz bombs sawed into English cities, and a group of crackpot professors invented the atomic bomb in the stands of an American football stadium. The war brought the thriller back with a vengeance and some of the old detective writers adapted to it as Blake did with *Smiler with a*

Knife or Cox in *Death in the House*. Michael Innes, in fact, wrote the whole change in the world and the change in its fictions into his *Case of the Journeying Boy* (1947). Here an adolescent's perception of reality, colored by Sapper's Bulldog Drummond books and films like "The Plutonium Blonde," is much more accurate than that of his reasonable tutor (Mr. Thew-less) who simply cannot understand the world into which they have been shot. Global travel, fiendish weapons, doomsday, and unalloyed patriotism were simply more relevant to the 1940's and 1950's than grace, wit, and reason.

A few writers like Marsh, Christie, and Allingham went back to the detective story after the war, but their share of the limelight shrank. Although some intellectuals defended the form in the forties, most sophisticated readers, immersed in cocktail party existentialism, were won over to Chandler's naive manhandling of the form in "The Simple Art of Murder," and asked with Edmund Wilson "Who Cares Who Killed Roger Ackroyd?" There was an exodus to gloomy, serious writers like Kafka, Sartre, and Thomas Mann. Much of the rest of the detective story's audience was drawn away by the radio and cinema, and then by television. To keep people reading, publishers turned to sensational literature, and the American hard-boiled tradition merged with the tradition of Sapper and gave the public violent, sexually active heroes like Mike Hammer, Shell Scott, and James Bond. The phenomenal sales of Spillane, Prather, and Fleming eclipsed much of the interest which publishers had in novels written in the old fashion. Also some writers, like Colin Watson and Julian Symons, carried the detective story to the end which Cox projected but could not quite bring himself to do: they left the fun and unreality behind and wrote crime novels full of bitterness and unpleasantness. Then too came the police procedural novel which disposed of the hero, the puzzle, the game, the wit, and the relief which the older writers had striven to create. In spite of all this, Hiroshima and Mike Hammer, there still remain people in corners of Britain, America, and Brazil—and goodness knows where else—who relish the quiet laughs and quaint complexities of a good detective story.

Appendix I

Detective Plots

One of the objections which some writers of the thirties voiced about the detective novel was that it was all plot to the exclusion of the other elements of fiction. Although I do not altogether agree with this, plot is vitally important to the form. It is one of the ways in which the detective novel can be defined. Detective writers in the twenties and thirties developed a plot formula which at the same time is simple and highly complex and we need to come to terms with it before we can fully understand the genre. Before going into this formula, however, there are several preliminary considerations, premises, which need to be understood.

It would be well to note that detective novels between the two world wars are in some ways like all detective stories which came before. The-y, in fact, depend on certain known traditions and assume a common background and specific expectations. Detective novelists assume that we know Poe, Conan Doyle, Freeman and the rest—they allude to their predecessors frequently—and that we expect the plot to include a problem and the detective's solution to it. This is the theme upon which they base their variations. Before Bentley, however, the detective tale was largely confined to short stories (with the exception of *The Moonstone)* which had very little in them besides the problem at the beginning and the solution at the end. Therefore, in addition to playing with the traditions of problem and solution, detective novelists in the twenties and thirties needed to develop a whole range of middle tactics to flesh out the short story into the short novel.

The detective novel is unique among forms of popular fiction in that it is self-conscious and that it developed its own prescriptive criticism while the form was still alive and growing. In the 1920's there appeared a number of sets of so-called "rules of the game" which were voiced in critical articles and in the novels themselves. Milne, Sayers, Christie, Van Dine, Knox and others set down various prescriptions about exactly what the detective novel was to be and what it was not to be. As interesting as these rules may be, however, they do not really advance our understanding of detective novel plots. What they boil down to are 1) admonitions that the detective novel is a reader-writer game in which there needs to be fair play in setting out clues and presenting characters—admonitions which were disregraded by most writers, 2) prescriptions about the subject matter of the detective story, and 3) warnings about a number of cliches which ought not be used because they were shopworn or the property of other, lesser kinds of fiction—the romance or the thriller. These do not give us much to go on and do not get us any closer to isolating the formula of the detective novel, but they do help to narrow the subject matter which fuels the formula.

Subject Matter

Regarding subject matter Van Dine is very clear. His seventh rule dictates that

> There simply must be a corpse in a detective novel, and the deader the corpse the better. Three-hundred pages is far too much pother [sic] for a crime other than murder. After all, the reader's trouble and expenditure of energy must be rewarded.[1]

This, unlike some of his other pronouncements, is not simply Van Dine's own practice made into law for everyone else. Mysterious death provided fuel for virtually all detective novels written in the twenties and thirties. Murder is the norm and plots which resolve in suicide and accident surprise because they do not contain murders. Even the Dodd and Mead Red Badge Eight Point Test for budding detective writers told the aspirant that

> On the *gravity* of the crime depends, in large measure, the reader's interest in the identity of the criminal. For this reason the crime should be murder or potential murder.[2]

Dollars to doughnuts if you open any detective novel of the era you will find a violent death before page one hundred. Before 1920 this was not the case. Edwardian short stories treat a variety of crimes; the Sherlock Holmes stories, for instance, include fraud, theft, blackmail, scandal, counterfeiting, and kidnapping as well as murder. The same with the Dr. Thorndyke stories.

Not only was violent death a prime ingredient in the detective novel, but a certain kind of violent death. As a rule the norm was "cold-blooded, deliberate murder." Consequently, as Poirot says in *Peril at End House,* "we exclude...homocidal mania...[and] we also exclude killing done on the spur of the moment under the impulse of an ungovernable temper."[3] Not only these but also gangland murders by "secret societies, cammorras, mafias, *et al,* have no place in the detective story." Most writers stay away from mass murder too. Why: The detective novel centers on cold-blooded, premeditated murder done by one, or at most two individuals because it is tamer and more analyzable than the other sorts. For one thing it fits in with the concept of the mental problem which some detective writers tried to sell their readers. This sort of crime also isolates two individuals working against one another for victory—the criminal and the detective—giving the readers the basic fable of good versus evil in the purest form. C.P. Snow's Aloysius Birrell says, in this connection, that

> Years ago they used to write ballads about war and brute force and lust...now they write detective stories in which all of men's energies are concentrated in seeking out wrong.[4]

Further, the good and evil in the detective novel are more domestic and more believable than in its alternative, the thriller. It is easier to credit that one person can solve one crime than it is to believe that one man can save the world. Call it a retreat from optimism or a move toward realism, it is what happened.

To ring in conspiracies or mental illness would sully the purity of the underlying fable and jumble the abstract problem. Besides, cold-blooded murder perpetrated by one person is more comfortable than its alternatives. As part of its business, the detective novel always assures its readers that their material world is nice and comfortable. Terror and pity do not enter, for what happens in the book is just that—something that happens in a book. *In Cold Blood* is not a detective novel. In reading a detective novel of our vintage readers are assured that their reason is stable and in control of their fate; they read these books to admire the writers' mental gymnastics. In the crime they see something completely alien happen: a twisted person makes pseudo-rational judgments and commits murder. This, however, can never happen to us; we cannot be the murderer or the victim because the story is not real. Once writers leave premeditated murder things change, they get uglier. The crime of passion shows us that our emotions can get the best of us—or those of our wives, husbands, children, friends, or even complete strangers—and we wind up in the soup. We become the criminal or the victim. Likewise, the crime of a deranged person who takes to randomly butchering innocent people turns our world inside out. Not much comfort can be derived from considering that we might be the victims of a diseased person who shoots passersby from a university library with a high powered rifle without any logical, rational motive. It might be thrilling to see this sort of crime happen and brought to justice but it disturbs us to know that it happens. In Golden Age novels, therefore, these things do not happen.

They do not happen because they disturb us, and they do not happen because of a snobbery. The detective novel assures us again and again that it is not the thriller, which is full of wild improbabilities and the grosser fable of one man saving the world. Detective novels do not present a world fraught with danger which constantly piques us with the hero's narrow escapes from death at the hands of the Master Criminal and his grimy myrmidons. Its readers are not adolescents who thrive on this sort of thing—or they have sublimated the part of them which does. On the other hand the detective novel is not the opposite extreme, the police procedural novel or its predecessor, the tale of scientific detection. These forms in their early manifestations seemed too dreary, too humdrum. The detective novel steers between them with enough detail and excitement to satisfy readers who see themselves as intelligent and civilized.

With these limitations placed on the kinds of crimes which the detective novel should treat, in theory and practice writers of the Golden Age had only ten options of subject matter. It will be simplest to give them in a list.

1. One murder committed by one person. Most detective stories of the period chose this, and the force of the remaining choices of subject matter comes largely from the fact that they are not this standard type.

2. One murder committed by two people acting jointly. Although this smacks of the thriller and Van Dine scorned it in his rules, murder with an accomplice appears regularly in certain writers like Christie and Carr.

3. One murder committed by two people acting separately. Although this is a technical impossibility, since one can only die once, this choice appears in a small class of stories. It works two ways: either there is an attempted murder which is believed to be successful but is not, followed by the real murder, or there is a murder by one person and a second party merely desecrates the corpse. See Cox's *Jumping Jenny,* Carr's *Four False Weapons,* and Christie's *Murder on the Calais Coach.*

4. One murder committed by an individual acting as the unwitting tool of another. This relatively small group actually spins off from *The Moonstone.* Here murder can be committed under the influence of hypnotism, drugs, ignorance, or the articulation of a death trap. Most of Marsh's books fall into this group.

5. Two or more murders committed by one person. Stories in which the murderer finds it necessary to silence a witness or accomplice or to hide his motives by covering his crimes in a series belong here as well as vendettas against groups of people. Van Dine uses this choice regularly.

6. Two or more murders committed by two connected people. Occasionally a murderer and his accomplice find it necessary to kill more than one individual for the same reasons as those cited above.

7. Two or more murders committed by unconnected people. This is a rare choice but it is used once during the period (at least) by Carr.

8. Suicide which accidentally looks like murder.

9. Suicide which looks like murder because the victim wished to

revenge himself on another (following Conan Doyle's "The Problem of Thor Bridge") or gain something for his family or friends. See Philip MacDonald's *The Joke*.
10. Accident which looks like murder.
Writers very, very seldom stray from these ten choices of subject matter. When they do so, they vary consciously and go to some pains to make clear to readers that they should not expect a regular detective novel. For instance Philip MacDonald notes that his novel dealing with mass murder, *Murder Gone Mad* (1931), is not a "whodoneit" but a "howcatchem."

Detection and witnesses comprise the other part of the initial choices for the detective story writer—initial in the abstract sense which is not the same as the order in which a book forms in an author's mind. These increase the complications of the formula. With each of the ten crime choices the writer can decide to include suspects/witnesses or to do without them entirely. For the detective novel between the wars this choice was not terribly operative as much of the middle of the mystery story needs to consist of character interaction and analysis. Further, there was a heavily anti-Thorndykean reaction in the twenties against the scientific detective tale (see Milne's introduction to *The Red House Mystery*). Still, writers could and did sometimes choose to concentrate exclusively on material evidence without bringing in suspects or witnesses. The other variant in the writer's initial choice lies with the choice of detectives, not with their characters or appearance, which is of course open, but in their number. There can be any number of detectives introduced but in practical terms most writers, not wishing to write 87th Precinct novels, chose three: Poirot, Hastings, Japp; Alleyn, Fox, Bathgate; Wimsey, Bunter, Parker; Dr. Fell, Hadley, the narrator; Vance, Markham, Van Dine, and so on. One is usually a police official who has available to him all of the technical machinery of scientific detective. He has the crime lab as well as plenty of burly constables to roam about making door-to-door inquiries. The second detective fills the role of the straight man, coming from Watson's family. Last there is the main detective who is the hero of the story and who usually solves the problem. Although three is the standard number, each writer when arranging materials can choose any number of detectives to probe about. This means, given the possibilities for variety in presentation of detectives and suspects, that the formula becomes more complicated.

The Ending

Detective stories prove things; most often they prove guilt but sometimes they simply find out the truth about facts of a certain environment. That is their business and it is unique in popular fiction. Other forms, like the romance, the thriller, and the western, show guilt in action—a bad person does bad things while a good person does good things—or they assume that labels will suffice for most readers to prove someone nasty—the traitor, the communist, or the outlaw. The detective novel has as its first responsibility to prove guilt in a quasi-legal manner, to show opportunity and motive. This part of the formula never varies. Detective stories must end with some sort of demonstration of the facts behind the enigma posed by the beginning. Further, writers can only accomplish this ending in a limited number of ways. The standard plot finds the detective uncovering the facts and stating the solution somewhere near the end of the story. Sometimes, however, when the detectives are particularly inept, as in Cox's novels, the narrator intrudes into the story to show what the investigators have missed, or he may show the same thing by giving an isolated bit of dialogue at the end of the novel—as in *Jumping Jenny*. Also, as in Carr's *The Crooked Hinge*, the solution can be substantiated through the mails from a culprit who has flown the coop. The last possibility—and it exists only in a tiny class of books as well as pseudo-books like *Murder Off Miami*—has the readers arrive at their own solutions based on the materials supplied by the text.

Typically the recitation of facts does not come quite at the end of the novel, and there is some room for writers to maneuver between the proof of guilt and the last word. Some novels do, in fact, end with the recitation of facts. It is really all that the form demands, but in order to insure the validity of the detective's solution, to complete the picture of the parallel fictional world, and to stay within the traditions of the novel there are six closing gambits available: 1) the murderer gets off after confessing to the detective and the crime is covered up, 2) the criminal confesses after the recitation of facts and the curtain drops, 3) the police arrest the murderer, 4) the police kill the criminal as he tries to escape or to commit another crime, 5) the criminal makes his escape good in spite of the efforts of the detectives, 6) the murderer commits suicide. In only one case that I can recall—Sayers' *Busman's Honeymoon*—does the writer dwell on what happens to the criminal after capture. The majority of writers care little about what happens to the criminal after he has admitted his guilt through word or deed. Few wish to take the readers into the moral and ethical shock of the process of trial and execution of another human being, since this would rupture the stylized game world of the novel. Instead most drop the curtain on the confessed murderer or remove him with suicide. One other closing technique needs to be mentioned before I move on. Cox and Carr both typically close their novels with multiple solutions. They both serve up a number of solutions which are possible but false before they come to the final, true, solution at the close of the novel. This too mitigates the moral considerations of the novel by making the final solution simply one in a series of ingenious constructs.

The Middle

When writing a detective novel, the writer has only a limited number of choices predicated by the fact that the beginning and the end are given: there must be a mysterious death and a solution. These choices reduce writers' options largely to issues of timing, for they can provide the body in the opening pages or anywhere in the first half of the book. The solution, likewise, can come after a number of erroneous conclusions or by itself near the end of the novel. The finish of the novel can also follow a number of courses to dispose of the criminal. All of thes parts of the formula govern the way in which detective novels open and close. The formula of the complete detective novel, however, goes further: it controls the exposition of the middle of the story. With the middle writers have far more options open for development and choice, but they are still within a formula. Middle tactics in fact offer so many permutations that it would take a computer to count them up. The best way that I have found to explain the middle of the detective novel plot is through the following flow charts which express, as far as I know, all of the plot elements and choices which writers of the twenties and thirties used to make their detective stories into novels. The charts, I hope, will explain themselves, but I will provide a few explanations to help readers along.

I. The Problem
   A. The Body
      1. The situation

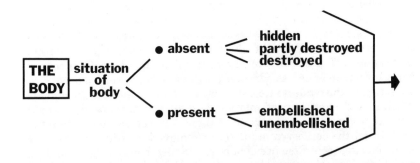

No matter where it occurs, every detective novel begins with a body or evidence of mysterious death just as in Common Law one must have a corpse or real evidence of foul play to initiate murder proceedings. Writers can choose to make finding the body a central part of the problem or they can embellish the corpse with zany accoutrements.

One can find the former in Blake's *There's Trouble Brewing* and the latter in Carr's *The Mad Hatter Mystery*.

I. The Problem
  A. The Body
    2. Identity

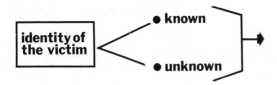

The second stage in fictional and real murders is to establish the identity of the victim. This is done by the coroner's jury in life as well as fiction. Some novelists make identifying the corpse the central issue in their books. See Sayers' *Whose Body?*

I. The Problem
  B. The efficient cause of death

In spite of the simplicity of this part of the chart, one of the things one learns from reading Golden Age detective novels is that almost anything material, as well as a few immaterial things, can be used as murder weapons.

I. The Problem
  C. Physical environmental evidence

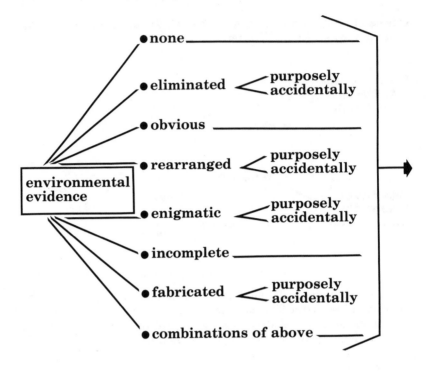

Here the number of choices multiplies rapidly, especially considering the last item, combinations of above. This means that writers can combine any of the items which can combine (obviously "none" cannot combine). There is a mathematical formula to figure out the precise number of combinations available, but it probably suffices to say that there are a lot. Physical evidence can be anything from fingerprints to lost bits of clothing to broken pieces of Ming vases: it depends on the ingenuity and interests of the writer. Edwardian detective stories, especially the Thorndyke tales, tend to stop at this point. Once minute bits of dust have been identified the solution becomes apparent. Golden Age writers generally treat evidence as something which is incomplete or enigmatic which cannot be interpreted until collated with the observations of witnesses and the psychological reactions of suspects. Without this complication, there would rarely be enough material to make a novel.

I. The Problem
  D. Identify suspects/witnesses

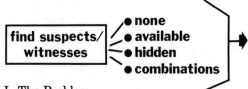

find suspects/ witnesses
- none
- available
- hidden
- combinations

I. The Problem
  E. Testimony of suspects

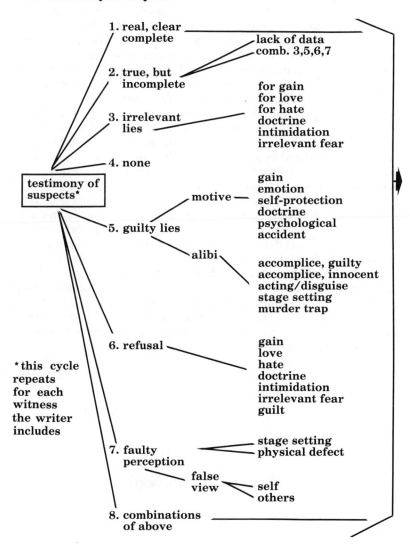

testimony of suspects*

1. real, clear complete
   lack of data
   comb. 3,5,6,7

2. true, but incomplete

3. irrelevant lies
   for gain
   for love
   for hate
   doctrine
   intimidation
   irrelevant fear

4. none

5. guilty lies
   motive —
   gain
   emotion
   self-protection
   doctrine
   psychological
   accident

   alibi
   accomplice, guilty
   accomplice, innocent
   acting/disguise
   stage setting
   murder trap

6. refusal
   gain
   love
   hate
   doctrine
   intimidation
   irrelevant fear
   guilt

*this cycle repeats for each witness the writer includes

7. faulty perception
   stage setting
   physical defect

   false view
   self
   others

8. combinations of above

At this stage the complications multiply and the writers' choices about how to deal with witnesses and suspects likewise multiply. In the simplest stories, which are never written, real and clear observations of the witnesses lead directly to the solution of the problem. Some novels bring in no witnesses—although this seldom happens since even a locked room must have witnesses to demonstrate that it is a locked room (which it is not, ever.) Writers have the option of having witnesses make enigmatic statements about the death which they in turn have the detective explain as the novel proceeds. Witnesses in detective novels often lie. This wholesale mendacity results from numerous personal motives unrelated to the events in question: witnesses hope to gain from lies, they may cover up guilty secrets which are irrevelant to the case, or they may lie because of love or hatred of another party. Witnesses sometimes lie because of their adherence to some sort of religious, philosophic, political, or economic doctrine—for example a communist might find it necessary to lie to agents of a capitalistic system who are trying to uncover the murderer of a grasping industrialist. Refusal to testify runs on the same lines as the motives for lying. Since novelists frequently wish to go beyond the testimony of witnesses, often one finds witnesses who have incorrectly perceived the events which have taken place before them. Sometimes this is due to stage-setting by the culprit who, like a conjuror, makes something appear to happen which actually does not. Faulty perception also stems from physical defects of the observer (e.g. being short sighted), or environmental conditions, and it can come from the witness' faulty perception of others whom he hates and consequently sees them perform what they did not, or faulty perception of himself which makes him believe that he committed a crime which he did not. Writers can use any or all of these schemes for creating witnesses in order to fill out the middle—and can emphasize any which seem appropriate or interesting.

I. The Problem
  E. The alibis

(See chart on next page)

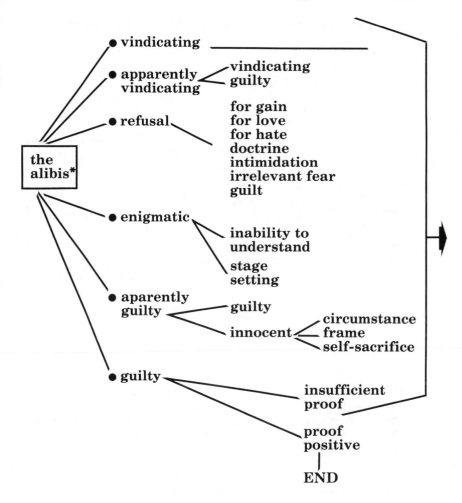

*this cycle repeats

Testimony about alibis is frequently the most mechanical item in detective novels bringing with it as it does clocks, maps, and time tables. The psychological motives for alibi making are much the same as those seen in the testimony of witnesses/suspects about the crime and their relations with the victim seen in the previous section of the chart. Because they are so mechanical, however, one finds that they rarely throw much light on the problem at this stage of the plot development. Either all characters have what seem to be good alibis or none has or innocent people have none while guilty people have cast iron answers.

II. The Solution
   A. Interpret immediate circumstances

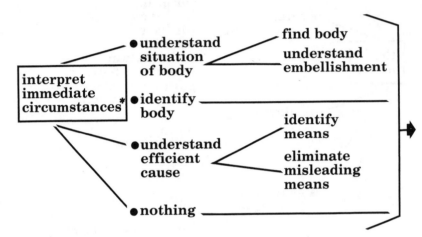

*this cycle repeats

All of this keys back to I.A., and I.B. It is almost impossible to really solve the problem here but it is the necessary starting place for the solution. In many cases the option of "nothing" takes effect here as the things which are discovered in this section were apparent from the very beginning.

II. The Solution
   B. Understand environmental evidence

(See chart on next page)

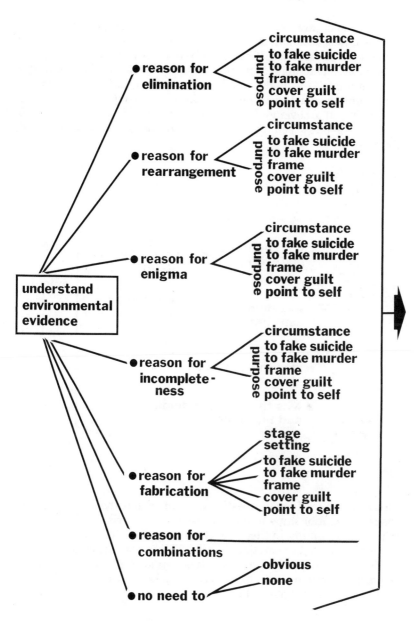

In Golden Age novels the material evidence has often been tampered with: things are added, subtracted, modified, etc. The reasons for this in the books are manifold. First there is the possibility that circumstance, accident, or nature has altered somehow the condition of the scene of the crime. When it is altered with a purpose the possible reasons are: 1) to make a murder look like suicide and thereby stop investigation, 2) to make a suicide look like murder for benign or malignant reasons, 3) to make an innocent party seem guilty, i.e. frame him, 4) to cover guilt by taking away one's fingerprints, etc., 5) to point to one's self out of conscience or out of overconfident playfulness.

II. The Solution
  C. Understand victim

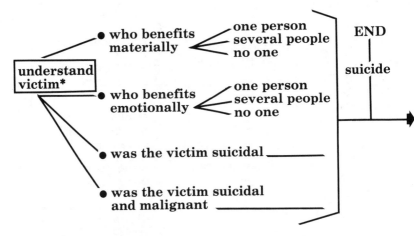

*this cycle repeats

This is where the famous question *qui bono* enters the formula, for the suspects' relationships to the deceased play a pivotal role given the criteria that murder in these novels must be done for understandable motives (material or emotional gain.) This is also the stage at which the first practical ending appears: if novels are built on suicide which accidentally or purposely has appeared to be murder it is understood at this point and the novel ends.

II. The Solution
  D. Psychological evidence
    1. Understand suspects

This is the point that we discover that Poindexter, the victim's nephew and husband of Alice, the vamp, who is obsessively tidy and constantly worried, and who once was kicked out of his club at his uncle's request, is right up there at the top of the list of suspects.

II. The Solution
    D. Psychological evidence
        2. Understand effects

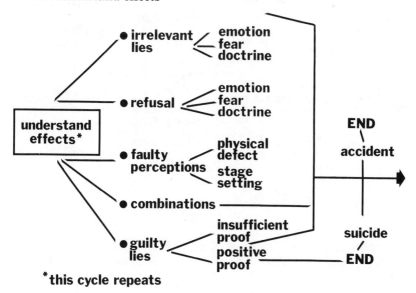

Here the detective understands motives. He understands how the suspects' minds work and what effect this has had on their testimony gathered in part I. Detective novels sometimes end at this point. In most cases, however, the psychological evidence lacks the strength to finish off the problem, as does the assembled material evidence. Finbow in C.P. Snow's *Death Under Sail* states what is the essence of the situation:

> People talk about material truth and psychological truth as though, if you are interested in one, you can't be interested in the other. Of course that's nonsense. If I had all of the material facts, I shouldn't want any psychological facts.... In exactly the same way, if you knew all the psychological facts about—say Aloysius Birrell—and they made it quite certain that he was bound to kill Roger, then I should believe that, though it seems to me materially impossible. But the point is, one never has *all* the material facts or *all* the psychological facts. One has to do what one can with an incomplete mixture of the two.[5]

II. The Solution
  E. The alibis

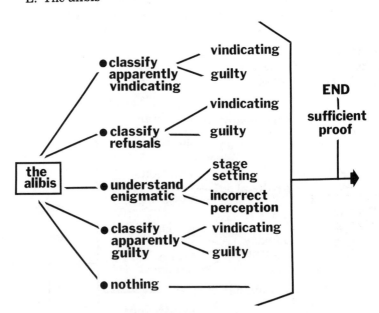

Clearing away the question of alibis is necessary in those novels which dwell upon them. This is another point at which the plot can end.

II. The Solution
   F. Combine material and psychological evidence

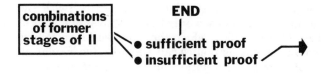

In the Ellery Queen novels this stage takes the form of the narrator stepping in and telling the readers that all of the facts are in their possession. Other writers give their detectives the nasty habit of telling their cronies that they know who did it but will not reveal this informaion because they need to be sure. At this point all plots revolving on accident and suicide must end. In fact most detective plots *could* end at this point but they don't. There is a need for one final dramatic scene to finish the whole problem with a flourish instead of a whimper.

II. The Solution
   G. Forcing the issue

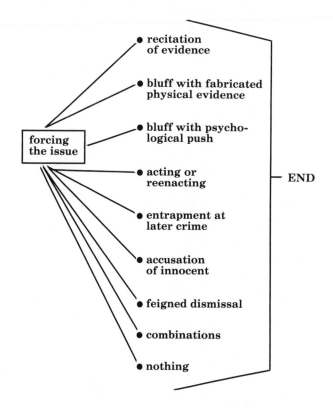

This stage brings us to the end of the detective plot and returns to those possibilities for conclusions which I outlined earlier. Here writers give their readers final proof in action of the guilt of one of the characters in the novel for almost all of these tactics (with the exception of "nothing" which is used only in a tiny class of novels in which the crime is not solved or in which the detective does not solve the crime, and even then closing tactics can and are often employed) evoke some sort of dramatic revelation on the part of one of the characters which surprises the readers and unravels the crime.

This formula describes a tremendous number of detective plots, many of which were used in the detective novels of the twenties and thirties. It does not, however, shed light on how writers actually conceived the ideas for their detective stories. Practically everyone knows that detective plots are created backwards, beginning with the clever solution and then backtracking to create the situation and crime to fit it. In this resepct they are like jokes, as I have suggested earlier. What I have outlined above is the steps which detective writers took to flesh out their novels and to write the beginnings for their endings. Perhaps the most significant point about the formula which I have outlined is that it is reasonably simple, that is it has clearly defined stages, but it is also capable of multitudinous variations. It is for this reason that the detective novel is such a viable form: it comforts readers in that it relies on a known pattern but it also piques them because the pattern is capable of almost infinite variation.

Appendix II

Chronology And Titles

For a number of reasons, best known to copyright lawyers and advertising departments of publishers, many of the novels which I have talked about appear under several different titles. Hence the following list should enable readers to make sure that we are thinking about the same books.

Margery Allingham
1928   *The White Cottage Mystery*
1929   *The Crime at Black Dudley/The Black Dudley Murder*
1929   *Mystery Mile*
1931   *The Gyrth Chalice Mystery/Look to the Lady*
1931   *Police at the Funeral*
1933   *Sweet Danger/The Kingdom of Death/The Fear Sign*
1934   *Death of a Ghost*
1936   *Flowers for the Judge*
1937   *The Case of the Late Pig*
1937   *Dancers in Mourning/Who Killed Chloe?*
1938   *Fashion in Shrouds*
1941   *Traitor's Purse*

John Dickson Carr
1930   *It Walks by Night*
1931   *The Lost Gallows*
1931   *Castle Skull*
1932   *The Corpse in the Waxworks/The Waxworks Murder*
1932   *Poison in Jest*
1933   *Hag's Nook*
1933   *The Mad Hatter Mystery*
1934   *The Blind Barber*
1934   *The Eight of Swords*
1935   *Death Watch*
1935   *The Hollow Man/The Three Coffins*
1936   *The Arabian Nights Murder*
1937   *The Burning Court*
1937   *Four False Weapons*
1937   *To Wake the Dead*

1938   *The Crooked Hinge*
1939   *The Problem of the Green Capsule/The Black Spectacles*
1939   *The Problem of the Wire Cage*

as Carr Dickson
1933   *Bowstring Murders*

as Carter Dickson
1934   *The Plague Court Murders*
1934   *The White Priory Murders*
1935   *The Red Widow Murders*
1935   *The Unicorn Murders*
1936   *Magic Lantern Murders/The Punch and Judy Murders*
1937   *The Peacock Feather Murders/The Ten Teacups*
1938   *Death in Five Boxes*
1938   *The Judas Window/The Crossbow Murder*
1939   *The Reader is Warned*

Carter Dickson and John Rhode
1939   *Fatal Descent/Drop to his Death*

Agatha Christie
1920   *The Mysterious Affair at Styles*
1922   *The Secret Adversary*
1923   *The Murder on the Links*
1924   *The Man in the Brown Suit*
1925   *The Secret of Chimneys*
1926   *The Murder of Roger Ackroyd*
1927   *The Big Four*
1928   *The Mystery of the Blue Train*
1929   *The Seven Dials Mystery*
1930   *Murder at the Vicarage*
1931   *Murder at Hazlemoor/The Sittaford Mystery*
1932   *Peril at End House*
1933   *Thirteen at Dinner/Lord Edgware Dies*
1934   *The Boomerang Clue/Why Didn't They Ask Evans?*
1934   *Murder on the Calais Coach/Murder on the Orient Express*
1935   *The A.B.C. Murders*
1935   *Murder in Three Acts/Three Act Tragedy*
1936   *Cards on the Table*
1936   *Murder in Mesopotamia*
1937   *Death on the Nile*
1937   *Poirot Loses a Client/Dumb Witness*
1938   *Appointment with Death*
1938   *Murder for Christmas/A Holiday for Murder/Hercule Poirot's Christmas*

1939   *Easy to Kill/Murder is Easy*
1939   *And Then There Were None/Ten Little Niggers/Ten
Little Indians*

Anthony Berkeley Cox
  as Anthony Berkeley
1926   *The Layton Court Mystery*
1926   *The Wychford Poisoning Case*
1927   *Mr. Priestley's Problem*
1927   *Roger Sherringham and the Vane Mystery/Mystery at
        Lover's Cave*
1928   *Silk Stocking Murders*
1929   *Piccadilly Murder*
1929   *The Poisoned Chocolates Case*
1931   *Top Storey Murder/Top Story Murder*
1931   *The Second Shot*
1932   *Murder in the Basement*
1933   *Jumping Jenny/The Dead Mrs. Stratton*
1934   *Panic Party/Mr. Pidgeon's Island*
1937   *Trial and Error*
1938   *Not to be Taken/A Puzzle in Poison*
1939   *Death in the House*

  as Francis Iles
1931   *Malice Aforethought*
1932   *Murder Story for Ladies/Before the Fact*
1939   *As For the Woman*

Ngaio Marsh
1934   *A Man Lay Dead*
1935   *Enter a Murderer*
1936   *The Nursing Home Murder*
1936   *Death in Ecstasy*
1937   *Vintage Murder*
1938   *Artists in Crime*
1939   *Overture to Death*
1940   *Death at the Bar*

Dorothy Sayers
1923   *Whose Body?*
1926   *Clouds of Witness*
1927   *The Dawson Pedigree/ Unnatural Death*
1928   *The Unpleasantness at the Bellona Club*
1930   *Strong Poison*
1931   *The Five Red Herrings/ Suspicious Characters*
1932   *Have His Carcase*

1933   *Murder Must Advertise*
1934   *The Nine Tailors*
1935   *Gaudy Night*
1936   *Busman's Honeymoon*

Notes

Notes to Chapter 1

[1]Patrick Howarth, *Play Up and Play the Game: Heroes of Popular Fiction* (London: Eyre Methuen, 1973), pp.13-14.

[2]John G. Cawelti, *Adventure, Mystery, and Romance* (Chicago: University of Chicago Press, 1976), p.40.

[3]Dorothy Sayers, *Have His Carcase* (New York: Avon Books, 1968), pp.152-3.

[4]See, for instance, my article in *Poe Studies*, 10 (1977), 39-41.

[5]Jerry M. Suls, "A Two Stage Model for Appreciation of Jokes and Cartoons," in *The Psychology of Humor*, eds. Jeffrey Goldstein and Paul McGee (New York: Academic Press, 1972), p.82.

[6]Ed McBain, *Jigsaw*, in *Three From the 87th* (New York: Nelson Doubleday, 1972), p.274.

[7]A.A. Milne, *The Red House Mystery* (New York: Dutton, 1965), p.viii.

[8]Warren Sussman, *Culture and Commitment: 1929-45* (New York: Brazillier, 1973), p.82.

[9]Milne, p.88, *The Wychford Poisoning Case* (New York: Doubleday and Doran, 1930), p.48, *The Roman Hat Mystery* (New York: International Reader's League, 1930), p.176,*The Eight of Swords* (New York: Harper and Row, 1971), p.213.

Notes to Chapter 2

[1]P.N. Furbank, "Chesterton the Edwardian," in *G.K. Chesterton*, ed. John Sullivan (New York: Barnes and Noble, 1974), p.16.

[1a] *Trent's Last Case* (Bungay: Penguin, 1944), p.15.

[2]Ibid., p.19.

[3]*Ibid.*, p.33.

[4]"A Defense of Detective Stories," in *Detective Fiction: Crime and Compromise*, eds. Dick Allen and David Chacko (New York: Harcourt Brace Jovanovitch, 1974), p.385.

[5]*Trent*, p.100.

[6]*Trent*, p.17.

Notes to Chapter 3

[1]In *Sleeping Murder* there is an allusion to Gielgud's performance of *The Duchess of Malfi* which took place in London shortly after the end of the war.

[2]Jacques Barzun and Wendell Taylor, *A Catalogue of Crime* (New York:

Harper and Row, 1971), p.119.
3*Passenger to Frankfurt* (New York: Dodd and Mead, 1970), p.51.
4*The Seven Dials Mystery* (New York: Books Inc., 1944), p.256.
5*Death in the Air* (New York: Popular Library, 1962), p.177.
6*Ibid.*, p.120.
7*Cards on the Table* (New York: Dodd and Mead, 1963), p.71.
8*Peril at End House* (New York: Grosset and Dunlap, 1932), p.67.
9*The Boomerang Clue* (New York: Grossett and Dunlap, 1935), pp.53-4.
10*The Mystery of the Blue Train* (New York: Pocket Books, 1966), p.53.
11*Ibid.*, p.134.
12*Peril at End House*, pp.109-110.
13*Boomerang Clue*, pp.58-9.
14*Ibid.*, p.60.
15*Thirteen at Dinner*, in *Murder-Go-Round* (New York: Dodd and Mead, 1972), p.111.
16*Appointment with Death* (New York: Dodd and Mead, 1938), p.215.
17*The Mysterious Affair at Styles* (New York: Avon, 1951), p.20.
18*Murder in Mesopotamia*, in *The Perilous Journeys of Hercule Poirot* (New York: Dodd and Mead, 1954), p.99.
19*Murder on the Calais Coach* (New York: Dodd and Mead, 1934), p.7.
20*Cards on the Table*, p.108.
21*Poirot Loses a Client* (New York: Dodd and Mead, 1937), pp.45-6,
22*Come, Tell Me How You Live* (New York: Dodd and Mead, 1974), p.i.

Notes to Chapter 4

1W.H. Auden, "The Guilty Vicarage," *Harpers* (May, 1945), p.408.
2*The Red House Mystery*, p.1.
3*Ibid.*, 63, 78, 95, 120, 120, 121, 121, 144, 145.
4*Ibid.*, p.103.
5*Ibid.*, p.187.
6*Ibid.*, p.69.
7*Ibid.*, p.147.
8*Ibid.*, p.13.
9*Ibid.*, p.89.
10*Ibid.*, p.ix.
11Raymond Chandler, "The Simple Art of Murder," in *The Simple Art of Murder* (New York: Ballantine, 1972), p.26.
12*Ibid.*, p.1.

Notes to Chapter 5

1Janet Hitchman, *Such A Strange Lady* (London: New English Library, 1975), p.62.
2*Whose Body?* (New York: Avon, 1961), p.7.
3*Ibid.*, p.20.
4*Ibid.*, p.110.
5*Unnatural Death* (New York: Avon, 1964), p.21.
6P.G. Wodehouse, *The World of Psmith* (London: Barrie and Jenkins, 1974), p.v.

[7]Hitchman, p.94.
[8]*Ibid.,* p.94.
[9]*Whose Body?* p.74.
[10]*Ibid.,* 127.
[11]Hitchman, p.88.
[12]*Clouds of Witness and The Unpleasantness at the Bellona Club* (New York: Harper and Row, n.d.), pp.105-6.
[13]*Unnatural Death,* p.158.
[14]"Problem Picture," in *Christian Letters to a Post-Christian World,* ed. Roderick Jellema (Grand Rapids: Eerdmans, 1969), p.117.
[15]*Unnatural Death,* p.163.
[16]*The Unpleasantness at the Bellona Club,* p.274.
[17]*Ibid.,* p.277.
[18]*Have His Carcase,* p.15.
[19]*Ibid.,* p.15.
[20]*Ibid.,* p.36.
[21]*Gaudy Night* (New York: Avon, 1968), p.178.
[22]*Strong Poison* (New York: Avon, 1967), p.95.
[23]*Ibid.,* p.71.
[24]*Tales of Mystery and Detection from the Omnibus of Crime* (New York: MacFadden, 1967), p.37.
[25]Hitchman, p.94.
[26]*The Five Red Herrings,* (New York: Avon, 1968), pp.24-5.
[27]Hitchman, p.100.
[28]Charles Dickens, *Pickwick Papers* (Boston: Estes and Lauriat, 1883), p.632.
[29]*Have His Carcase,* p.337.
[30]*Ibid.,* p.351.
[31]*Unnatural Death,* p.64.
[32]*Murder Must Advertise* (New York: Avon, 1967), p.246.
[33]*Tales of Mystery,* p.37.
[34]*Murder Must Advertise,* pp.78-9.
[35]*Gaudy Night,* p.178.
[36]*Ibid.,* p.256.

Notes to Chapter 6

[1]*Have His Carcase,* p.337.
[2]*The Layton Court Mystery* (New York: Grossett and Dunlap, n.d.), p.v.
[3]as quoted in Chris Steinbrunner, Otto Penzler, *et al, Encyclopedia of Mystery and Detection* (New York: McGraw Hill, 1976), p.362.
[4]*The Layton Court Mystery,* p.5.
[5]Steinbrunner, p.362.
[6]*The Piccadilly Murder* (New York: Doubleday and Doran, 1930), pp.100-1.
[7]*The Wychford Poisoning Case* (New York: Doubleday and Doran, 1926), p.i.
[8]*Ibid.,* p.12.
[9]*The Second Shot* (New York: Doubleday and Doran, 1931), pp.5-6.
[10]*The Mystery at Lover's Cave* (New York: Doubleday and Doran, 1927), p.179.

[11]*The Poisoned Chocolates Case* (New York : Doubleday and Doran, 1929), p.159.

Notes to Chapter 7

[1]*The Allingham Case Book* (New York: Mannor Books, 1977), p.9.
[2]*Castle Skull* (New York: Berkley, 1968), p.77.
[3]*The Allingham Case Book*, p.12; p.13.
[4]*The Mysterious Mr. Campion*, p.11.
[5]Allingham claimed that her novels fell into groups of threes, but this is not really true in the twenties and thirties. The way I see the groups is:

Thriller: *Black Dudley, Mystery Mile, Gyrth, Chalice, Sweet Danger.*
Regular Detective Novels: *Police at the Funeral, Death of a Ghost, Flowers for the Judge.*
Reevaluation: *The Case of the Late Pig*
Romances: *Dancers in Mourning, Fashion in Shrouds, Traitor's Purse.*
[6]*The Mysterious Mr. Campion*, p.11.
[7]*Ibid.*, p.9.
[8]*The Allingham Case Book*, p.15.
[9]*The Mysterious Mr. Campion*, p.11.
[10]*The Crime at Black Dudley* (Harmondsworth: Penguin, 1973), p.135.
[11]*Ibid.*, p.22.
[12]*Mystery Mile* (New York: Mannor Books, 1973), p.43.
[13]*Sweet Danger* (Harmondsworth: Penguin, 1976), p.125.
[14]*Ibid.*, p.95.
[15]*The Case of the Late Pig* (New York: Doubleday and Doran, 1937), p.16.
[16]*Ibid.*, p.70.
[17]*The Mysterious Mr. Campion*, p.12.

Notes to Chapter 8

[1]*It Walks By Night* (New York: Harper Brothers, 1930), p.101.
[2]*Castle Skull* (New York: Berkley, 1968), p.7.
[3]*The Four False Weapons* (New York: Collier, 1962), p.59.
[4]Frank Swinnerton, *The Georgean Scene* (New York: Farrar and Rinehart, 1935), p.94.
[5]*Ibid.*, p.95.
[6]*Hag's Nook* (Harmondsworth: Penguin, 1941), p.10.
[7]*The Life of Sir Arthur Conan Doyle* (New York: Harper and Brothers, 1948), p.215.
[8]*The Problem of the Green Capsule* (New York: Bantam, 1964), p.86.
[9]*The Crooked Hinge* (New York: Collier, 1971), p.219.
[10]*The Plague Court Murders* (New York: Belmont, 1974), pp.16-7.
[11]"The Adventure of the Bruce-Partington Plans," in *The Annotated Sherlock Holmes* (New York: Potter, 1967), II, 433.
[12]*The Reader is Warned* (London: Heinemann, 1939), p.306.
[13]*The White Priory Murders* (New York: Belmont, 1973), p.191.
[14]*The Eight of Swords* (New York: Harper and Row, 1971), p.93.
[15]*The Plague Court Murders*, p.73.

[16]Nevil Maskelyne and David Devant, *Our Magic* (New York: Dutton, 1911), p.176.

[17]*It Walks By Night,* p.118.

[18]Maskelyne and Devant, pp.182-4.

[19]*The Plague Court Murders,* p.13.

[20]*The Eight of Swords,* p.147.

[21]*The Plague Court Murders,* p.180.

[22]*The Eight of Swords,* p.212-3.

[23]*The Lost Gallows* (New York: Collier, n.d.), 121-2.

Notes to Chapter 9

[1]*A Man Lay Dead* (Cleveland: World, 1942), p.215.

[2]*Death in Ecstasy* (London: Bles, 1955), p.233.

[3]*Ibid.,* p.105.

[4]*Death in a White Tie* (New York: Furman, 1938), p.289.

[5]*A Man Lay Dead,* p.210.

[6]*Enter a Murderer* (New York: Berkley, 1974), p.159.

[7]*Death at the Bar* (Boston: Little, Brown, 1940), p.182.

Notes to Appendix I

[1]S.S. Van Dine, "The Rules of the Game," in Howard Haycraft, ed., *The Art of the Mystery Story* (New York: Grosset and Dunlap, 1961), p.190.

[2]Courtesy of Dodd and Mead.

[3]Agatha Christie, *The Peril at End House* (New York: Grosset and Dunlap, 1932), p.111.

[4]C.P. Snow, *Death Under Sail* (London: Heinemann, 1959), p.44.

[5]*Ibid.,* p.78.

Index

A

Alleyn, Roderick, see N. Marsh
Allingham, M., 12, 13, 18, 21, 27,
    126, 144, 194, 197, 198
The Case of the Late Pig, 135, 136,
    137, 139, 140, 144
The Crime at Black Dudley, 17, 127,
    128, 129, 130, 132, 133
Dancers in Mourning, 27, 135, 136,
    137, 138, 141, 142
Death of a Ghost, 135, 136, 138, 139
Fashion in Shrouds, 27, 135, 137,
    138, 141, 142, 143
Flowers for the Judge, 135, 138, 141,
    143, 144
The Gyrth Chalice Mystery, 128,
    129, 132, 136, 142
Mystery Mile, 128, 129, 130, 132, 134,
    137, 143
The Oaken Heart, 144
Police at the Funeral, 135, 136, 137,
    138, 139, 141, 143, 144
Sweet Danger, 128, 134, 142, 144
The Tiger in the Smoke, 144
Traitor's Purse, 27, 141, 142
The White Cottage Mystery, 127
Armstrong, H.R., 122
Auden, W.H., 64, 71

B

The Baffle Book, 25
Bailey, H.C., 17
Ballantyne, R.M., 6
Barton, R.E., 81, 90
Barzun, J., 39, 64
Bencolin, Henri, see J.D. Carr
Bentley, E.C., 11, 12, 20, 29-37, 38, 72,
    74, 112, 118, 124, 132, 133, 201
Berkeley, A., see A.B. Cox

The Black Tower of Bransdorf, 6
Blake, N., see C. Day Lewis
Blake, Sexton, 9, 30, 126, 127
Boys Own Paper, 6
Boucher, A., 28
Bramah, E., 8, 30, 35
Buchan, J., 5, 8-9, 12, 129
Byrne, L. St. C., 108

C

Campion, Albert, see M. Allingham
Carr, J.D., 10, 12, 25, 27, 145-184
Arabian Nights Murder, 151, 155,
    158, 183
The Blind Barber, 151, 155, 157, 158,
    167
The Bowstring Murders, 149, 150-1,
    152, 161
The Burning Court, 149, 156, 169,
    174, 182
Castle Skull, 145, 146, 147, 155, 176
The Crooked Hinge, 151, 156, 159,
    171, 175, 205
Death in Five Boxes, 160, 167
Death Watch, 151, 155, 158, 171
The Eight of Swords, 18, 20, 151, 154,
    157, 159, 160, 161, 165, 168, 174,
    179, 183
Fatal Descent, 160, 174, 179
The Four False Weapons, 145, 146-7,
    173, 203
Graveyard to Let, 155
Hag's Nook, 151, 152, 155, 156, 157,
    158, 178
It Walks by Night, 145, 147, 148, 170,
    176, 181
The Judas Window, 160, 163, 165,
    167

The Life of Sir Arthur Conan Doyle, 154

The Lost Gallows, 145, 146, 148, 178, 183

The Mad Hatter Mystery, 18, 151, 156, 157, 159, 207

The Murder of Sir Edmund Godfrey, 178

The Plague Court Murders, 160, 161-2, 165, 167, 169, 176, 178, 183

Poison in Jest, 147, 149-50, 158, 177

The Problem of the Green Capsule, 151, 155, 159, 175, 176

The Problem of the Wire Cage, 151, 156, 157, 158, 159, 181

The Punch and Judy Murders, 160

The Reader is Warned, 160, 163-5, 167, 170

The Red Widow Murders, 160, 166, 178

The Ten Teacups, 17, 160, 181

The Three Coffins, 151, 155, 156, 157, 170, 171, 176, 181, 183

To Wake the Dead, 17, 151, 158, 159, 177

The Unicorn Murders, 160, 163, 164, 172, 174

The Waxworks Murders, 145, 146, 147, 148

The White Priory Murders, 160, 164, 167, 181, 182

Cawelti, J., 9

Chandler, R., 17, 19, 24, 64, 70-1, 199

Charteris, L., 32

Chesterton, G.K., 5, 8, 29, 32, 77, 152-3

Christie, A., 11, 12, 18, 19, 26, 38-63, 69, 93, 132, 198, 199, 200

The ABC Murders, 46, 52, 55, 59, 60, 63

And Then There Were None, 38, 49, 52, 53-56, 62

Appointment with Death, 49, 55, 62, 81

The Big Four, 39, 42-43, 50, 60, 61

The Boomerang Clue, 42, 46, 47, 48, 50, 52, 55, 56, 61

Cards on the Table, 44-45, 49, 54, 55, 57, 59, 60

Come, Tell Me How You Live, 62

Curtain, 38, 60

Death in the Air, 44, 46, 50, 52, 55, 56

Death on the Nile, 49, 50, 55, 60, 61, 62

Easy to Kill, 38, 46, 52, 55, 56, 61, 62

Giant's Bread, 61

Holiday for Murder, 52

The Man in the Brown Suit, 39, 40-41, 49, 50, 52, 56, 62, 119

The Mousetrap, 56

Murder at Hazlemoor, 56

Murder at the Vicarage, 39, 47, 48, 49, 50, 56

Murder in Mesopotamia, 49, 50, 55, 57, 60, 61, 62

Murder in Three Acts, 46, 50, 52, 55, 60, 61, 62

The Murder of Roger Ackroyd, 23, 38, 39, 41, 52

Murder on the Calais Coach, 46, 49, 50, 52, 56, 57, 203

Murder on the Links, 39, 58, 60, 61

The Mysterious Affair at Styles, 17, 39, 46, 49, 50, 56, 60, 61, 62

Mystery of the Blue Train, 39, 46, 47, 50

Passenger to Frankfort, 41

Peril at End House, 38, 47, 48, 49, 52, 55, 60, 201

Poirot Loses a Client, 54, 55, 56, 58, 59, 60

The Secret Adversary, 39, 40, 50, 51-2, 56, 61

The Secret of Chimneys, 39, 41-42, 50, 56

The Seven Dials Mystery, 39, 50, 56

Sleeping Murder, 38

Thirteen at Dinner, 48, 50, 55, 60

Unfinished Portrait, 61

Cole, G.D.H. and M.I., 12

Collins, W., 27, 28, 29, 33, 35-36, 42, 48, 79, 81, 83, 88, 108

Cox, A.B., 12, 13, 18, 19, 59, 69, 90, 95, 98, 111-125, 180, 194, 198

As For the Woman, 119, 120, 125

Before the Fact, 26, 111, 119, 120-122, *Death in the House,* 125, 199

Jumping Jenny, 112, 125, 203, 205

Layton Court Murders, 112, 116, 124

Malice Aforethought, 26, 119, 120, 121-122

Mr. Priestley's Problem, 114, 116, 124

Murder in the Basement, 112
Panic Party, 112, 113, 122
Piccadilly Murder, 115
The Poisoned Chocolates Case, 112, 115, 123, 124
Puzzle in Poison, 116
Roger Sherringham and the Vane Mystery, 112, 123
The Second Shot, 26, 112, 115, 118, 119
The Silk Stocking Murders, 112, 114
Top Storey Murder, 112, 124
Trial and Error, 115, 116, 122, 125
The Wychford Poisoning Case, 112, 117
Crofts, F.W., 12
crossword puzzles, 22, 47

D_____
Dell, E.M., 27
Detection Club, 21, 111, 115
Dickens, C., 73, 81, 96, 184
Dickson, Carr, see J.D. Carr
Dickson, Carter, see J.D. Carr
diction, 31, 68-69, 73-74, 133-134, 166-167
Doyle, A.C., 5, 7-8, 10, 19, 20, 22, 29, 30, 35, 67, 112, 126, 135, 154-155, 161-62, 200, 201
Drummond, Bulldog, see H.C. McNeile

E_____
Eliot, T.S., 109
Eustace, R., see R.E. Barton

F_____
Fell, Gideon, see J.D. Carr
Fleming, I., 8, 199
Freeman, R.A., 5, 8, 19, 20, 23, 30, 34, 56, 69, 74-75, 77, 88, 116, 191, 200, 201, 204
Freud, S., 26, 81, 89

G_____
Gaboriau, E., 5, 20
games, see play
Glyn, E., 27
Graves, R., 11, 71

H_____
Haggard, H.R., 5, 7-8
Hammett, D., 19, 24
Hannay, Richard, see J. Buchan
hard-boiled detectives, 24, 32
Haycraft, H., 5, 21
Hitchcock, A., 26, 111
Holmes, Sherlock, see A.C. Doyle
Hope, A., 5, 7, 41-42
Howarth, P., 7
Hughes, T., 6
Huizinga, J., 17, 18-19, 20
Hull, E.M., 27
Huxley, A., 89
Huxley, J., 76

I_____
Iles, F., see A.B. Cox
In Cold Blood, 202
Innes, M., see J.I.M. Stewart

J_____
jigsaw puzzle, 22
jokes, 14-15
Joyce, J., 81, 105, 109

K_____
Kennedy, Craig, 30
Knox, R., 12, 13, 18, 21, 69, 132, 198 200

L_____
Lawrence, D.H., 26, 81, 87, 92, 105
LeFannu, S., 104
LeQueux, W., 5, 8-9, 12
Lewis, C.D., 12, 13, 17, 198-9, 207
locked room mysteries, 180-183
Lowndes. M.B., 26

M_____
McBain, E., 16
MacDonald, P., 12, 13, 20, 26, 198, 20
MacDonald, R., 19
McNeile, H.C., 8, 40
magic, 175-177
Manchu, Fu, see A.H.S. Ward
Marsh, N., 12, 13, 25, 27, 185-197, 198 199
A Man Lay Dead, 185, 186, 189, 191 192, 195, 196
Artists in Crime, 187, 188, 192, 193

196
Artists in Crime, 187, 188, 192, 193, 196
Death at the Bar, 191
Death in a White Tie, 27, 187, 188, 189, 190
Death in Ecstasy, 187, 189, 191, 192
Enter a Murderer, 17, 190, 192, 195, 196
Nursing Home Murder, 192, 193, 194
Overture to Death, 188, 192, 193, 195
Vintage Murder, 27, 187, 191, 192, 195
Merrivale, Henry, see J.D. Carr
Milne, A.A., 16-17, 19, 64-71, 117, 204
multiple solution plot, 95, 122-123, 179-180
Murch, A., 5
murder game, 17, 24-25

N_____
Nayland-Smith, Dennis, see A.H.S. Ward
Newbolt Man, 7, 12

O_____
Oppenheim, E.P., 5, 8-9, 11, 12, 38, 40, 75, 77
Orczy, E., 8, 30, 35, 133

P_____
Palmer, W., 122
penny dreadfuls, 6
Penny Sunday Times, 6
play, 16-21
Poe, E.A., 5, 14, 19, 20, 22, 29, 31, 35, 200
Poirot, Hercule, see A. Christie
Prather, R., 199
Priestley, J.B., 26
Psmith, R., see P.G. Wodehouse
puzzle story, 21-26, 94, 169-170

Q_____
Queen, E., 20, 24, 25, 27, 52, 81, 217

R_____
The Red House Mystery, see A.A. Milne
Rhode, J., see C.J.C. Street
Richwine, K.N., 152

Ripley, H.A., 25
Rohmer, S., see A.H.S. Ward
rules of the game, 13, 21, 42, 69-70, 93, 200, 201

S_____
Sapper, see H.C. McNeile
Sayers, D., 11, 12, 13, 20, 26, 27, 72-110, 132, 186-187, 194, 197, 198, 200
Busman's Honeymoon, 27, 90, 107-110, 205
Clouds of Witness, 77-81, 87, 105, 108
Documents in the Case, 87-90
Five Red Herrings, 24, 91, 94-96, 97, 99, 103, 104-105
Gaudy Night, 27, 90, 96, 105-107, 109
Have His Carcase, 13, 90, 91, 96-99, 101, 102, 105, 111
Murder Must Advertise, 17, 27, 97, 98, 99-102, 105
The Nine Tailors, 97, 102-105
The Omnibus of Crime, 21, 26, 85, 87, 93, 94, 97, 100-101, 105, 117
Strong Poison, 90-94, 95, 97
Unnatural Death, 23, 24, 81-85, 86, 87, 90, 94, 97, 100
Unpleasantness at the Bellona Club, 85-7, 97
Whose Body? 72-77, 78, 81, 82, 87, 96, 118, 207
schoolboy novels, 7
Sherringham, Roger, see A.B. Cox
Six Against Scotland Yard, 111, 198
Snow, C.P., 12, 107, 202, 216
Spillane, M., 19, 199
Stevenson, R.L., 5, 129
Stewart, J.I.M., 12, 13, 24, 27, 195
Street, C.J.C., 12, 161, 175, 180
Stout, R., 12
Suls, J., 15
Symons, J., 12, 199

T_____
Templar, Simon, see L. Charteris
Tey, J., 12, 15
Thompson, H.D., 25
Thorndyke, Dr., see R.A. Freeman
thrillers, 5-11, 128, 129-30
Trent's Last Case, see E.C. Bentley
Twain, M., 30, 184

V＿＿＿＿＿＿
Van Dine, S.S., see W.H. Wright
Vane, Harriet, see D. Sayers
Varney the Vampire, 6
Vidocq, F.E., 8

W＿＿＿＿＿＿
Wagner the Wehrwolf, 6
Wallace, E., 5, 8-9, 10-11, 12, 13, 38, 77,
    97
Ward, A.H.S., 5, 8-9, 10, 12, 30, 42-3

Watson, C., 199
Wells, C., 21
Westmacott, M., 38, 39, 61, see also A.
    Christie
Wheatley, D., 25
Wilson, E., 64, 199
Wimsey, Lord Peter, see D. Sayers
Wodehouse, P.G., 8, 13, 43, 74, 84, 141
Wooster, Bertie, see P.G. Wodehouse
Wright, W.H., 18, 20, 21, 24, 27, 46, 69,
    93, 98, 200, 201, 203